THE
WORLD OF HARLEQUIN

returned on or bef

A

5 A

A

THE
WORLD OF
HARLEQUIN

A Critical Study of the Commedia dell'Arte

BY

ALLARDYCE NICOLL

CAMBRIDGE UNIVERSITY PRESS

CAMBRIDGE

LONDON · NEW YORK · MELBOURNE

Published by the Syndics of the Cambridge University Press
The Pitt Building, Trumpington Street, Cambridge CB2 IRP
Bentley House, 200 Euston Road, London NWI 2DB
32 East 57th Street, New York, NY 10022, USA
296 Beaconsfield Parade, Middle Park, Melbourne 3206, Australia

Library of Congress catalogue card number: 76–18411

ISBN 0 521 05834 1 hard covers
ISBN 0 521 29132 1 paperback

First published 1963
First paperback edition 1976

Printed in Great Britain
at the
University Printing House, Cambridge
(Euan Phillips, University Printer)

39682.

792. 3

To the memory of a great Harlequin
MARCELLO MORETTI

PREFACE

OF necessity, any book on the commedia dell'arte must to a certain extent be 'historical'. It should, however, be emphasised that the prime aim of the present volume is not to survey the extant factual records concerning the activities of the Italian players but critically to explore the question posed in its opening pages: what was the basic force which kept this particular kind of theatrical presentation vital for more than two centuries and which, even after it had vanished, has caused many of its characters to live in our memories?

In seeking for an answer to this question, an attempt has been made to place all reliance upon the original sources of information, considered as objectively as possible. The commedia dell'arte has attracted to itself a considerable amount of colourful writing by enthusiasts who, untrained in handling evidence, have tended to repeat unsubstantiated assertions and who have been inclined to impose upon the ascertainable facts their own romantically inspired concepts. During recent years, moreover, among more scholarly essays on the subject, it has inspired the expression of extreme opinions, so that sometimes partial evidence has been selected for the purpose of 'proving' this theory or that. So far as possible I have sought here to take no statements on trust unless they have a basis in contemporary documents and to avoid approaching the evidence with preconceived opinions. Thus on several controversial issues I have found myself compelled to take a middle course. We may, for example, discover documentary support for the view that 'improvisation' was something largely meaningless when interpreted strictly; we may with equal ease discover support for a view diametrically opposed. We may read the scenarios with a fixed idea of how such a character as Pantalone was treated and ignore evidence which indicates a different conception of his role. We may argue, and quote support for, the theory that Goldoni killed the commedia dell'arte; we may use other quotations to demonstrate that the commedia lives more vitally in his work than it does in the plays of Gozzi. We may romantically acclaim the verve of the Neapolitan figures and close our eyes to the disturbing elements introduced into the commedia dell'arte from the South. With all these controversial issues, it would seem that the only hope of reaching the truth rests in pursuing an even path.

Nothing is said here concerning the origins of the commedia dell'arte or of its characters—partly because that theme has already attracted too much attention and partly because it throws but little light on the qualities inherent in the Italian improvised theatre from 1550 onwards. Historically, there is much of interest in determining the genealogy of Harlequin, but, quite apart from the inevitable uncertainty concerning that genealogy, no information on the subject can aid us materially in assessing Harlequin's power from the end of the sixteenth century up to the twentieth. And it must be insisted that the analysis of this power forms the theme of the present book.

Obviously, the rich pictorial evidence relating to the commedia dell'arte is of very special importance, and fortunately reproductions of many contemporary prints, drawings and paintings are readily available. In this book I have sought to give preference to illustrative material which, for the most part, has not been reproduced or which is to be found only with difficulty.

For assistance in various matters my sincere thanks are presented to: Ellis Waterhouse and his staff at the Barber Institute; Gabriele Baldini; Giorgio Brunacci; Giuliano Pellegrini; Mario Apollonio; Nico Pepe; Vito Pandolfi; Léon Chancerel; Michel Poirier; Arnold Szyfman; Mieczysław Brahmer; Grigori Kozintsev; Yuri Shvedov; Zdenek Střībrný; Heinz Kindermann; Agne Beijer; as well as those in charge of many libraries, especially the Biblioteca Corsiniana and the Museo Burcardo in Rome, the Hermitage in Leningrad and McGill University Library in Montreal. The task of reading and comparing the original manuscript scenarios would have proved virtually impossible had it not been for the almost complete microfilm reproductions assembled in the Shakespeare Institute; and the effort to reconstruct an image of what the commedia dell'arte once stood for would have lacked much without the opportunity of seeing Marcello Moretti as Arlecchino and Nico Pepe as Pantalone in the lively production of *Arlecchino servitore di due padroni* by the Piccolo Teatro della Città di Milano.

ALLARDYCE NICOLL

CONTENTS

ILLUSTRATIONS

xiv

ACKNOWLEDGEMENTS

Acknowledgement is gratefully made to the owners named above for permission to make reproductions, and thanks are also expressed to the following: Bulloz (jacket/cover and 3, 88, 108); Vivarelli & Gullà (9, 10); Bayer, Nationalmuseum (11): Beata Bergström (16, 17, 18, 21); Giraudon (22, 29); Caeco (24); Fotoodděleni Zk-Čsav (25, 58, 61, 117, 119); Enciclopedia dello Spettacolo, Rome (46, 84, 85); Alinari (47, 48); A. C. Cooper (66, 112); A. Dingjan (71); Max Erlanger de Rosen (122); Staatliche Porzellan-Manufactur, Nymphenburg (127); Ledino Pozzetti (129).

The photograph for figure 2 was kindly supplied by Valentino Bompiani, Milan.

Asterisks refer the reader to the notes
contained on pp. 229 — 233

PROLOGUE:
HAMLET AND HARLEQUIN

By a somewhat strange coincidence a short period of a dozen years at the beginning of the seventeenth century saw the appearance of three great and important drama folios. In 1623 were issued Shakespeare's collected comedies, histories and tragedies; seven years earlier, in 1616, that volume had been preceded by Ben Jonson's *Workes*; and five years earlier still, in 1611, had been published Flaminio Scala's *Il teatro delle favole rappresentative*, containing fifty dramatic pieces.

The first of these is so famous that familiarly it is known simply as The First Folio. Most of its component plays are of frequent recurrence in theatres all over the world; some of them have been given a wider dissemination in film form; the names of numerous characters created by Shakespeare's imagination—Romeo and Juliet, Falstaff, Portia, Lear, Macbeth, Othello—are known to millions of people, and still further millions of men and women, less lettered and possibly quite uninterested in the stage, recognise in Hamlet a proverbial figure.

To students, the second volume finds acceptance as a collection of plays possessing genuine quality and wide historical significance, but even students might find it difficult to list more than one or two of Jonson's characters. Volpone—yes, he would be mentioned; after that, there would probably be much stumbling. Among the general public almost complete ignorance reigns concerning the titles and contents of these plays; and, although some of them remained stock-pieces up to the end of the eighteenth century, not a single one of Jonson's characters has so impressed itself on the popular imagination as to be remembered. A casual reference to Lear, even perhaps to Pistol, would be generally appreciated and its significance comprehended; a casual reference to Macilente or to Bobadill would leave all but scholars at a loss.

The third volume has been perused only by a few specialists, and barely a hundred persons might be expected to have any knowledge whatsoever concerning its author, Flaminio Scala; yet it is in this collection that Harlequin—Arlecchino, Arlequin, Harlekin, call him what we will—first makes his entry within the framework of a printed play. Immediately we utter the word 'Harlequin', we realise we are on familiar ground, and in these plays Harlequin does not stand alone. Those to whom Lear and Othello are recognisable names will almost certainly display equal awareness of Pantalone (or Pantaloon) and Pulcinella (or Punch). And so far as Arlecchino is concerned, we may aver with assurance that the two theatrical characters most universally known today are Harlequin and Hamlet.

✻   ✻   ✻   ✻   ✻

Still another thing may be observed. It is not only that Hamlet and Harlequin are names familiar to vast millions of people, many of whom are in no way interested in the stage and among whom considerable numbers might find it a hard task to say anything pertinent about these two characters; there is also the fact that Hamlet, with the drama of which he forms a part, and Harlequin, with the comedy in which he reigned, possess certain salient qualities in common. Hamlet and his creator Shakespeare have had the almost unaccountable power of passing over all frontiers; they have been incorporated into scores of different ideologies, so that classicist and romantic alike have been their enthusiastic admirers, so that recent years have seen Hamlet hailed both as a supreme creation of existentialism and as a kind of Marxist hero; and these recent years have witnessed an intense upsurge of interest in Shake-

speare's dramas which goes far beyond any bardic idolatry of the past. Much the same may be said of Harlequin and his theatre. The decades from the twenties of our century down to the present have seen the publication of dozens of books, hundreds of articles on this subject, some devoted to Harlequin himself, some expounding the stage from which he sprang; and numerous experiments have been made in an attempt to revive that stage's spirit. If the books and articles had been confined to Italy, where Harlequin's theatre was born, or to France, where it early became acclimatised, no particular surprise need have been experienced, but the range of modern interest here spreads to the most distant lands. Furthermore, such interest reveals that this theatre has the same power of lending itself to incorporation into the most diverse ideological realms. One historian emphasises the early association of Harlequin with Renaissance courts and, sadly, traces his decline to the gradual vulgarisation of his art at times when he was forced to appeal to less intelligent spectators; another applies a Marxist interpretation, insisting that at the start Harlequin was created by the common people and owed his decrepitude to his entering ducal and princely palaces. The differences in interpretation are of less significance than the eager admiration displayed by both exponents; each anxiously seeks to bring this theatre, alongside Shakespeare's dramas, within the orbit of his own life's philosophy. No one has sufficient esteem for Volpone to be other than coldly objective towards him: as a character he has no vigour sufficient to make a more active appeal. But Hamlet, born of Warwickshire and London mists, and Harlequin, creature of the Tuscan sun—these we seek to make our own.

⁂　⁂　⁂　⁂　⁂

The intimate conjunction of these two persons must seem strange, despite the curious fact that the same year, 1601, saw the first datable portrait of Harlequin and the composition of Shakespeare's *Hamlet*.* At first glance—indeed on further reflection—the two characters appear to inhabit utterly different worlds. That the former starts out as the hero of a tragedy while the latter is the centre of a play of merriment matters hardly at all; what attracts our attention more closely is the fact that they appear distinct in kind, as though they were denizens of two separate planets.

In the first place, Hamlet exists for us in one drama only; his very being is confined within the bounds of the three thousand nine hundred lines of the play to which he gives his name. Our knowledge, our conceptions, of Harlequin derive either from no single comedy to which we can give a title or else from dozens of pieces wherein he makes an appearance.

Puzzling though Hamlet's character may be, we feel we know him, but no one could describe what he looks like; Harlequin's appearance we could immediately present in detail. If we turn to any collections of prints and photographs showing a range of famous stage Hamlets of the past, we find figures tall and figures thin, princes fat and princes lean, dressed variously all the way from eighteenth-century brocades to later Georgian plus fours, from ancient Danish garments to the garments of fantasy; among them we shall, alas, probably discover even some female Hamlets, as though this hero's very sex were uncertain. Hardly two are the same; several we could not have recognised without the aid of descriptive captions. For Harlequin all is different. True, his costume changed, changed from a dress of irregular patchwork to the formal ribbon-bound triangles and lozenges he flaunted during the eighteenth century; yet we can always be sure of his identity, not only from the costume but also, and more importantly, from his bodily attitudes. Among his very first portraits

3

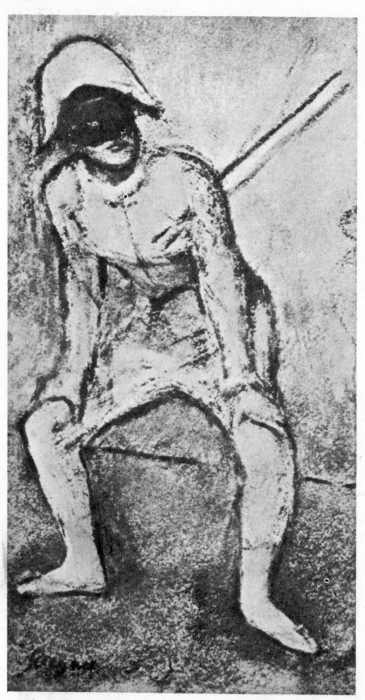

are those in the pamphlet composed by Tristano Martinelli in 1601, and the figure depicted there is easily recognisable as the same presented in scores of prints issued during the following three hundred years. No modern artist could paint a 'Hamlet' which would be immediately discerned as such, but Cézanne and Picasso and Degas and Dérain have all created sketches or canvases which need no title to tell us the name of their sitter.

In spite of the strong mental image of Hamlet, we are prepared to allow, indeed we expect, individual actors to vary their interpretations of the part; individual performances of Harlequin naturally have varied too, yet there is a much greater measure of uniformity in his histrionic presentation. We are prepared to accept Hamlet in a series of startlingly different conceptions—now as an adolescent in a sentimentally conceived romantic strain, now as a typical Renaissance prince, now

4 HARLEQUIN
5 HARLEQUIN'S EARLY COSTUME
6 HARLEQUIN'S LATER COSTUME

6

even as a figure of darkness, a symbol of the death wish. No such uncertainty is associated with the figure of Harlequin. Unquestionably, the early Arlecchino was unlike the Arlequin dreamed of by Marivaux, yet the connection between these is immeasurably firmer and closer than that between the various Hamlets who have been portrayed on the stage. While we do not object to a certain amount of variety in the presentation of Harlequin, we should be disturbed were he to be given to us in such vastly diverse guises as operate in Hamlet's world.

A further mark of distinction becomes apparent when we consider that we do not look for Hamlet elsewhere than in Shakespeare's tragedy; indeed, on the few occasions when one dramatist or another attempts the writing of a play introducing him as a character we experience a measure of discomfort. Harlequin, on the other hand, happily takes his place in scores, in hundreds, of dramatic pieces. This means that the one character has been delineated once and for all, set down immutably by Shakespeare, whereas Harlequin is a character infinitely repeated, theatrically pervasive. In many countries poet-dramatists have created roles clearly based on awareness of Shakespeare's masterpiece, but in almost every instance an attempt has been made to conceal the likeness, or at least to use every endeavour to draw readers and spectators away from making any formal comparisons. Harlequin

7 HARLEQUIN   8 'L'HARLEQUINO BERGAMASCO'

easily steps into comedies distinct from the kind to which he is more properly accustomed.

All of these differences between the poetically conceived hero of Shakespeare's tragedy and this elusive creature of the stage clearly raise important dramatic questions. Concerning the source of Hamlet's power there is no real basic problem; he stands forward before us as a character born of the penetrating imagination of a supreme playwright, expressing himself with that author's passionate eloquence. Having served his immediate purpose for comparison, he may now be dismissed from the present enquiry; we accept him as a paramount creation of the poetic inspiration, and, although the subtlety with which he is delineated may be hard to define, we all understand in general terms why he should so have impressed his personality upon us. But whence derives Harlequin's strength? We can quote Hamlet's words, but what lines can we ascribe to the other? Here unquestionably is a puzzle—a puzzle the solution for which demands not merely a consideration of the particular form of theatrical expression out of which he grew but also an examination of fundamental dramatic problems.

9 'LA RÉVÉRENCE D'ARLEQUIN'   10 'ARLEQUIN SOUPIRANT'

THE COMEDY OF SKILL

Harlequin's theatre, called by various names during earlier years, has now become familiarly distinguished by its eighteenth-century title, the 'commedia dell'arte'. Originating about the year 1550, it spread rapidly through almost all the countries of Europe, reaching even as far as Moscow and establishing a permanent Théâtre Italien in Paris; for well over two centuries it endured as a potent force, continued thereafter in Italy a less distinguished career for a further hundred and fifty years, and, during the course of its activity, left a strong mark not only on popular stages in many other lands but also on some of the greatest playwrights of that era, among whom are to be numbered Shakespeare, Lope de Vega and Molière. Clearly, it is important to determine precisely wherein its virtue consisted, and equally clearly such an enquiry must begin by at least a rapid glance at some of its typical offerings.

THREE SCENARIOS

Three examples, all taken from Scala's collection, may at present serve for this purpose. The first is *Il pellegrino fido amante*. Set in Genoa, the plot introduces us to Pantalone, with his daughter Flaminia and his servant Franceschina. Flaminia is loved by Orazio, a young gentleman whose servant is Fabrizio. It soon turns out,

---

❧ *Il Pellegrino Fido Amante* ❧

PANTALONE, a merchant
  FLAMINIA, his daughter
  FRANCESCHINA, his maid-servant

ORAZIO, a young gentleman in love
    with Flaminia
  FABRIZIO, his servant (ISABELLA in
    disguise)

CAPITANO SPAVENTO,
    a vainglorious soldier
  PEDROLINO, his servant

PILGRIM, really FLAVIO in disguise,
    following Isabella whom he loves
  ARLECCHINO, his servant

DOCTOR GRAZIANO, father of Isabella

9

however, that this Fabrizio is really a girl in disguise—Isabella, daughter of Graziano, a Milanese doctor, who, having been wooed by a certain Flavio and not wishing to marry, has thus fled her father's house. Flavio shows himself the perfect lover and comes as a pilgrim, attended by his servant Arlecchino, to Genoa in search of her. Complications are introduced through a Capitano Spavento and his astute servant Pedrolino, but the course of true love ends happily; Isabella's heart is touched by Flavio's fidelity; she gives him her hand; and at the same time Orazio wins his Flaminia.

Merriment there is in plenty, mainly provided by Arlecchino, Pedrolino and Franceschina, but the general atmosphere breathes the air of pleasant romance, not too far removed from that of such a play as *Twelfth Night*. Most of the same

---

❧ Il Vecchio Geloso ❧

PANTALONE, a Venetian merchant
  ISABELLA, his young wife
  PEDROLINO, his servant

DOCTOR GRAZIANO, Pantalone's
    friend, in love with Flaminia

CAPITANO SPAVENTO,
      also in love with Flaminia

ORAZIO, a young gentleman in love
           with Isabella

FLAVIO, his friend

BURATTINO, a market-gardener
  PASQUELLA, his wife
  OLIVETTA, his daughter

CAVICCHIO, a peasant

FLAMINIA, a widow, Isabella's sister, in
      love with Capitano Spavento

---

characters, with others, appear in *Il vecchio geloso*, although here Isabella is Pantalone's wife, Pedrolino is his servant and Graziano his friend; Orazio and Flavio are two young gentlemen, Flaminia is Isabella's sister and Capitano Spavento sports as a huntsman. Arlecchino does not come on stage, his place being taken by Burattino, a market-gardener, who has a wife Pasquella and a daughter Olivetta. The country air suggested by Burattino's occupation receives further emphasis from the introduction of a peasant, Cavicchio—for this play, as distinct from the other, is set in rural surroundings. Pantalone, knowing that his beautiful young Isabella is pursued by Orazio, has taken her to his villa some six miles from Venice. Much to his annoyance, however, the lover and his friend have followed them and courtesy demands that they should be invited to join in an open-air banquet. The first scene presents the group in relaxed ease. Graziano, invited by the company, tells them a story from Boccaccio's *Decamerone*; the sound of music can be heard; Cavicchio enters to add to the entertainment by playing some melodies and later by narrating an amusing tale. Gradually, in the midst of this group atmosphere, the personalities of individuals begin to become apparent; rascally Pedrolino offers to aid young

Orazio, Isabella shows herself attracted by her lover, Pantalone urges her to guard her honour and, when she becomes angry, humbly begs her pardon, Graziano makes advances to Flaminia, Burattino is all intent on teaching his daughter Olivetta how to tend the garden. The act comes to an end with the laying of Pedrolino's trick to hoodwink the jealous husband and aid the lovers; he persuades Pasquella, when the time comes, to take Isabella into a room of her cottage (where Orazio will be concealed) and he bribes Burattino to present a basket of figs to Orazio as though these were a present from a neighbouring friend named Tofano, so that the young lover may be given a convincing story to explain his leaving the party: Pantalone will be fully prepared to believe he has gone off to Tofano's house and his suspicions will be lulled.

The stage thus set, the play proceeds. Wandering singers perform; benches and chairs are set out, and an entertainment of dancing follows, provided by Olivetta and some village girls. Horns sound without; Capitano Spavento, who loves Flaminia, enters with his fellow-huntsmen. Confections of all kinds, fruit and wine, are brought in; the merriment becomes more and more hilarious, while Graziano grows more than a little tipsy. At last, when Pedrolino gives her the signal, Isabella tells her husband she must retire for a little; she is led by Pasquella into the cottage, where of course she meets her Orazio, while Pantalone jealously holds the door.

The music still plays in the final act. Isabella begs Orazio to play a Roman tune on his guitar. Pantalone agrees to give Flaminia in marriage to the Capitano, and then, tired out, dozes off in his chair. Pedrolino, indefatigable, cheats Graziano into going to bed in the cottage with Pasquella instead of, as he thinks, with Flaminia; Pasquella rushes in, crying out that she has been raped—whereupon her husband, Burattino, naïvely enquires from Pantalone whether through Graziano's escapade he must now consider himself a cuckold. On Pantalone's answering in the affirmative, Burattino declares that, in that case, he is not alone; he then proceeds to tell a story about a jealous husband who held the door for his wife and her lover. The story so closely parallels what has actually happened that poor Pantalone—as was of course intended—cannot help but realise how he has been cheated. His outraged cries are, however, finally stilled when Orazio assures him that Isabella has been the true sufferer; Pantalone had married her as a young girl at a time when he knew that he himself was impotent. Confessing the truth, the old man gives up his wife to Orazio, the Capitano marries Flaminia and Olivetta is released from her garden cares to become Pedrolino's bride.

La Fortuna di Flavio

PANTALONE, a Venetian merchant living in Rome

FLAMINIA, his daughter
FRANCESCHINA, his maid-servant
GRILLO, his servant

ORAZIO, a Turkish gentleman converted to Christianity, in love with Flaminia
PEDROLINO, his servant

CAPITANO SPAVENTO, formerly betrothed to Lidia, now in love with Flaminia

MORAT, his slave, really FLAVIO, Pantalone's long lost son

GRAZIANO, a charlatan
ARLECCHINO, his associate
TURCHETTO, a singer, really a Turkish girl ALIFFA, Orazio's sister

BURATTINO, an innkeeper

CINZIO, the Governor's nephew

LIDIA, in love with Capitano Spavento, disguised as a pilgrim

---

The admixture here of cuckolding comedy and country delights may well be contrasted with the romantic spirit of the third example, *La fortuna di Flavio*. Once more, the same essential characters appear—Pantalone, with his daughter Flaminia and his servant Franceschina; Orazio, a Turkish gentleman turned Christian, with Pedrolino; Capitano Spavento with his slave Morat; Burattino, an innkeeper; a young gentleman Cinzio, and Lidia disguised as a pilgrim. For good measure

12

13 A PLAY WITHIN A PLAY

15   ZANNI DELIVERS A LETTER

Graziano comes in, not as a Doctor but as a wandering charlatan, accompanied by his accomplice Arlecchino and by Turchetto, a singer and dancer.

The plot tells of confusions and misunderstandings and romantic passions. Capitano Spavento is misled into thinking Flaminia is a courtesan and her father Pantalone a pander; Orazio falls in love with her, and weeps to hear how desolate her father, Pantalone, is over the loss of his son; this son is discovered in the slave Morat, who, however, is plunged from joy into mental distress because he had promised his sister, Flaminia, to Orazio, and now finds her the object of the Capitano's attentions—and to the Capitano he owes his life; fortunately at this moment the military gentleman receives information from Arlecchino that his neglected sweetheart, Lidia, has followed him to the city disguised as a pilgrim, and his wonder at her fidelity leads him to give up his new love. In the midst of all this series of adventures Graziano, like the hero of Jonson's *Volpone*, sets up his bench in the open square, endeavouring to attract an audience by the aid of Arlecchino's jests and Turchetto's singing. All ends happily, the Capitano reunited to Lidia, the noble Orazio winning Flaminia and Pedrolino espousing Franceschina.

Still another quite delightful romance, by no means dissimilar in its variegated episodes from Shakespeare's romantic comedies.

WORDS AND ACTIONS

Obviously, the scope of the Italian comedy must later be more closely examined, but for the moment these three examples may serve as a foundation on which to base some general observations.

In the first place, all the three pieces are clearly fully developed comedies, and here it has to be emphasised firmly that, although clownish tricks played a considerable part in the commedia dell'arte and although certainly such clownish tricks appeared in more blatantly extended forms among the poorer troupes, the typical dramatic works with which we are at present concerned were indeed comedies and not, as some puritanically minded contemporaries declared, merely collections of buffooneries. Those who were experts in the theatrical realm realised this truth without any doubt and were precise in their instructions. Pier Maria Cecchini, who created the role of Fritellino, declared that laughter in these performances should be like salt with food and that the aim should be to produce a 'commedia', not a 'buffoneria'. His companion, Niccolò Barbieri, known as Beltrame, similarly stresses that the true commedia dell'arte play is 'not a piece of buffoonery' but a tasteful entertainment, 'well-balanced and sober, witty and not full of impertinent trivialities.... Laughter arising from comedy and laughter born of buffoonery are alike laughter, but the one derives from wit or clever dialogue, the other from excessive agility.... The comedian produces laughter as the sauce to his skilful speeches; the stupid buffoon makes it the be-all and end-all of his display.'* We may, therefore, base any

15

further observations on recognition of the fact that the core of the commedia dell'arte was a play in which clownish episodes might and did assuredly occur but which was not designed simply as an assemblage of largely unconnected farcical incidents. There is no reason for regarding it differently from, let us say, the Stratford-upon-Avon *Tempest* when Peter Brook justifiably introduced a great deal of rough-and-tumble business for Stephano and Trinculo; the play remained a play, and the rough-and-tumble business must have been precisely similar in commedia dell'arte productions of the better kind.

A second fundamental fact must also be firmly grasped. This comedy was based on a combination of language and action, not on pantomime alone. Often those who, in our own times, make an attempt to describe commedia dell'arte performances tend to stress the movements of the actors and to insist upon their purely physical tricks; yet this is a false view. When Casanova, himself the son of an actress and always an admirer of the commedia dell'arte style, turned to analyse the interpretation of Arlecchino given by a skilled contemporary actor—apparently Antonio Sacchi—he concentrated not on the performer's admirable acrobatic skill but on his words. 'The substance of his witty speeches,' he said, 'always fresh and spontaneous, is so disjointed and confused, its strange phrases composed of such a collection of words suited for themes of an entirely different kind and so unexpectedly applied to what he is talking about, so replete with divers ridiculous metaphors, that it would seem as though the whole must prove but a formless chaos; yet this method finds full justification in the very disorder of the style he alone knows how to manage....The intelligent spectator must recognise that this actor is gifted with a most lively imagination and a mind stocked with a medley of divers notions and dissociated ideas which at the moment of action revel confusedly in his head but which he controls and utilises with a mastery so skilful as, by a kind of magic, to compel even the most sophisticated members of his audience to submit to the illusion and in spite of themselves to laugh, applaud and acknowledge their admiration. This actor has the unique and inimitable gift of being able to make his audience share in the entanglements of those speeches: he plunges in and emerges with the wittiest confusions of intricate rhetoric; boldly he goes on, appears so lost that he cannot get out again, then in a moment wriggles out of his predicament and issues from the labyrinth just as the most attentive spectator, duped by his desperate circumlocutions, is at last convinced that he cannot escape. Finally he stops without having reached any conclusion—indeed having demonstrated that no conclusion could possibly be reached: he has carried the confusion to its absolute limits. Arlecchino then appears to be in despair and in a torment of exasperation: no one can refrain from laughing, confronted by this constant bubbling up of images enlivened by a sublime genius which thus can utilise them in a manner beyond description.'*

If this is true for such a character as Arlecchino, by tradition a stage figure whose

16 THE CAPTAIN, THE MAIDSERVANT, THE HEROINE, PANTALONE AND ZANNI

art relies greatly upon his acrobatic skill, it is obviously still more so for his companions—the loquacious Dottore, the Capitano with his outlandish bombast, the lovers with their lyrical ecstasies. Without the use of words, those scenes of 'equivoque' which formed so significant a part of many plays would have been impossible. Somewhat to our surprise we find that much even of the farcical business, where we should expect action alone, is in fact based on words. It may be, as some have supposed, that at the start such pieces of stage business did depend entirely, or almost entirely, upon physical movement, but certainly the catalogue of those stage tricks prepared by Placido Adriani indicates free use of dialogue.* The trick which he calls 'Pulcinella's kindness' shows the Capitano, who at the moment does not recognise with whom he is speaking, saying he would like to kill Pulcinella; the latter immediately starts to praise himself, declaring, 'Pulcinella is a pleasant fellow, simple and good-natured'. So the trick of the fly finds Pulcinella ordered by Pantalone to stay on guard outside his master's house; Pantalone comes in, asks if anyone is there and

Pulcinella assures him not a fly is stirring. When Pantalone enters he finds his house full of people; he comes out in a passion, and is told, 'But you didn't find any flies there, only men and women'. This dependence upon words needs constant emphasis precisely because it is constantly overlooked. In several recent books on the commedia dell'arte the name of Charlie Chaplin has been familiarly invoked as though he were the living embodiment of this style of theatre. Nothing could be more in error. Everyone recognises Charlie Chaplin's genius as a pantomimic actor; everyone equally recognises that his skill evaporates when he turns to dialogue. The truly talented exponents of the commedia dell'arte depended upon both.

In still another respect the invoking of Charlie Chaplin's name may lead us astray—and this brings us to a consideration of the third fundamental quality in the Italian comedy. Although Chaplin appears with other actors in his films, quite clearly he is dominant; the others hardly matter at all. But the plays which have been briefly summarised above demonstrate that they are not vehicles for a single star; their effect arises from their presentation of a closely intertwined group of characters. The emphasis in all these plays is upon the entire company brought upon the stage; in none of the three selected instances, which are thoroughly typical of the half-a-hundred dramas in the Scala collection, does the author single out one figure and make him the chief. Confirmation from those who were actively engaged in such productions may be found in a diversity of places. Sufficient be it here to note Cecchini's basic rules: all the various parts, he insists, bring delight to the audience, but the actors must be careful to see that they do not, by exploiting their individual roles, 'snap the thread of the comedy' and so, 'by their digressions, make the audience forget the plot'.* Every actor must remember that, when a second player enters, he should at once give him place; he should not interrupt this second player, and especially, if he is taking a comic role, he should not engage in ridiculous business while a serious speech is being delivered—this 'may amuse a hundred boobies in the audience, but it will offend ten more intelligent spectators', and the latter are 'more to be esteemed than all the rest'.

Serious speeches and ridiculous clowning, merry servants and fervent lovers, old men and young, all have their apportioned parts in this comedy, all contribute to the general symphony, the art of all is controlled by the purpose of the play in which they appear.

CHARACTERISATION

Having thus glanced at these fundamentals, we may turn to consider the kinds of character, or rather the particular methods employed in presenting the characters, peculiar to the commedia dell'arte plays, and here perhaps for the moment it may be wise to concentrate mainly upon one person—the figure of Pantalone.

The three selected comedies show that for the most part the same individuals are presented in each. Arlecchino is absent from one play, Burattino from another; Cavicchio makes an entry only in *Il vecchio geloso*; but in all three the rest of the cast are basically the same, and in all three Pantalone heads the list of dramatis personae. In the first he displays himself merely as the father-head of a household, in the second he jealously tries to keep his young wife from a young lover, in the last he is a parent grieving bitterly over the loss of a son. The several situations are entirely distinct, yet his name and appearance are identical, and, although the various plots call for the expression of distinct emotions, the expression of these emotions is proper to the one character. Obviously this utilisation of identical theatrical figures over and over again is peculiar; and its very peculiarity necessitates at least a brief consideration of a wider question—the ways in which a playwright can present the persons whom he calls into being for the conduct of his plot.

In a drama no opportunity offers itself for such detailed analysis of personality as, for example, exists in the modern psychological novel: the restricted length of a play absolutely forbids anything of such a kind. The dramatist, therefore, is compelled to work for rapid and bold effects, and commonly the greater playwrights of the past have selected one or other of two devices.

The first might be called the 'Shakespearian'. Here the author endeavours to create the effect of a personality, employing all possible stylistic methods to build up the illusion that a single character in one of his plays, to whom perhaps can be given no more than a few score or at most a few hundred lines, is a living being. In Shakespeare's works the illusion derives largely from the poetic medium itself, in Chekhov and Ibsen its source often may be discovered in a kind of concealed symbolism whereby through the interrelations of the various persons in the drama much more is suggested to the audience than can formally be expressed. In addition to this source of the illusion, however, another, less immediately apparent and often neglected, exhibits itself when we look at these dramas more carefully. The characters are no doubt consistently delineated, but the author allows himself, of set purpose, to introduce at times what might be called unexpectednesses, the effect of which is, paradoxically, to emphasise the illusion of a vital personality. Rosalind, herself fathoms deep in love, thus surprisingly utters her love's heresy: 'The poor world is almost six thousand years old, and in all this time there was not any man died in his own person, videlicet, in a love cause. Troilus had his brains dash'd out with a Grecian club; yet he did what he could to die before, and he is one of the patterns of love. Leander, he would have liv'd many a fair year, though Hero had turn'd nun, if it had not been for a hot midsummer-night; for, good youth, he went but forth to wash him in the Hellespont, and, being taken with cramp, was drown'd; and the foolish chroniclers of that age found it was—Hero of Sestos. But these are all lies: men have died from time to time, and worms have eaten them, but not for love.' This is not what we should have looked for from Rosalind, animated by her passion for Orlando; indeed, when we stop to consider the speech, we might well be tempted to think its sentiments more proper for the cynical Jaques. The plain fact is, however, that in real life we are constantly being surprised by seeing or hearing those we know breaking away from an expected norm, and doing or saying things we should not have anticipated. Men and women are not machines, hour by hour, day by day, going through exactly the same motions; their very vitality, their livingness and the essence which differentiates them from the mechanical, rests ultimately in this quality. Thus the playwright who introduces elements of the unexpected shows himself not guilty of inconsistency but simply keenly aware of a basic element in human life which he can exploit, usually, as is proper to the theatre, in a peculiarly bold and effective manner.

Rosalind's speech may stand for scores of other similar speeches in Shakespeare's works, sometimes direct utterances such as this one, sometimes unexpectednesses in behaviour, like the action of the girls in *Love's Labour's Lost* when they bring the shadow of the hospital across the sunshine of courtly badinage, or unexpectednesses of description, like that peculiarly effective and life-giving comment on Sir Nathaniel: 'There, an't shall please you, a foolish mild man; an honest man, look you, and soon dash'd. He is a marvellous good neighbour, faith, and a very good bowler.' Precisely such unexpectednesses abound in the greater Elizabethan plays. These should not be regarded as inconsistencies, resulting from the playwrights' carelessness or incompetence. Evadne in *The Maid's Tragedy*, Vittoria Corombona in *The White Devil*, Hippolito in *The Honest Whore*, have thus been cited as examples of a veering from character consistency; the truth is that their very life depends upon their lapses from a mechanical pattern. The 'Shakespearian' method of character presentation, the illusion it gives of inner reality, depends partly, sometimes largely, upon this device.

Opposed to this 'Shakespearian' method stands the 'Jonsonian'. Here the author strips away from his dramatic character all but a few salient qualities and presents him as a type. Even in that masterpiece, *Volpone*, we can speak only of the hero's lyrical passion for gold, of his savage delight in gulling fools, of his lustfulness—and nothing else. While it is true that such a method of displaying 'humours' properly recognises the extreme restrictions of the stage, clearly the recognition itself finds accompaniment in the abandoning of any real attempt to create an illusion similar to that in Shakespeare's plays. The types are boldly conceived, and they have vigour; but never are we led to view them as real men and women.

A variant in this display of types appears in the melodramas so popular in the early nineteenth century—and here maybe we seem to be approaching closer to the commedia dell'arte. The appearance, however, is deceptive. No doubt in melodrama after melodrama we encounter the same stock types—hero, hero's friend, heroine, villain—but these stock types are, in fact, utilised in a manner directly

contrary to that which distinguishes the three plays we are considering. Each melo-drama introduces essentially identical stock characters under different names and with different costumes, while the sentiments expressed by all are unvarying. Thus the villain will be exhibited now as a country squire, now as a factory owner, now as an eastern potentate, now as the Wandering Dutchman, and every one of these will use the same language, display the same hate and anger, without the slightest variation. The hero's friend may be ploughman, soldier, sailor, clerk, and no possibility exists of distinguishing one from another save through their names and dress.

What the commedia dell'arte discovered was something entirely different. Here a single person, Pantalone let us say, retains his name, costume and essential basic characteristics in successive plays, but he is made to appear in diverse circumstances and in diverse relationships with his companions. The Pantalone of *Il pellegrino fido amante* acts a not very important role as a father with a daughter Flaminia; in *La fortuna di Flavio* he has the same daughter, and he is shown grieving over the loss of his son; in *Il vecchio geloso* he is a central figure, suffering jealousy on account of his wife Isabella. Isabella herself, who is a wife here in love with a young gallant,

21

becomes in *Il pellegrino fido amante* a girl who unexpectedly runs away from her faithful admirer because she does not want to marry. In one play Graziano appears as a Milanese doctor, in another his profession is not clearly specified—he is simply a friend of Pantalone's, easily made drunk, easily hoodwinked—while in a third he appears as a charlatan. Whatever his particular circumstances, his essential personality remains the same; the impression we get is of an individual revealed in different ways through the varying connections he has with his fellows and through the particular positions in life which have been accorded to him. Here, therefore, there is not simply the introduction of stock figures, constantly expressing the same sentiments and always fulfilling the same roles in different plots, as in melodrama; nor is there here the exhibition of definitely limited 'humours' of the Jonsonian sort; rather is there the dramatic presentation of accumulative personalities. If the story is true that Queen Elizabeth asked Shakespeare to show her Falstaff in love and thus brought *The Merry Wives of Windsor* into being, she was seeking precisely what the commedia dell'arte gave to its audiences. Already Shakespeare had introduced Falstaff into two plays, the twin parts of *Henry IV*, but in these the settings, the characters and the relationships of the characters were unvaried, so that in effect the two parts are not separate; instead of two plays, we have only one very long drama of ten acts. But when Falstaff was set, in *The Merry Wives*, within a different framework, a definite approach was being made towards the commedia dell'arte method. The basic differences were that this was an isolated experiment, whereas in the other it was regular practice, and that, with a few exceptions, the characters in *The Merry Wives* were distinct from those in *Henry IV*, whereas in the commedia dell'arte plays the whole collection of theatrical persons were transferred from one piece to another.

We shall be in error, therefore, if we dismiss the commedia characters as 'types'. That they are types in one sense is true, but by their repetition in different circumstances they create the illusion that they are living beings. Had they been merely stock figures, they certainly never would have appealed as they did, nor would they have endured over their stretch of time. What really happened was that the impression of vitality effected within the course of a single Shakespearian play by means of poetic dialogue and the use of the unexpected was built up in the commedia dell'arte through the almost infinite variations rendered possible in long series of plays. Rosalind's surprisingly clear-eyed view of love is paralleled in Isabella's reluctance to marry, and as we watch her from comedy to comedy we are continually being afforded fresh glimpses, sometimes startling, of her vital personality.

This discovery of those concerned with the commedia dell'arte was truly a discovery. Although suggestions of its virtue may be found occasionally here and there, the long history of the drama, with the possible exception of early Roman farces, exhibits nothing comparable with it. Only in some non-dramatic literary areas can a kind of parallel be found. If those scholars are correct who believe that the *Iliad* and the *Odyssey* originally took shape in the form of a multitude of independent lays, then the building-up of Hector, Achilles and Odysseus was effected in this manner. Certainly the personality of Robin Hood came, not from one single work, but from the dozens of ballads celebrating his adventures. Should we seek for a modern example, that may be found in Sherlock Holmes and Dr Watson. Both of these seem to be 'real'—so real that biographies of each have been written; but the illusion of reality results from the accumulative method. A single Sherlock Holmes story may be effective in itself, but the characters must seem flat; it is only as we read on and on that the presentation of diverse facets transforms the two-dimensional into the three-dimensional.

True, all of these examples deviate from the commedia dell'arte plays in that the settings and relationships of the characters remain constant; we usually find Holmes in Baker Street, and his connections with Dr Watson hardly vary. On the other hand, despite this, the method employed is fundamentally the same, and that this method possesses peculiar potency becomes evident when we observe that all the persons to whom reference has been made have impressed themselves strongly on the popular imagination. Robin Hood, like Harlequin, is a figure of international fame, and in many a country the mere sight of an illustration showing a lean-faced man with Inverness cape and deerstalker cap serves for instant perception of a known friend. Cartoonists can use Harlequin, Robin Hood and Holmes freely, and without captions, knowing that these persons will immediately be recognised.

Still a further aspect of this method of character presentation needs to be noticed. By the accumulative process, the various persons may be shown, as it were, in growth. Odysseus, in full vigour at the siege of Troy, becomes older during his years of wandering; Robin Hood is shown both at the beginning of his outlaw's career and at its melancholy end; in the commedia dell'arte plays Isabella and her companions are now younger, now slightly older, from comedy to comedy. Besides this, the long endurance of the commedia dell'arte permitted another kind of growth, the nearest parallel to which might perhaps be found in the changing popular conceptions of Robin Hood from medieval times to modern. While it is undoubtedly true, as will later be seen, that one cause of the commedia dell'arte's decline during the late seventeenth and early eighteenth centuries may be traced to the fundamental changes made by some eccentric actors in their time-honoured roles, it is also true that gradual development and expansion were fully in keeping with this peculiar theatrical style. Significant here is the title of one of Marivaux's plays, *Arlequin poli par l'amour*; 'Harlequin refined by love' truly embodies the concept which that author had in view—and it was a concept which harmonised with the previous career of Harlequin. As has already been noted, when we first meet him he appears in a costume heavily and irregularly patched; during the seventeenth century the patches become formalised, and in the century following his characteristic costume becomes ever neater and more elegant. So, too, with his personality: the actor Giuseppe Biancolelli endows him with wit, Antonio Visentini makes his acrobatic agility finer and more delicate, and Marivaux's view of him exactly corresponds with such a natural growth in his being. Yet, in spite of all, Casanova's description of Antonio Sacchi's Arlecchino is not basically at variance with what we know of Tristano Martinelli's in 1600, and if we compare portraits of these two, separated by a century and a half, there can be no doubt concerning their identity. So, too, Goldoni was fully justified in making his Pantalone more staid and sober, thus adapting him to his own purposes; the fundamental Pantalone remains, only time has laid a spell on him and made him gentler. The change that Shakespeare shows in Lear is precisely the same, foreshortened time and violent incident achieving an effect more rapid than, but not different in kind from, that wrought over the years in the old father of the commedia.

Occasionally, of course, an originally well-established character might go completely, but in such instances a new figure was apt to take the place of that which had vanished. A typical example of this is the substitution of the French Pierrot for an original Pedrolino. In Scala's plays Pedrolino pushes himself forward as a gay-witted confident intriguer; Pierrot becomes the very image of sad-eyed simplicity. That the one took his name from the other seems certain; yet the two are completely distinct. Such developments, however, are rare, and in their rarity throw emphasis upon the more enduring features of the commedia dell'arte's style. Nor are they in essence entirely alien to that style itself, since they testify to the power inherent in this theatrical form to admit dynamic growth.

IMPROVISATION

The three plays selected from Scala's collection illustrate still another, and very important, feature of the commedia dell'arte. Unlike other dramatic works, they offer no dialogue for the characters introduced; all that the author provides is a series of entries and exits, with indications of the 'business' of the various scenes. This 'business' involves, not merely instructions concerning what the characters are to do, but also instructions as to what they are to say. A typical example of a second-act opening will make this clear:

OLIVETTA: sent by Flaminia to speak to Isabella about Orazio:

at this

PEDROLINO, from Isabella's house, learns from Olivetta how she has come to talk to Isabella on Orazio's and the Capitano's account. Pedrolino sends her indoors, saying she should leave everything in his hands: she goes in and he remains.

What the commedia dell'arte discovered, in addition to the invention of a special method of portraying dramatic characters, was the virtue of improvisation, whereby

24

the actors became themselves their own authors. At various times, in different companies and among individual players, the amount of improvisation certainly fluctuated, but from beginning to end improvisation was what determined the special quality of the Italian style and distinguished it from other stage methods. Recently, some attempts have been made to deny this truth; yet truth it remains.

Quite clearly, skill in improvisation is not granted to everyone, and clearly, also, it depends ultimately upon native ability, even although training can play its part in bringing it to perfection. Hence we need not be surprised to find talented amateurs winning esteem alongside of professionals. The common interpretation of the term, commedia dell'arte, assumes that 'arte' means what 'the quality' did in Elizabethan theatrical parlance, what 'the profession' means today. The existence of these amateurs, however, suggests that another sense must be attached to the word. The very first full description of a commedia dell'arte performance refers to an amateur production; during the mid-seventeenth century at Rome the artist Salvator Rosa often left his easel to act improvised comedies with his fellow painters; at Warsaw in 1640 the papal nuncio Filomardi was scandalised to learn that some ecclesiastics were behind the costumes and masks in performances sponsored by Ladisław IV;

had this worthy cleric lived on to about 1720 he would have been still more scandalised to find Dom Placido Adriani, Benedictine monk of San Severino near Naples, not only devoting time and labour to collecting and composing such pieces but actually encouraging fellow monks and priests to present the plays—himself winning distinction in the part of Pulcinella. Dozens of similar records have come down to us, and in several there is evident not simply a hesitant aping of the professional style, but even a confident contempt of those who engaged in these things for purposes of gain.* In view of the evidence, the common interpretation of the meaning of 'commedia dell'arte' will not serve; rather must we think of 'arte' in what was in early times a familiar connotation, as 'special ability' or 'singular talent'. Thus the kind of theatrical entertainment with which we are concerned may fittingly be regarded as the 'comedy of skill'.

At the same time, our attention must clearly be concentrated mainly on the work of the professionals, since, despite the activities of the amateurs, the professional actors were responsible for carrying on this tradition through its long career and since constant practice in addition to native ability was required to bring the art to its fullest perfection. We need not, in fact, be surprised to find that the names of many among those most famous in the pursuit of this theatrical style were repeated over many generations. The Biancolelli family may serve as an example. The first of this name known to us is a Francesco during the first half of the seventeenth century: he married Colombina, the daughter of a Pantalone. Their son, born in 1636, became a far-famed Arlecchino and was affectionately nicknamed 'Dominique'; he married a Eularia, daughter of Florinda. One of his own daughters won success in the role of Isabella, another was even more popular for her Colombina, while his son acted first as Arlecchino and later as Pierrot and Trivellino. This son's wife also came from the profession, a Colombina, daughter of a Scaramuccia and his wife, Marinetta, and the tradition was carried on by his daughter, Maria Teresa, who was on the stage as late as 1762. Similar records of family traditions and ramifications abound during the two hundred and fifty years of the commedia dell'arte's history, a symbol of the inherited skill and strict training necessary for those who aimed at true success in this profession.

Here, however, we must be on our guard: the work of these actors has to be viewed objectively if we are to reach the truth; all kinds of sentimentality have to be laid aside. First, we are compelled to accept the facts that many of those who earned their livings by assuming commedia dell'arte roles were little more than charlatans' accomplices and that many others who took their places in regular companies lacked the skill necessary to give distinction to their performances. In 1585 a vivid if dismal picture is presented of such a troupe. They arrive at a small town and an audience assembles: 'There is an orchestra that sounds like the braying of asses and the drone of hornets; then comes a prologue fit for a charlatan's harangue.... There

is a tiresome plot which bores you to distraction, villainously bad intermezzi; a Pantalone not worth a farthing; a Zanni who looks like a goose; a Graziano who vomits out his words; a Bawd stupid and insipid; a Lover whose speeches are a torment to listen to; a Spanish Captain, with nothing to say save '*mi vida*' and '*mi corazon*'; a Pedant who stumbles over his Tuscan phrases every minute; a Burattino whose whole humour consists in putting his cap on his head; a Signora, with a monstrous voice, with the speech of the dead, and the movements of a sleep-walker, one who has an eternal quarrel with the Graces and a mortal dissension with beauty.'*
And from this year 1585 onwards numerous accounts of similar poverty-stricken performances crowd in upon us. While, however, due weight must be given to such evidence, it should not attract our attention away from the truly talented actors of the time. After all, we do not despise and neglect Shakespeare because the decades during which he lived produced numerous dull, stupid and worthless comedies and tragedies, and because several contemporaries condemned the English stage of that time in terms hardly less severe.

Our attention, then, must be focused on the more important companies, but even

27

here caution is demanded. It would be false to think of groups of dedicated artists, all eager to give of their best to the public, all intent on perfecting their peculiar form of theatrical entertainment. Scores of letters are extant written by the most famous players of the seventeenth century; in not one of these appears a single sentence, even a single fragmentary phrase, alluding to their art. What does confront us is a record of personal complaints directed against their fellows, of petty rivalries, of contending passions among the actresses, of husbands and lovers drawn into bitter back-stage conflicts. Says G. B. Andreini to the Duke of Mantua in 1614: 'The whole of this company was in arms, although they fought each other more with sharp words than swords.... Thank God I managed to pacify them—but who knows for how long? I am precisely like a man who succeeds for a moment in blocking up a torrent; in another moment the dam will be shattered and the water will come gushing and flooding out more fiercely than before.'*

20 ISABELLA AND ORAZIO

'The great rivalries which disunite this company', a lament uttered by Francesco Calderoni in 1664, is a phrase echoed again and again throughout these years. Sometimes only two actors were involved, as in the violent name-callings between Carlo Cantù and his fellow-player, the Dottore, in 1647. Usually, a whole company was swept into the fight, and usually, too, the source of the trouble lay in the actresses, animated both by professional jealousy and by personal attachments. As Gozzi wryly remarks in his memoirs, 'among actresses, the term friendship is something fabulous; for this term they immediately substitute the word love, and refuse to admit any distinctions. They refer to friendship triflingly only when they are by themselves, and then it is accompanied by a deluge of protestations and Judas

28

kisses.' In 1609 Virginia Andreini wrote to Cardinal Gonzaga, informing him that she had 'hurled to the ground every trophy set up by Signora Flaminia' and had 'pulled her nose down just as much as she had stuck it up in her pride'; she further reports that this Flaminia, although supported by her husband, 'is loathed because of the affair she is having with Cinzio'. Typical of the kind of confusion which could, and often did, rage behind the scenes is the affair that disrupted the great company of the 'Confidenti' in 1618. The two chief actresses, Lavinia and Valeria, hated each other, and the former's outstanding success in a particular play brought matters to a head. The whole affair thrust into the open a tangled web of conflicting emotions. Ortensio, Lavinia's husband, takes her part, but the effectiveness of his aid becomes lessened when that lady energetically accuses him of carrying on an intrigue with Nespola, while Valeria draws in Fulvio, her own particular admirer. The battle rages merrily, Lavinia declaring that she would rather starve or 'eat roots' than step on the same stage as Nespola, her husband wretchedly lamenting that he is forced to live 'in a constant inferno', Valeria, with the aid of Fulvio, desperately trying to outwit her rival. Reading records such as these, we can fully appreciate the heart-felt sigh breathed by Francesco Allori when he reported to the Duke of Mantua in 1675: 'Here we have just finished our season with good houses and general acclaim—and what is more important, with excellent concord in the company.'

Occasionally, these troubles refused to remain back-stage. As early as 1567 we hear of a kind of Capulets-and-Montagues strife in Mantua over the rival claims of Flaminia and Vincenza—no doubt stimulated largely by the ladies themselves; about a century later, in 1651, the Modena company, then in Bologna, received letters warning them not to proceed to Padua as they had intended, since that city was divided into two camps, one supporting the Modena troupe's Angiolina, the other supporting a rival Armellina; the poor actors were told that they would risk life and limb were they to enter into this arena.

A third point may be made here. Our knowledge of these troubles derives largely from letters sent by the actors themselves to the noble dukes and princes who were their patrons. From the very start such patronage was widespread and intimate; the greater companies moved from court to court, and at times anxious missives were despatched from one chancellery to another, begging that particular players should be given leave to proceed to give delectation to the courts concerned. The Emperor Matthias in 1614 commanded a patent of nobility to be issued to Pier Maria Cecchini, the creator of the role of Fritellino, thus putting him 'in the ranks of gentlemen and peers, as if he had been born a nobleman from gentle grandsires both on his father's and on his mother's side'. Thus, dismissing from our minds the motley array of charlatans' accomplices and the pitiful meaner troupes which set up their trestle-stages in market squares or inns, we are sometimes tempted to think of the larger and more distinguished actors as enjoying a glorious career, befriended

21 THE CAPTAIN, HARLEQUIN, THE HEROINE AND LUCIA

by princes and speaking to them in terms of surprising familiarity. Such a picture requires to be qualified by consideration of two things. First, the whims of princes in those days were apt to be somewhat arbitrary and eccentric. Angelo Costantini, the famous Mezzettino, was also ennobled when he went to serve the Elector August II, but, having dared to offer his attentions to that monarch's mistress, he was promptly arrested and remained for over twenty years immured in the castle of Königstein. Apart from such mishaps, when comedian-nobles overstepped their privileges, thought must be given to the general run of what Domenico Bruni, in one of his prologues, styled 'the miseries of the actors'. For them 'the delights of travelling about the world' were 'rainstorms, ice-storms, snow-storms, wretched inns, surly innkeepers, knock-kneed horses, broken-down carriages, impertinent boatmen, importunate coachmen, inquisitive port officials and custom-house in-spectors—all the other similar delights which are the constant accompaniments of theatrical joys'. And the miseries were increased when, for one reason or another, the company's receipts ran low. In 1690, the important Modena troupe was constrained to despatch a pitiful letter from Brescia addressed to their lord. Because of the 'inclement winter weather' they found themselves 'in deplorable misery', with 'takings not enough to pay for lodgings'. If aid were not to arrive, they asserted, 'the company will not be able to leave the town without pawning their costumes'.*

Nevertheless, despite the presence of scores of incompetent actors, despite the trials, the petty jealousies and the internecine feuds, the testimony of contemporaries bears full witness to the brilliance achieved in many of the performances; while the careful instructions given by such players as Barbieri and Cecchini prove that this brilliance was based, first, on an inborn dexterity and talent, and, secondly, on a training stricter and more exacting than that which would ordinarily be demanded of a player whose business was merely the interpretation of a dramatist's lines— a training which could be secured only within the circuit of a compact professionalism.

LITERARY DISCIPLINE

All those, both the practising experts and the observers, who turned to comment on the style of the commedia dell'arte were agreed that a sharp distinction had to be drawn between the qualities necessary for success in an interpreter of written dramatic texts, and the very special qualities which alone could produce an effective exponent of this particular style.

Concerning the primal requirements there was no matter of doubt: both suppleness of body and a lively imagination were demanded. Evaristo Gherardi speaks of 'a good actor in the Italian style', explaining that by a good actor in the Italian style is meant a man who is resilient, who uses his imagination more than his memory, who composes, during the very moment of his action, whatever dialogue he utters. Added to this, an ability to act in concert with others was positively essential: 'Above all, the actor must see that he does not speak while another is speaking, lest he create an objectionable confusion in the minds of the audience'; this actor must 'support anyone with whom he is playing, harmonising his words and actions so well with those of his companion that he responds perfectly in his whole performance, in all his movements, to whatever his fellow-actor demands, in such a manner as to give the impression to the audience that the pair have worked out their business beforehand'.*

Promptitude, therefore, imagination and adaptability were all prerequisites, and these in no mean measure. 'This kind of comedy', remarks one commentator, 'does not admit of mediocrity in the actors; it is absolutely necessary that they should be excellent.'* Naturally, such excellence was rare: 'The Italian actors learn nothing by heart.... To act in a play all they need do is to look at the plot a minute or two before going on stage. Thus the greatest beauty of their pieces is inseparable from the action, the success of their comedies depending absolutely upon the actors who give them their charm, greater or less according to the skill of the players themselves and to the

31

situation, bad or good, in which they happen to be performing. It is this necessity of playing on the spot which makes it so difficult to replace a good Italian actor when unhappily a vacancy occurs in a company. Everyone can learn by heart and repeat on the stage what he has memorised, which is quite another thing from what an Italian actor does.'* 'In this art', declares Niccolò Barbieri, 'there is required a talent granted to but few; out of a hundred who try their hands at it, not ten prove successful.'*

Imagination in itself, of course, was not enough; the actors had to study hard, but instead of reading plays they read the best literature of the time, especially those books which might have been familiar to the kinds of character they represented. In one of his prologues Domenico Bruni writes an address intended to be spoken by the Servetta, the Maidservant; the lines are penned in character, so that the Maidservant of the play pretends she is also the servant of her fellow actors. A new piece is to be performed. 'Just listen,' she cries to the audience, 'this morning the Prima Donna calls me: "Ricciolina, bring me Boccaccio's *Fiammetta*; I want to study it." Pantalone asks me for Calmo's *Letters*, the Capitano for *Le bravure di Capitano Spavento*, the Zanni for Bertoldo's *Jests*, the *Book of Pastimes* and *The Hours of Recreation*, Graziano for the *Sayings of the Philosophers* and for the latest *Anthology*; Franceschina wants the *Celestina* to help her play the bawd, and the Lover calls for Plato's *Works*.'* The picture thus presented is a fascinating one. Instead of seeing the members of a company all intent on memorising their lines from parts or printed texts, we watch each one seeking to stimulate the imagination by leafing through non-dramatic writings of a kind appropriate to the role. The only works mentioned which might provide actual dialogue are the *Celestina* and Francesco Andreini's series of extravagant rodomontades supposed to be uttered by Capitano Spavento; the rest are poems, letters, philosophical disquisitions.

The Lover's choice, the *Works* of Plato, does not enter here as a jest. Many modern actors, especially perhaps English and American, are afraid of books; the best commedia dell'arte players were truly learned and, in best Stanislavski method, steeped themselves in the literary pursuits of those they portrayed; furthermore, the critical part of the audience expected this of them. Today, we should not expect a reviewer, in introducing a new actress, to rest her claims to distinction upon the facts that she was a Ph.D. and freely associated with literary societies; but that is precisely what Nicolas Boindin did in welcoming Elena Balletti to Paris in 1716. 'This', he wrote, 'is a woman of great wit and a fine actress: one proof of her wit is that she has been deemed worthy of election to four academies, in Rome, Ferrara, Bologna and Venice.'* His conclusion is that therefore her skill in improvisation must be excellent.

'The actors of today', writes Niccolò Barbieri, 'are such that there is not a good book they have not read, a witty conceit they have not appropriated, a fine piece of description they have not imitated, a deep thought they have not made their own; they are always reading, always gathering beauties from books.'* Particularly, of course, was this necessary for the cultured Lovers: they had, indeed, to go far beyond mere reading. In his instructions to actors intending to play these parts, Andrea Perrucci starts by advising them to study good books written in perfect Tuscan, but he soon proceeds further to tell them that, in addition, they require to master all 'the figures of speech and tropes used in rhetoric'. 'But', he interjects, 'you will say to me: "Oh, you want the actor to be so learned that it will be exceedingly hard to find anyone of such capability." "That may be so," I reply, "but the more he studies rhetoric the better actor he will be."' Hence he insists that the player who aims to shine in this profession must make himself thoroughly familiar with the meanings and applications of 'metaphor, metonymy, synecdoche, autonomasy, catachresis, metathesis, allegory and irony—protasis, aphorism, syncope, comparison, apocope, antithesis, systole'—and so on through a long list of rhetorical devices. And, not content with that, he later provides a series of specimen speeches, inserting footnote references to the rhetorical devices exemplified. Thus, his soliloquy for a despairing Lover begins: 'Look not for any peace, my heart; having become a slave to this beauty's tyranny, you are dazzled by the sun's rays and your torments cannot be assuaged.' In order to make Perrucci's comments clear, this must be given in the original Italian: 'Non isperar[a] pace, cuor mio; sendo[b] soggetto alla tirannide del bello, t'abbarbaglio[c] la luce d'un sole, nè puoi temprare[d] le tue pene.' The notes explain: (a) 'protasis, adding letters at the beginning of a word: "isperare" for "sperare"; (b) apheresis, cutting off letters at the beginning of a word: "sendo" for "essendo"; (c) epenthesis, adding letters in the middle of a word: "abbarbagliare" for "abbagliare"; (d) syncope, cutting out something from the middle of a word: "temprare" for "temperare".'*

Some of the actors, no doubt, had but sketchy educations, but numbers of them were like Pier Francesco Biancolelli, who before he came to the stage had been given by his father, the great Arlecchino, a profound classical education under the Jesuits. Perrucci's instructions, therefore, are not to be regarded as the impractical meanderings of a mere theorist. He was writing with full knowledge of what the commedia dell'arte demanded and of what could be found among its more distinguished practitioners.

The younger Biancolelli followed his father in taking the part of Arlecchino, and this reminds us that it was not only the Lovers who benefited from their learning. Casanova, in praising Antonio Sacchi, spoke of 'the grace' inherent in the 'elegant inculture' of his speeches, and Goldoni explains its source: 'Antonio Sacchi possessed a keen and brilliant imagination, and he was a marvellous commedia dell'arte player. Where other Harlequins merely repeated the same things over and over again, he always penetrated deeply into the scenes he acted, by means of continually fresh witticisms and unexpected replies, thus ever keeping the action lively....His comic tricks and his facetious lines were not drawn from popular speech nor from that of other actors. He put to use the works of dramatists, poets, orators, philosophers; in his improvised speeches could be recognised thoughts worthy of Seneca, Cicero, Montaigne; and he had the skill to adapt the deepest concepts of these great men to the simplicity of the foolish character he represented, so that the thought itself, worthy of admiration in a serious author, became thoroughly laughable when it issued from the mouth of this excellent actor.'*

No surprise need be felt, therefore, when we observe that dozens of the more famous players applied themselves to the literary art during such leisure as their acting careers allowed them, and that the range of such works occupies a by no means unimportant place in seventeenth-century writing. As might be expected, some of them turned to the penning of plays; G. B. Andreini, for example, has a long series of dramatic compositions, among them the *Adamo* (1614) which well may have formed part of Milton's inspiration when he was planning *Paradise Lost*. More significant are the almost innumerable poems and prose-works penned by the comedians from the time when Isabella Andreini composed her *Lettere* (published 1607) and *Rime* (collected in one volume 1696), winning for these writings no less than for her acting the promise of that 'Aeterna Fama' assured her on the medal struck in her honour. It is significant that when her husband, Francesco, prepared the *Lettere* for publication he described her on the title page as 'Member of the Company of the "Gelosi" and of the Accademia degli Intenti'.

Isabella Andreini and Elena Balletti were certainly not the only players to become members of well-known learned and literary academies, and occasionally the distinctions were higher still. The 'academic' affiliations of these actors and actresses find ample illustration in two particular ways. First, the names given to the early sixteenth- and seventeenth-century companies—the 'Gelosi', the 'Desiosi', the 'Confidenti' and the like—are clearly modelled on the names of similar type adopted by the associations of the learned in so many Italian cities. This means that the actors themselves, in the pursuit of their art, aspired to enter into the academic orbit. And, secondly, the learned academies themselves not only took a lively interest in the affairs of their theatrical companions but also freely acknowledged their admiration. Typical of this is the declaration of the famous Accademia degli Intronati of Siena that the actress Vincenza Armani in her improvised speeches composed more exquisitely than could the most skilful authors seated at their desks.*

ACTORS AND PARTS

Towards making this improvisation effective the actors were aided in two distinct and different ways. It is obvious that, at the very start, they possessed a double advantage—the parts which they took were normally the same, and with these parts the spectators were familiar. Occasionally, an individual actor abandoned one role to assume another, as Francesco Andreini did when he set aside the Lover in order to devote himself to the Captain, or modified the role, as Giuseppe Domenico Biancolelli altered the nature of his Harlequin, or invented a fresh role, as Angelo Costantini created Mezzettino; but as a general rule a player, having adopted a character, stayed with that character throughout his whole life. G. B. Andreini played the part of Lelio until he retired aged about 73; Tiberio Fiorilli was Scaramuccia well into his eighties, and Pellesini was still acting Pedrolino when he was 87. Thus, the actor did not have the task of creating dialogue suitable for several entirely separate stage-figures, but could concentrate entirely upon those words which would prove most effective for the character of his choice. Apart from this, as soon as he came upon the stage, he could have the assurance that the public would meet him halfway. In any ordinary play the dramatis personae are unknown to the spectators and on the playwright is imposed the necessity of providing words calculated not only to inform the public concerning the positions in life, the relationships, the interests of the creatures of his imagination but also concerning their natures. In a commedia dell'arte performance, on the other hand, the very costumes worn by the comedians immediately told the audience who they were, and accordingly these actors did not have to seek for lines to explain and establish something utterly unknown. The basic elements of Pantalone's nature had already been fixed; all his interpreter was asked to do was to provide the necessary vitality, to give effective touches to the already familiar person, and, of course, to adjust his Pantalone to the requirements of the various plots.

The second aid provided for the actors may seem to carry them away from the area of improvisation. When they were advised to read books of a style suited to their roles, we realise that this was designed simply to whet their imagination, so that on the basis of such reading they could create their own improvised speech; but in addition to that they were specifically instructed to pen out and to learn by heart a variety of passages which might serve them in good stead during their performances. Each actor thus might well have a notebook filled with suitable material—the 'zibaldone', 'repertorio', 'generici', 'doni', 'dote', or 'squarci', to which we have frequent allusion. Books of practical information such as Perrucci's could provide them with numerous specimens; others such as the *Bravure* (Venice, 1607) written by Francesco Andreini or Antonio Pardi's *Le stupende forze, e bravure del Capitano Spezza Capo* (Bologna, 1606) could be adapted to their particular requirements; still others might be provided by friendly authors, as Gozzi furnished the members of the Sacchi company 'with a long series of stock passages suitable for, and most essential to, my actors'.*

The kinds of stock passages were various. First there came the tags, 'uscite' and 'chiusette', which actors might have on tap to give them sharp and effective conclusions to their scenes. Generally these assumed couplet form, although Perrucci carefully advises the players not to indulge too much in verse, since such verse will seem unrealistic; the couplet endings for the lovers he does, however, permit, since it is quite 'realistic' for those in love to become lyrical. Thus quite appropriately a young gallant, after an unfortunate conversation with his mistress, can leave the stage with

> *Amor, angue tu sei, se il tuo veleno*
> *sen corre al cor mentre mi serpe in seno,*

or some other convenient sentiment.*

More extended are single speeches, devised to serve either as part of a dialogue scene or as soliloquies. At this point, however, several experts are at pains to insist that such memorised passages must not stand out from the rest of the improvised speech. Such a warning applied with particular force when the speech itself was not a soliloquy but part of a dialogue in which another player was involved. A single actor might, for example, have considered the several scenes in which he was due to appear; he might have 'sought out the diverse means by which he could harmonise his dialogue with the action'. But the other actor in one of these scenes might have done precisely the same, planning for himself an entirely different course for the dialogue: 'Here then are the two actors on the stage, each with his concept of his character and situation. Both try to get to the same point—but, compelled

22 HARLEQUIN AND COLOMBINE DANCING

36

to reply sensibly to each other and bound necessarily to the same objectives, each is gradually forced to abandon the path he had planned out, in order to harmonise with his companion.' This seems obvious, and we can only assume that the numerous written dialogues for two persons were, in practice, concerted beforehand. Such dialogues cover all the various principal situations with which lovers might be expected to become involved. Isabella Andreini offers her 'Amorous debate concerning the worthiness of lovers' or her disquisition 'concerning true love' or her discussion 'of the passions of love and hate'. Among Domenico Bruni's offerings are enquiries 'Whether distance aids love' and 'Whether the senses or the intellect are of most importance in love'; here too are an 'Amorous war', a 'Sun and moon', and a 'Parting'.*

For the most part the written scenes are highly mannered according to the literary fashion of the time, and, as Perrucci insists, depend largely on formal patterns and on the extended use of metaphors: 'among these', he remarks, 'I give highest esteem to the long-drawn-out metaphor because there one can see the subtleties of a wit which is able to discover so many varied conceits based on one object'. The lover and his lady talk:

> *Man.* How lucky I am to meet you here!
> *Woman.* What ill luck for me!
> *Man.* See how I adore you.
> *Woman.* See how I despise you.
> *Man.* I shall draw nearer to speak to you.
> *Woman.* I am leaving so as not to look on you.

Here she drops her handkerchief, and the handkerchief itself now forms the focus for a lengthy debate. The lover picks it up, and refuses to return it. On the lady's enquiring what use it can be to him, he replies that it will cure his wounds; 'But there is no balsam on it', she objects; 'That', he says, 'I shall hope for from your pity'. So the game goes on. The handkerchief's whiteness is interpreted by the lover as a symbol of happy peace; it will become a sail of his good fortune, a bandage for _____ e lady for her part stresses its frailty, something _____ whiteness is a symbol of icy chill. Eventually _____ h he likens it to a canvas on which her cruelty _____ ith a piece of paper on which his importunity _____ t as an image of his eternal faith, while she _____ ssion consumed.*

_____ rio calls them, were common, and generally _____ often indeed adding the trick of repeated _____ calls for a 'dialogue'—whether improvised _____ vers 'in which every speech of hers ends

37

"Valerio, you do not love me", and every speech of his "Lucinda, you do not love me".'* The style may seem absurd, but not if we think of these passages as being like arias, and so delivered.

Nor was it only the lovers who had dialogues in this style. We have also a 'Dialogue of a servant and a serving-maid concerning the illness of a lover'—'with a ridiculous extended metaphor' and with much innuendo—beginning:

> *Man.* Hullo there! Anyone at home?
> *Woman.* Who's knocking?
> *Man.* A poor invalid.
> *Woman.* This is not a hospital.
> *Man.* But it's where I can regain my health.
> *Woman.* Who do you think can help you here?
> *Man.* You, my gentle doctor—

and so on, and so on.*

Concerning these memorised passages and the difficulty of reconciling their presence within the improvised style a middle course must be taken. We may agree that, as the commedia dell'arte pursued its course, written scenes more and more intruded. We may also agree that in the passage of time new actors inherited from their predecessors many stock scenes, which they repeated by rote. 'When the same piece is being played', says an observer in the latter part of the eighteenth century, 'the comedians take great care to remember those passages which were effective on the first night, and do not hesitate to make use of them.... The play remains in the repertory; a hundred different comedians come one after another playing the parts; each one brings in something fresh, and at the end the scenes are so filled with business that one is surprised at the amount of witticisms and stage tricks which are presented to us. The actor, to make a success, needs no more than a wide knowledge of theatrical tradition, and thus the improvisation becomes basically an affair of memory, whereby the actor only provides the links between part and part, together with well-arranged dialogue.'*

While this is assuredly true, it is true more for the period of decline in the commedia dell'arte than for the early period when the actors were fresh and when the theatrical tradition had not become so overladen; and we are concerned with the commedia dell'arte rather in its strength than in its weakness. Even so, the descriptions of Sacchi's performance of Arlecchino leave us in no doubt whatsoever that the more talented players even of later times still founded their art basically and deeply upon their skill in improvisation.

During the earlier period we receive the impression that the memorised parts were not so numerous and that they were restricted for the most part to lyrical or rhetorical passages which could stand out independently by themselves apart from the main dialogue of the plays. Thus, for example, in Scala's *La pazzia d'Isabella*, the heroine, being told that her Orazio is dead, loses her wits. She draws Burattino and Franceschina aside, saying she has something of importance to report to them—and at this point the author feels it necessary to depart from his normal practice and to write down the precise words of her lunatic aria. Thus, too, the Capitano could have his solo of blustering boasts and the Dottore his meandering disquisitions—show pieces to be spoken when these characters remained alone or virtually alone upon the stage, without the necessity of combining with others in moving the plot along. Leaving such passages aside, we may believe that improvisation ruled in the main conduct of the plays.

In any event, contemporary comment clearly demonstrates that the more skilled actors were gifted with the power of incorporating any things they had memorised within the fabric of their own words. If Niccolò Barbieri is absolutely correct in stating that 'the comedians study and store their memories with a great mass of things—philosophical sayings, poetic conceits, pleas of love, reproofs, despairs and frenzies—which they have on hand for various occasions', Perrucci is also in the right when he asserts that the better players 'have so great skill in making use of such conceits that what has been carefully memorised seems to be wholly the result of their improvisation'.* They had the skill, too, of continually altering and adjusting what they gave to the public. 'Improvisation', declares Luigi Riccoboni, 'offers scope for variety in the action; you can go again and again to see the same play and each time it will be different. The improvising actor plays more vividly and more naturally than the actor who learns his part.' The 'naturalness' of the Italian plays was constantly being referred to by contemporaries, and we may suspect that what these contemporaries really meant was vitality, liveliness and freshness. 'Gestures and inflections of the voice', according to Charles de Brosses, were here always 'married to the theme'. 'The actors come and go, speak and move as though they were at home.' It was this which gave this theatre 'a naturalness and truth which the very finest playwrights rarely attain'.*

THE FOUR MASKS

It is now time to become better acquainted with the company. The three plays selected as examples have already introduced us to several of the basic figures and have demonstrated that basic figures are those with which we are concerned. Shakespeare's troupe, the Lord Chamberlain's or King's Men, was composed of about a dozen actors; roughly the same number of players composed a typical commedia dell'arte company. Whereas, however, Shakespeare's fellows were accustomed, if need be, to double or treble their roles, with the result that a single play might introduce some twenty-five to thirty characters, doubling in commedia dell'arte performances was, in general, unknown; and consequently, except for a few unusual productions, the number of characters in each play corresponded with the number of actors included in the troupe presenting it. If, therefore, our attention is for the moment focused on the comedies, we are confronted with a group of roughly ten or twelve staple persons.

In the very centre of these are 'the four masks' so frequently referred to by contemporaries, two 'vecchi' or older men and two 'zanni' or servants. One of the very first references to commedia dell'arte performances alludes to 'Magnifichi e Zanni'—Pantalones and their serving-men; a century and a half later Riccoboni speaks of 'the four masked actors of our theatre, the Venetian Pantalone, the Bolognese Dottore and the two servants, Harlequin the Bergamask and Scapin the Lombard';* later still the four figures were named by Goldoni as Pantalone, Dottore, Harlequin and Brighella.

All these characters appeared with masks on their faces, and here again we must pause to observe a further invention of the commedia dell'arte. Masks, of course, had for many ages been frequently associated with stage performances, and it is clear that they possessed certain definite advantages. Primarily they served to stress the essential theatricality of the production itself. The use of the mask, declares a prominent modern director, 'testifies that this is authentic theatre, not a dull reproduction of real life, which is the absurd aim of so much current stage endeavour'.

40

This does not mean, however, that the use of the mask is designed to effect an escape from reality and to lead us into the realm of the artificial: 'for the actor', continues this director, 'the mask serves to create a surreal type' and 'to facilitate a journey into the world of the imagination'.* As another modern author has put it, 'religiously, philosophically and aesthetically the mask consecrates the effacement of immediate reality for the benefit of a vaster reality'.*

In introducing masks into its plays, therefore, the Italian comedians were simply keeping true to the spirit of the theatre they served. At the same time, they found that these masks had a special value for their own kind of performances. A mask has a personality of its own. 'The actor who performs under a mask', insists Jacques Copeau, 'receives from this papier-maché object the reality of his part. He is controlled by it and has to obey it unreservedly. Hardly has he put it on when he feels a new being flowing into himself, a being the existence of which he had before never even suspected. It is not only his face that has changed, it is all his personality, it is the very nature of his reactions, so that he experiences emotions he could neither have felt nor feigned without its aid. If he is a dancer, the whole style of his dance, if he is an actor, the very tones of his voice, will be dictated by this mask—the Latin "persona"—a being, without life till he adopts it, which comes from without to seize upon him and proceeds to substitute itself for him.'* In the light of such a statement, we realise that the employment of masks for at least the more dynamic characters in the commedia dell'arte plays possessed considerable value, and it had the further virtue of placing emphasis on the actor's whole body. Harlequin's personality depends partly on his suppleness; since he is masked, our eyes are intent upon him in his entirety, not merely upon his features; as a result a witticism emanating from that eternally fixed countenance has a flavour quite different from the same witticism issuing out of lips which are part of a living face; and a gesture which might easily be missed when our attention is directed towards a comedian's features suddenly assumes an unwonted and even strange significance.

In its particular use of masks, however, the commedia dell'arte made a special double discovery. Two usual disadvantages of the mask are, first, that, covering the whole face, it may seem to be an inanimate object set on top of a mobile body and, secondly, that the voice may become muffled. Habitually, however, the Italian players avoided the employment of full masks and, instead, wore either half-masks which left the mouth free or else partial masks covering only the nose and part of the cheeks. Thus full freedom for the voice was secured—still further proof that the comedians regarded the dialogue of their plays as being of prime importance—while the inanimate was more effectively combined with the animate.

In addition to this form of the masks employed, the Italian actors introduced a characteristic method in the adapting of those masks to the requirements of their plays. The commedia dell'arte is almost unique in mixing together some actors

41

whose faces are thus concealed and other actors whose faces are open to view. If the masks had been complete, a somewhat awkward cleavage would have resulted, as though we were being confronted by beings from two separate worlds; as it is, the half-masks allowed just the measure of distinction desired without making an absolutely firm line between the one group and the other. The 'four masks' are, accordingly, at once a community of their own and yet not too far removed from their companions: and anyone who has had the opportunity of witnessing a performance in the commedia dell'arte manner will agree that a great part of the effect created depends upon the sharp, and yet not too sharp, juxtaposition of the two sets of dramatic figures.

PATTERNING

We start, then, with these four central characters, with the pair of elderly masters and their servants. The arrangement in pairs is by no means fortuitous. While the immediate practical value is the opportunity offered for the carrying on of dialogue, another and a deeper value consists in the fact that by this means a kind of twin-sided mirror is provided for each couple; Pantalone differs from the Dottore, yet they are sufficiently close to each other to reflect, and by reflecting to enrich, the personalities of each; Harlequin has a nature far removed from that of Scapin, yet Scapin's inner being reveals itself in Harlequin's actions and Harlequin's in Scapin's.* While, however, such doubling is unquestionably characteristic of much of the commedia dell'arte's structure, we must be careful to observe that it was not unvaryingly so. Indeed, close scrutiny of the extant scenarios demonstrates that in these plays there is a constant ringing of changes on the numbers one to five, almost like the art of campanology. If the elderly men, the lovers and the servants often, indeed usually, come in pairs, the Captain stands generally alone, and the two servants are not balanced by two maid-servants but by a single Franceschina or Colombina. Sometimes the Captain becomes one of a trio of lovers; sometimes the introduction of a third elderly man, even a fourth, varies the pattern. And the action of the plays harmonises with the arrangement of the persons. In, for example, Flaminio Scala's *La caccia* there are four elderly heads of households—Pantalone, Burattino, Graziano, Claudio; the first has a daughter, Isabella, and a servant, Pedrolino; the second has a daughter, Flaminia, and a maid-servant, Franceschina; the third has a son, Flavio, and a servant, Arlecchino; the fourth has only a son, Orazio. In this play, apart and distinct from these characters, Capitano Spavento appears alone and pursues his own path. Thus, there is parallelism, yet each group differs from the others, and the mathematical patterning of one, two, three and four stands out clearly. When we turn to the text, we see how these numbers are further played upon. The action begins with the appearance of Pantalone at his window, blowing his horn for the start of the hunt; a second window opens and Graziano sounds his horn; a third is

42

similarly opened by Claudio, a fourth by Burattino. For a moment, after the echoes have died away, the stage is empty: then a new movement starts. Isabella at her window speaks of her love of Flavio; Flaminia throws her casement open and loudly curses her fate, whereupon Isabella, thinking the words are addressed to her, retires. This appears to be a movement of two, instead of the opening movement of four; but suddenly Pedrolino appears at another window cursing Franceschina, and Flaminia in her turn takes his words as directed at her, and she, too, retires. Now Franceschina comes in, is reconciled to Pedrolino; and that pair goes off. The whole movement, therefore, consists of a series of variations on the basic numbers. Immediately after this, still another variation is introduced: Arlecchino, Graziano, Claudio and Burattino enter, dressed for the hunt—a quartet which, when Pantalone joins them, changes itself into a quintet and which further becomes modified by the addition of a pair, Pedrolino and Franceschina.

The whole of the patterning is exact and carefully contrived, almost as formal as a piece of choreography. Such designs receive constant modulations from play to play. In Scala's *Li tappeti alessandrini*, for example, the elderly fathers are, not four, but three, and each has his own distinctive household: Pantalone's consists of a son, Orazio, and two servants, Pedrolino and Olivetta; Graziano has only a son, Flavio; for Claudio there is no child but a maid-servant, Franceschina. An approach towards the four families of *La caccia* is, however, suggested by the presentation of Fabrizio (really Isabella in disguise), with a servant of her own, Arlecchino. There is no Capitano, but Flaminia makes her entry by herself. Once more, the mathematical patterning is obvious. How far this patterning can be carried may be exemplified by one other selected play, *La fortunata Isabella*. Here the one-two-three arrangement is especially interesting. Pantalone and Graziano are the elderly men— a pair—but the former's house has only one daughter, Flaminia, while the latter's has two sons, Orazio and Flavio. Three other pairs are presented—Pedrolino, an innkeeper, with his wife, Franceschina; Isabella, pretending to be a maid-servant, with

---

✥ *La Fortunata Isabella* ✥

PANTALONE, a Venetian merchant, in love with Franceschina

FLAMINIA, his daughter, in love with Flavio

GRAZIANO, in love with Franceschina

ORAZIO ⎰ his sons, the one in love
FLAVIO ⎱ with Isabella, the other with Flaminia

PEDROLINO, an innkeeper

FRANCESCHINA, his wife, loved by Pantalone and Graziano

ISABELLA, betrothed to Capitano Spavento but deserted by him

BURATTINO, her servant

CAPITANO SPAVENTO, betrothed to Isabella

ARLECCHINO, his servant

CINZIO, Isabella's brother

43

Burattino; and Capitano Spavento, with his servant Arlecchino. By himself stands Cinzio, but, since he is Isabella's brother, he links up with his sister and incidentally with Burattino.

The continual variations thus introduced into the commedia dell'arte plays must be fully appreciated when we turn to consider the characters. To think of these characters simply in pairs means that we shall impose upon an art of infinite modulations a dull and static design which ill suggests what these performances had to offer.

PANTALONE

By far the most constant, and in a sense the most important, of all the characters is Pantalone. As we examine any one of the comedies, we realise that its spirit is animated by a series of focal points of interest. The main story is generally one of love, and hence the young Orazios and Isabellas are centrally significant. On the other hand, the love story is usually directed by the clever tricks and stupidities of a Pedrolino and an Arlecchino—and so they form a second dynamic centre. The Capitano generally is drawn into the lovers' circle, and very often the conduct of the plot depends upon his actions—and thus still a third focal point is established. Apart from all of these is the focal point provided by Pantalone. In many plays this character's actions may be negative rather than positive; he may serve merely as an obstacle which the lovers must surmount; but his importance is shown by the fact that hardly any single comedy fails to place him at the head of the dramatis personae, while the majority of the plays start their action with his entry upon the stage. There is, therefore, every reason for treating him first.

He is constant in that his costume remained almost the same from the beginning to the close of his career. About this there can be no disagreement. His tights (or short breeches and stockings) and his jacket were red; at his belt were usually a dagger or sword and a handkerchief; almost always he had a black round hat, a long black sleeved gown and black slippers. His mask, darkish brown, with hooked nose and usually greying hair protruding from under the hat, was furnished with a pointed beard or moustache. The only variations to be found in his many portraits are the occasional additions of spectacles and a pouch, sometimes so placed as to suggest a phallus.

One further feature of his role is certain and uncontroversial. He was a Venetian, even if his habitat in many of the comedies lies outside Venice, and his speech was the dialect of that city. By his use of this dialect, Pantalone, who is the first to utter any lines in so many of these

23 PANTALONE

44

24 PANTALONE'S MASK

45

plays, introduces us at once to what was another prime feature of the Italian improvised drama. Not only was the dialogue improvised, it was also improvised in various forms of speech appropriate to the persons represented. Class distinctions, no doubt, played a small part here, so that Arlecchino's particular use of Bergamask set him out as an unlettered servant; but it is entirely false, on the basis of such employment of dialectal forms, to suggest that the commedia dell'arte was a 'class-conscious' form of theatre. During the period of the Renaissance national and local dialects had not been ironed out into the flat uniformity which in many countries is our present ideal; and it would be as absurd to find in the different speech forms in these comedies a division by class as it would be to argue that Sir Walter Raleigh's broad Devonshire at the court of Queen Elizabeth marked him out as a parvenu, or that King James I's strong Scots accent was a sign of his lack of culture. The fact is that these differences existed for all inhabitants, for all classes, living in the various Italian cities, just as to a certain extent they exist today within the range of the Germanic territories. Thus Pantalone's Venetian reflects his national or local origin, not the class to which he belongs.

The commedia dell'arte realised to the full the value of this variety in speech both for the purpose of enriching the total design and for that of offering characteristic qualities to the members of its company. Venetian, Bergamask, Bolognese, Neapolitan, Roman, Tuscan all made up a vocal symphony, and every opportunity was seized upon for adding other notes. Isabella, posing as a maid-servant in *La fortunata Isabella*, speaks French, and slaves brought from the east speak broken Turkish. Sometimes this tendency becomes so strong that we reach almost to the area of later 'dialect comedy' in the Goldoni style, as when G. B. Andreini pens *La Venetiana* (1619) under commedia dell'arte inspiration, peopling his stage with gondoliers and other inhabitants of the city; or else we move into a sphere wherein the use of dialects becomes, not merely one part of the design, but almost the whole of the pattern, as in another play inspired by the commedia dell'arte, Vergilio Verucci's *Li diversi linguaggi* (1609), wherein all attention is concentrated upon the forms of speech used by the characters—Claudio's French, Pantalone's Venetian, Zanni's Bergamask, the Pedant's Sicilian, the Captain's Neapolitan and Franceschina's Matriccian.

Pantalone, then, is a Venetian, and almost always, in the comedies, he is the head of a household. At this point, however, trouble starts. One thing which has bedevilled much of modern writings on the commedia dell'arte is a kind of sentimentalism through which the historians, dominated by romantic and other prejudices, have imposed on this stage their own ideas and conceptions; their eyes, to adapt Kant's pregnant phrase, have brought with them what they have determined to see. A typical example of such sentimentalism appears in a recent Russian study of the subject, where Pantalone is categorically described as 'a rich and almost always

25 PANTALONE   26 PANTALONE

miserly old merchant, always decrepit and stumbling. He limps and groans, he coughs, sneezes and continually blows his nose, or else is plagued with stomach-ache. Self-assured as he is, he is yet always being led by the nose. He thinks himself cleverer than anybody else, but at every step he becomes the butt for every conceivable kind of trick. Despite his age and decrepitude he makes advances to the women. Although he is always rejected, he remains an incorrigible suitor.... When he makes love, he tries to show how active he still is, indulges in lively pirouettes and thus tries to conceal his gout and rheumatism. Then, with pain-distorted face, he clutches his sore leg or sinks, moaning miserably, onto a chair.'*

'That', declares this author, 'is Pantalone.' But, of course, that is precisely what the true Pantalone was not. Apart from the facts that chairs on the commedia dell'arte stage were rare or non-existent, most of the action taking place out-of-doors,

47

27　PANTALONE WOOS HIS LADY

that a mask can hardly exhibit a 'pain-distorted face', and that we shall look in vain among the texts for any nose-blowings, coughs or sneezings, the description given here runs directly counter alike to the instructions provided by expert contemporaries, to much of the iconographical evidence and to that of the best scenarios.

It may be that such a caricature was presented on charlatans' stages before vulgar audiences; it is certainly true that, both early and late, numbers of lesser actors tended to debase this character and that numerous scenarios introduce him in situations unbecoming, absurd and even degrading; but good actors were specifically warned not to make of him a figure of laughter merely. Pantalone's role, insists Cecchini, 'is always a serious part, although it is connected with the comic roles because of the speech and dress'; and 'the actor interpreting this character must preserve that element of seriousness which is an integral part of the character in reproving, persuading, commanding, counselling and doing many other things fitting a keen-witted man'. The seriousness, according to this instructor, may be dropped a trifle 'when he talks to a servant about love, banquets, amusements and

48

28 PANTALONE IN A RAGE

29 PANTALONE RUNNING

other light matters, since all men of rank, however dignified and eminent, act just in that manner'.* Apart from such situations, Pantalone's behaviour should not be of a kind to arouse raucous laughter, should not depart from the serious norm.

He is, of course, a 'vecchio', an 'old man', but care must be taken to remember that in the Renaissance an 'old man' was not necessarily one descended far towards his grave. What is striking in many of his early portraits is Pantalone's remarkable physique. Certainly his very first representation, that in the frescoes at Trausnitz in Bavaria, shows him as an old man with straggling hair; and certainly, too, several later illustrations stress his frailty. At the same time, it must be remembered that the Trausnitz paintings are based on an amateur performance, and that the prints which display a thin and weak Pantalone are amply outweighed by others which exhibit under the red tights brawny thighs and limbs of which any athlete might well feel proud. And in these prints, although he sometimes appears in indecorous and ridiculous situations, his general presentation is either in dignified posture or else in violent action. When he is not standing as though he were delivering a homily, he appears in vigorous movement. In crouched attitude he circles, with almost animal ferocity, around the abject figure of a servant who has annoyed him; he displays the grace of a dancer as he leans sideways from a pointing companion or sweeps in courtly bow towards the object of his affections; even more vigorous, virile and masculinely active is his portrait as, arms widely outspread and cloak flying out behind him, he reaches forward with his right foot bent and left stretched out behind. There is nothing of decrepitude here.

30 STEFANELLO BOTTARGA (PANTALONE)

These pictures are amply supported by the Scala scenarios. Named Pantalone dei Bisognosi or, more simply, Magnifico, he is described not only as 'very rich', but also as a man of great distinction in his own community. In one play he is 'the chief citizen of Naples', in another 'a noble Venetian'.* True, he becomes foolish when he pretends to an adolescence he has lost; at times laughter is aroused when he abandons his dignity and rivals the lovers in their intrigues. As in Shakespeare's plays, a constant conflict between youth and age operates here, and many comedies end, as *L'amante astuto* expresses it, with the older men 'burlati', or cheated, and their sons happy. Sometimes, too, he finds himself absurdly cuckolded by sprightlier gallants. At the same time, it must be insisted that the stress which almost all historians of the commedia dell'arte have placed on such episodes offers a false impression of his dramatic role. He is far from decrepitude, and his lapses are effective and amusing rather because of the contrast between, on the one hand, a keen intelligence applied to the conduct of his business affairs, a normally dignified bearing and worthy sentiments, and, on the other hand, actions which might be easily condoned in one of lesser rank but which from him appear unfitting.

Obviously, the part was one which could be turned into a farcical scarecrow and it often was presented as such, but in many of the early comedies, indeed in the majority, Pantalone's role is 'serious' and his demeanour appropriately discreet. In one play he is a 'gentleman of honourable family' who has lived a 'quiet and happy life' until his daughter suddenly falls in love and so disrupts the serenity of his household; in another he is a worthy father whose 'tranquil peace and contented existence' have similarly been upset through no fault of his own.*

He does, of course, at times contribute to the disturbance of his own peace of mind, but once more decrepitude only occasionally finds mention. He can prove himself stingy, avaricious and credulous on occasion, and often he overdoes the advice which he freely imparts to others. Impotent he may sometimes be, but far more commonly he displays virility enough to seduce and get with child a Franceschina or an Olimpia; and, if his young wife inclines towards a lover, he provides justification for her actions by his own extra-marital adventures. Of special interest in this connection is the comedy of *Il pedante*. Although there he has a lovely young wife, Isabella, Pantalone spends his time with courtesans. Naturally, Isabella is angry, and after one quarrel with her husband she goes so far as to accept a ring from the Captain. In essence, however, she remains true to her husband, and when the tutor Cataldo, a kind of prototype of the hypocritical Tartuffe, tries to console her, she reveals his trickery, begs Pantalone to pretend to go off on business, traps the lover and has him thoroughly castigated. Far indeed from the caricature portrait is this Pantalone, and his wife Isabella seems quite contented with her lot. She is equally contented at the close of *Il ritratto*. There, when Pantalone deserts his house and makes love to a young actress, she does find solace in an affair with young Orazio, but the conclusion of the comedy is not quite what we might expect; when Pantalone at last sees the error of his ways, she does not go off with her lover but merely advises her husband to abandon such pursuits, to 'stay at home and govern his wife'.

Pantalone's bravery still further removes him from the knock-kneed rheumatic scarecrow erroneously described for us. Already, attention has been drawn to his dagger, and several scenes show that he knows well how to use both this weapon and a sword. In *La travagliata Isabella*, the Captain and his brother annoy Pantalone by continually serenading his daughter Flaminia; not in a sudden senile passion but following a careful plan, he attacks the brothers, masters them, leaves them for dead and flies to Rome so as to escape legal punishment for his deed. Even although at the end he shows abject terror on the reappearance of the revengeful Captain, this Pantalone is a valorous and sympathetic character. Much the same occurs in *Il portalettere* where the irate father, seeking to protect his daughter's honour, confronts and wounds a young Venetian gallant. It has been said that in the scenarios Pantalone 'is sometimes pathetic, but dignified, never': such a statement, however, must be seen as a distortion of the facts.

As we look at these examples, a character takes shape of a kind entirely removed from the person of the doddering old man who is often substituted for him; moreover, it is a character which may as readily be found in modern as in Renaissance society. Were we to seek his present-day counterpart we should not be far wrong in thinking of a middle-aged businessman, wealthy and well esteemed, apt at times to dally with ladies of doubtful virtue, at other times as apt to show himself the devoted father anxious to protect a young son or puzzled by the actions of a daughter he does not understand, courageous in his own way, and in his own way wise, even if sometimes his wisdom, valid in the general world of affairs, may seem folly to impetuous youths and maidens consumed by passion.

Here is something much more subtle dramatically than just an age-consumed old man. In thinking of Pantalone we should forget Shakespeare's lean and slippered pantaloon and see him as he actually was, or at least as he was intended to be, a vigorous and downright middle-aged merchant, with a fine career behind him, who has become involved in an emotional world with which he cannot always cope.

Pantalone was the earliest and the most enduring name of this character, already established in the sixteenth century—indeed, so well known then as to appear in popular rimes—and remaining fixed in the public mind until the days of Goldoni and later.* At the same time, other designations were at various times applied to or associated with him.

These fall into distinct categories. Actually one of the portraits of Pantalone referred to above is labelled 'Stephanel Bottarga', and here we are introduced to an interesting dramatic problem which confronted the Italian comedians. From time to time, the plot of some comedy necessitated the presentation of this character of the elderly merchant as a man living in disguise under another name; since, however, he wore the familiar stock dress and mask he could not be called anything save Pantalone, and consequently, in order to fit the requirements of the plot and to provide the audience with the necessary surprise, a kind of topsy-turvy procedure had to be adopted, the spectators being informed towards the conclusion of the piece that this Pantalone was in reality another. Thus, therefore, in one comedy Pantalone turns out to be Stefanello Bisognosi and in another Stefanello Bottarga. The same procedure is adopted in several other comedies where the Magnifico, accepted as such by the audience throughout the greater part of the action, is discovered at the end to be, in reality, a man named Tofano.* The first category accordingly consists, not of additional characters, but simply of variant names introduced to fit plot requirements.

Mention of Tofano, however, leads to consideration of a second category, since this Tofano appears elsewhere either as Pantalone's brother or as the head of a household distinct from his. Usually, like Pantalone, he is a Venetian merchant, although twice he figures as a physician. In general we may regard him as Pantalone's double when such a double was needed in a particular comedy. An even more interesting

31 PANTALONE AND HIS TWIN

story concerns the fortunes of Stefanello Bottarga. In 1585 Cesare Rao has a 'Lamento di Giovanni Ganassa con M. Stefanello suo padrone', and the linking of Ganassa and Stefanello in these verses reminds us that during the preceding year there is record of an Italian actor styled Estefanelo Bottarga who, apparently in association with Zan Ganassa (Alberto Naseli), was performing in the Iberian peninsula. So successful were these two players that 'ganassas' and 'botargas' became, and for long remained, popular Spanish carnival and tournament figures; even Lope de Vega appeared on one occasion before Philip III as a 'botarga', clad in Pantalone's familiar costume of red and black. It seems obvious that some actor, whose real name is unknown to us, adopted the character and appearance of the Magnifico, presented it under the name of his alias, Stefanello Bottarga, and, although his fame did not spread wide in Italy, succeeded in establishing this role and title among Spanish audiences.*

Leone Adorni of Genoa appears to have been a kindred type, and perhaps also Zanobio—although concerning him there is some doubt. There was an actor, Girolamo Salimbeni, who has been recorded as Zanobio da Piombino, as though that were the name of a single character, but Zanobio is introduced in one Scala

53

32 PIOMBINO

play and Piombino separately in another, while Francesco Andreini likewise keeps the two distinct.* We may assume that the first was a 'vecchio' akin to Pantalone and that the other, to judge from an illustration of 1618, was presented on the stage as a dumpy, almost dwarf-like, person of more comic appeal.

A third category of allied characters consists of those who are truly to be identified with Pantalone but to whom individual companies had given variant names. Thus, for example, Ubaldo Lanterni is substituted for Pantalone throughout one entire collection of scenarios; a second collection gives us the name of Ponsevere, still another that of Prospero; elsewhere Anselmo or Beltrano is used;* while among certain acting groups—particularly when the Neapolitan influence caused a breakdown of the clearly defined Tuscan patterns—persons such as Tartaglia who were characteristically servants could for the nonce step upwards to become heads of households and replace Pantalone in comic plots, even if they failed to reproduce his qualities. Discussion of such characters may, however, for the moment be postponed.

33 THE DOTTORE

34 DOTTOR SPACCA STRUMMOLO

THE DOTTORE

Pantalone's companion and neighbour, sometimes friend and sometimes enemy, was the Dottore, styled by successive interpreters in diverse ways—Dottor Graziano Scarpazon, or Partesana da Francolino, or Balanzoni, or Spaccastrummolo, or Brentino, or Baloardo, or Forbizone, or Graziano de' Violoni, or Scattalone, or

55

Lanternone.* As with Pantalone, however, one title proved both earliest and longest lasting, and in the scenarios his role is habitually signalised under the name of Gratiano or Graziano.

Like Pantalone, too, he wears a dress which varies only slightly through the years —a decorous black garb, with short cloak and doctoral bonnet, white ruff or collar, a pair of gloves in his hand and a handkerchief tucked into his belt. Over his face he wears, not so much a mask, as a large nose, sometimes provided with cheek-pads. Pantalone's coeval, he is depicted as a man about forty or forty-five years of age, and his characteristic speech is Bolognese.

In general, his role provided a foil for Pantalone, one which could stand alongside his and yet become at times rather less 'serious', deviating more frequently from the other's gravity. In particular, he generally shows himself as more lascivious than his companion, and his adventures with serving-maids and others are numerous. When kept in restraint, it was, according to P. M. Cecchini, a 'gracious part', that of a man 'who sought to be up-to-date despite his classical learning';* at the same time, it readily tempted its interpreters to exaggeration, so that even as early as 1628 warnings were issued against reducing the Dottore's person to the level of a clown's.

Fundamentally, the dramatic force of the role depended on the characteristic speech which the public expected from this character. In the comedies, Pantalone generally plays a dynamic part, whereas the Dottore wanders in and out ineffectually, rarely moving the action forwards, but continually talking. This talk has certain typical qualities. First, the Dottore, who is most commonly presented as a legal man, can never refrain from expressing his opinions or from giving his advice even in situations about which he knows nothing. Thus, for example, when Pantalone is in despair because his daughter has suddenly fallen sick, the Dottore cannot refrain, while they await the arrival of the physician, from lengthily proposing a series of balsams, pills and plasters suitable for the cure of horses, or, when Pantalone proposes to go on a voyage, from 'giving a ridiculously lengthy list of the names of the winds'. Secondly, his mind is so stored with expert book knowledge—mainly classical mythology, Latin tags and legal sentences—that he finds it impossible either to think or to speak in a simple logical manner. Sometimes the comic effect of his utterances comes from their inordinate length; sometimes, less effectively, it derives from ridiculous errors. And thirdly, he is apt to express the obvious with grave circumlocution—'You cannot make a sea-voyage without leaving dry land', or 'Whoever discusses a question says something or other', he announces gravely.*

Examples of his set speeches abound, but with them a difficulty arises. That they are expressed in his familiar Bolognese dialect offers no serious problem; it is easy to render this into standard Italian and thence, if need be, into English. But when we have so rendered and translated the 'Grazianesque' language, the result means nothing to us; it seems merely boring and childish with its accumulations of Latin phrases

56

35 DOTTOR CAMPANAZ

36 THE DOTTORE

and endless examples from classical legend, its twisted logic and its verbiage. Here, however, we must remember that the Dottore's method of talking was intimately related to the special tone of the learned within the Renaissance period; and, in order to appreciate what he once stood for, we must, as it were, translate not just his words but his whole being into modern terms. Wherever verbiage triumphs and expert knowledge prevents simple thought, there we shall find him. The civil service mind at its worst is, one might say, his modern spiritual home. A glance at the instructions provided for tax-payers by the Inland Revenue authorities reveals his presence. Or else we turn to the final paragraph of the National Insurance Bill, 1959, and read: 'For the purpose of this Part of this Schedule a person over pensionable age, not being an insured person, shall be treated as an employed person if he would be an insured person were he under pensionable age and would be an employed person were he an insured person.' This is authentic Graziano. If we wish to realise the force of his role, we must imagine him now clad in black jacket, striped trousers and stiff collar, with a furled umbrella crooked over his arm, a briefcase in his hand.

37   ZANNI AND THE DOTTORE

In the comedies his precise profession is but rarely mentioned; he is simply 'Dottore', 'Graziano' or 'Graziano Dottore'. There are suggestions that he is rich and, like Pantalone, of honourable family, but these are less frequent than they are with his companion, and he seems in general not so firmly placed in the social scale. Although normally a legal man, he can occasionally be a physician, but he can also be a charlatan, and in later plays, when a certain deterioration in the commedia dell'arte was setting in, his part sometimes degenerates from that of an innkeeper,

59

a schoolmaster, an actor, a judge, to a majordomo, a gardener and an ordinary servant.* Perhaps the most interesting of his odd appearances is in *Il Dottor bacchettone* where he plays the part of a scoundrelly Tartuffe. This Dottore asks his servant Stoppino if, after rising, he has given thanks to heaven; when Stoppino replies that first he had to have breakfast, his master sanctimoniously tells him he must think primarily not of the body but of the soul. He pretends to aid the poor, but, still posing as an other-worldly man, he tricks Pantalone of a large sum of money and even cruelly cheats a wretched and impoverished Corallina.

Such, however, is an aberration; for the most part Graziano takes a less dominant, and certainly a less dynamic, part in the action of the plays in which he appears.

Again like Pantalone, he once or twice turns out to be someone other than himself; thus, for example, in *Mala lingua* he is revealed at the conclusion of the comedy as Michelino or Michilino, and a character so named, presumably merely a variant of the Dottore, appears elsewhere as head of a household.* So, too, he occasionally makes his entry under other titles; the Merlino Pulpettone of *Flaminio disperato*, for example, is described as 'Graziano dottore' in the list of dramatis personae, while Graziano's part appears to be the same as that of Pandolfo Baccelli in the Bartoli scenarios and of Scartoccio in the Corsiniana series. Under whatever guise he makes his entry, however, his 'Grazianesque' features remain unimpaired and his loquaciousness unabated.

CASSANDRO AND CLAUDIO; COVIELLO AND COLA; PASQUARIELLO AND TARTAGLIA

Pantalone the merchant and Graziano the professional man make an excellent pair. They are sufficiently akin to act in concert, sufficiently different to avoid monotony. The virtues and vices of each are reflected in the other's words and actions. With sure awareness of dramatic values, the commedia dell'arte retained them to the end of its career.

At the same time, before we leave this realm of the older men, two observations must be made. The first is that, while the pair of fathers formed the staple in most comedies, variety was constantly being provided, as has been briefly noted above, by the occasional introduction of trios or quartets. In Scala's *La finta pazza*, for instance, Pantalone and Graziano are accompanied by both Cassandro and Zanobio, in *Li duo amanti furiosi* Graziano is absent but Pantalone has companions in Cassandro and Coviello. It becomes necessary, therefore, to consider the nature of some other elderly characters apart from the basic couple.

Of these Cassandro d'Aretusi is perhaps most important.* Concerning his costume we know nothing, and there is even uncertainty regarding his place of origin; he has been described as a Florentine, but elsewhere there are suggestions that he comes from Bologna, Rome or Siena. If such doubt exists, however, concerning his appearance and origin, we may be reasonably sure of his nature. Like Pantalone, he is a merchant and of honourable family, but from the part he takes in the plots it seems that he is even more 'serious' than his fellow businessman, more kindly and a less active participant in the movement of the comedies. Sometimes his mission, like that of Vincentio in *The Taming of the Shrew*, is merely to bring a tangled plot to rights. Nevertheless, his personality was forceful enough to keep him firmly on the boards for more than two hundred years; he is a character in several French plays of the eighteenth century, and when Jan Potocki wrote his *Parady* for performance in far-off Poland in 1792 he included the Dottore among his commedia dell'arte characters but in place of Pantalone he chose 'Kasander'.*

Another similar but less enduring figure was Claudio or Claudione,* evidently intended to be a Frenchman, but his role is so shadowy that it need not detain us. Of more importance is Coviello, and here we come to the second observation concerning these elderly men. For the most part Pantalone, Graziano, Tofano, Cassandro, Claudione and the rest are fixed in their positions; although Graziano may occasionally be degraded, he and Pantalone are usually heads of households and of good family. When, however, the Tuscan comedy was carried south to Naples and there inspired native actors to apply themselves to the practice of improvisation, a change entered in. The Neapolitans possessed great vitality and their high spirits brought to these comedies a magnificent verve—the quality which animates Callot's well-known plates in the *Balli di Sfessania*. Unfortunately, this vigour and effervescent gaiety were accompanied by another trend inimical to the spirit of the commedia dell'arte as that was exhibited in the north. The motto of the Neapolitan actors was 'Everything for a laugh', and consequently they tended to alter comedy into farce, to shift attention from character and to make such dramatic figures as they invented into clowns. Both the structure of the plays and the integrated, consistently drawn theatrical types were lost amid scenes which had no object save the arousing of laughter, and stock figures which had no firm dramatic foundation.

Coviello may here be regarded as typical. In the Neapolitan scenarios he appears mainly as a servant, the companion of Pulcinella, and an early print depicts him as a grotesque with a long-nosed mask and spectacles, dressed in tight trousers buttoned down the sides, a tight jacket and a short cloak. Elsewhere we find references which suggest that he has some of the characteristics of a comic Capitano; indeed, in some records he is actually styled Capitan Coviello. Were this all, he would not concern us here; we should find nothing which might justify our discussing him alongside the Magnifico and Graziano. To our surprise, however, he suddenly appears in a couple of the Neapolitan scenarios as the head of a household, once with a son and daughter, a maid-servant and a serving-man, and once with a wife and a bastard son, while in other collections of plays his part quite clearly is that of Pantalone's companion. Throughout the Venetian scenarios he is described variously as a merchant, a physician and a 'dottore'; in the Corsini and Locatelli collections he comes in once or twice as a servant but more frequently as one of the fathers. When we turn for aid to the various plays written in imitation of the commedia dell'arte, the same confusion is found to prevail: in one he is a servant, in one an inn-keeper, in one a merchant, in two a doctor, and in one he is named Spaccamontagna, a 'foreigner'.* All we can say is that in this uncertainty resides one of the signs of the commedia dell'arte's degeneration; what presents itself here is not a character, such as Pantalone, interpreted by divers actors, but a part in which the actor's skill becomes of more significance than the part he plays.

38   COVIELLO SINGING

It is even possible that the very costume of Coviello altered in accordance with the position he occupied. We can hardly imagine the grotesque liveried person shown in the print of 'Coviello singing' as a dignified father of a family, and there exists at least one piece of evidence which suggests that his costume may have changed for

62

39 CETRULLO AND BAGATINO

40 COLA

different roles. The vivacious pamphleteer G. C. Croce refers to Coviello as 'Coviello Cetrullo Cetrulli', and, although the name Cetrullo by itself appears elsewhere and also, in a couple of other records, seems to be associated with Pulcinella, Croce's identification of Coviello and Cetrullo gives us justification for believing that these were either the same person or at any rate closely allied.* Of Cetrullo we possess an illustration which shows a man decorously clad in breeches, jacket, cloak and ruff, just such as might be appropriate for the head of a household. If indeed Coviello and Cetrullo are one, then we must imagine a stage character quite distinct in essence from such persons as Pantalone and the Dottore, which permitted an actor to appear in various costumes, now as an intriguing servant, now as a braggadocio, now as an elderly gentleman—and such procedure ultimately spelt death for the commedia dell'arte.

This vulgarising and disintegrating influence was the more unfortunate in that the Neapolitan actors, with their verve and uninhibited joy in life, had much to give to the Italian theatre. The Tuscan players might be likened to those good modern Shakespearian producers who seek to derive their stage business from an appreciation of the qualities revealed in the persons of the plays; the Neapolitans were like those poor, but perhaps lively, producers who, not capable of appreciating Shakespeare fully, regard his works as mere raw material for display of their own ingenuity, disregard character value, have 'fun' with the texts, reduce comedy to the levels of farce, and make tragedy into spectacular melodrama.

The figure of Coviello does not stand alone: indeed, all the types invented by the Neapolitans exhibit the same vague vacillation and incertitude. Cola, or Cola-fronio, is listed by Perrucci among the elderly men, and he enters as such into several plays, yet his usual role is that of a servant, nor is he consistent even in that part, since sometimes he acts as a rascally acrobatic knave and sometimes as a dull-witted fool, stupidly jealous. How vague was his personality may be realised when we find one record, G. C. Croce's *Dispute fra Cola et Arlechino* (Bologna, 1628), which seems to suggest that he is Harlequin's master, and a second record of 1607 which proposes the substitution of the part of Cola for that of Arlecchino. Further evidence of a similar kind comes from some comedies written under the influence of the commedia dell'arte: there we find him as a doctor, a merchant, a Neapolitan knight, a lover and a common servant.* Dressed in slashed doublet and hose, with spectacles on a grotesquely elongated nose, and indulging in much acrobatic movement, he could assume all these roles; but in assuming them he obviously was unqualified to give to any one a distinctive and concerted spirit.

Two other associated persons may be mentioned briefly here. Like Cola, Pas-quariello's name appears listed among the elderly men, and he too has vague associations with the Capitano; but, again like him, his commonest entry is as a servant, though he also can play a part as a lover, a bravo or a gardener.* Dressed in breeches,

STRAMBOTTI 629
Di
PASCHARIELLO TRVONO
NAPOLETANO,

Stampata in Napoli. 1606.

Con Licenza de' Superiori.

jacket and cloak, with a sword at his side, he appears portrayed in a woodcut of 1606, while his later costume, with peculiar vertical stripes and a ruffed collar, can be seen in a French print of the end of the seventeenth century. A further kinship with Cola is his reputation for acrobatics: as the verses underneath his portrait put it,

> *Chacun admire mes Postures*
> *dans l'agitation de mon corps.*

And finally there is the irritating Tartaglia, whose sole constant characteristic seems to have been his stammering; the Neapolitan public apparently was mightily amused when he stuttered out his 'co-co-co-co', no one being sure whether he was trying to say 'content' or 'console' or 'comfort' or 'cuckold', but for us the trick has lost its savour. At one time, he wore a striped costume with a round hat, later he sported breeches, a laced waistcoat and cloak, with a curled-brim hat. Servant, gardener, innkeeper and father of a household, he has no more personality than his companions—a thing impossible for a person who enters at one moment as the Captain's comic attendant, at another as the companion of Pantalone and the Dottore, at another as a substitute for Pantalone himself.*

66

The number of the 'Four Masks' is made up by the addition of two serving-men, the zanni whom the Elizabethans called the zanies. It is somewhat ironic that these comic and irreverent figures should have aroused of late in amateurish and academic circles a considerable measure of serious debate and, in particular, that they should have become the centre of historical–philosophical controversy. The current fashionable view, reiterated at somewhat wearisome length by many modern writers, is that there were two zanni, one astute and one foolish, and that such an individually named character as Arlecchino is nothing more than a zanni of the second type.

For this statement there seems, at first glance, to be immediate support. In the seventeenth- and eighteenth-century writings on the subject reference is frequently made to the first and second zanni (although it may be observed that whereas, for example, in 1699 Perrucci speaks of 'il primo e secondo zanni', P. M. Cecchini, some seventy years earlier, refers to the 'primo e secondo servo'). Moreover, when the early scenarios, such as those in the Scala collection, are examined, it is clear that in numerous comedies, even when the word 'zanni' finds no mention, the comic business frequently derives from the contrasted activities of an astute intriguer and a simpleton.

Such, however, is not the whole of the picture, and two further facts require to be particularly observed. The first is that by no means all the plays contain the contrasting pair and that often measures of astuteness and folly are apportioned to both the servants. Sometimes a comedy will have two poltroons. In another the more foolish partner will suddenly turn the tables by cleverly cheating his apparently more astute companion, or else the intriguer, after the execution of several rascally tricks, will prove a fool in the end and so come to grief. Instead of thinking rigidly of clever and stupid, we should rather regard these characters as akin to Laurel and Hardy, concerning whom it is difficult to determine which partner is less foolish, which more astute. Variations of this kind are, however, not so important as the second fact—which is that numerous comedies in their listing of the two comic servants call one 'Zanni' and give to the second some specific name, while several early prints clearly make a distinction between, say, Harlequin on the one hand and Zanni on the other. The only possible conclusion seems to be that, while the word 'zanni' was often used in the generic sense of 'comic servant' or 'clown', as Zanni it was also applied to a particular character. If this is so, a corollary follows, that, although all the comic servants may in one sense be called zanni, it is wrong to attempt to confuse Zanni as a character with his companions. Both Harlequin and his variant Trivellino are thus among those who are made in several scenarios to appear alongside a Zanni, and who remain distinct from that comic type.

The whole question becomes, of course, hopelessly complicated by the bewildering complexity of names and qualities assumed by these serving-men. Some have

42   FRANCATRIPPA AND HARLEQUIN

43   ZANNI AND HARLEQUIN   44   ZAN MUZZINA

68

extended careers lasting over centuries, some suddenly spring up, have their moment of glory under one interpreter and as suddenly vanish. The rough rhymes from G. M. Raparini's *L'Arlichino* (Heidelberg, 1718) provide us with an amusing catalogue, and even it is by no means complete:

Arlichino, Trufaldino,	Trappolino, Zaccagnino,
Trivellino, Tracagnino,	Sia Pasquino, Tabarrino,
Tortellino, Naccherino,	Passerino, Bagatino,
Gradellino, Mezzettino,	Bagolino, Temellino,
Polpettino, Nespolino,	Fagottino, Pedrolino,
Bertolino, Fagiuolino,	Fritellino, Tabacchino.

Of these, a few are wholly unknown elsewhere, a few belong to one actor alone, a few had moderately extended careers, and one, Arlecchino, proved himself immortal.

How most effectively to survey these comic servants is hard to decide, but perhaps the best approach is to discuss them according to their appearance on the stage. What in effect the public saw were innumerable variations of three main types, each type being distinguished by a certain basic costume. One actor was sloppily dressed, a second had a more or less close-fitting attire, and a third, also with close-fitting garments, presented a colourful show of diversely coloured textures. These three basic costumes may be styled the loose, the tight and the patched, and according to such costumes, which seem to have had distinct origins, we may survey their wearers —bearing in mind, of course, that usually only two of them took part in the action of any single play.*

A start must be made with the typical wearer of the third kind of costume— Arlecchino, the character whom both Riccoboni and Goldoni signalised as chief of the zanni. By no means is his name the commonest in the extant scenarios, but from the time when he first stepped on to the stage at the close of the seventeenth century down to modern days he is the person who has most securely seized upon the imagination alike of the general public and of the intelligentsia.

During his career Harlequin changed: that is certain. His earliest costume, usually fitted close to the body, was marked by a series of irregularly placed patches; if we can trust the provenance assigned to a mask now preserved in the Parisian Musée de l'Opéra, his half-mask was rougher than that which he wore later, and was, moreover, furnished with bushy hair at the eyebrows and upper lip. There may have been intermediate developments, when the patches began to assume geometrical forms, but certainly by the second half of the seventeenth century the patches had developed into regular triangles or lozenges, arranged with precision all over his dress and often set off with strips of ribbon; and by that period his mask was innocent of any hirsute appendages. Throughout the century following, this was Harlequin's familiar uniform, modified only by being made ever neater and at times more colourful. With the dress, too, he changed spiritually. At the beginning he was less refined than he later became, and it would seem that he was definitely duller and less animated.

All this is true; yet it must be repeated that fundamentally Harlequin remained the same from the start of his career to the end, and that he is recognisable in all his guises. Partly the recognition comes from certain characteristic physical attributes. Harlequin excels in agility and acrobatics and, although some actors were more skilled than others, no one of his exponents could succeed unless he possessed at least a fair measure of suppleness of body. Few, it is true, could vie with Visentini who, when Harlequin gets a fright, was able to turn a back-somersault with a glass of wine in his hand, not a drop being spilled, and who on at least one occasion, to the anxious trepidation of the audience, crawled like a fly round the first, second and third galleries; yet every actor esteemed in the part was noted for exhibitions of physical skill, if not quite so out of the common, at least remarkable.*

Two or three special movements were commonly associated with him and set him off from his companions. The first was his way of entering the stage, with a sense of quick urgency, his legs held almost unbent and given a kind of strutting effect. In this there was created an impression of self-confidence, perhaps of impertinence, certainly of his own awareness of the humour of his role. The second was a strange trick by which he seemed to alter his height by lowering his head without moving his shoulders and then suddenly extending his neck concertina-wise, again without moving his body. And a third consisted in the elaborate manipulation of his cap and his wooden *batte*. All of these provided him with a characteristic set of actions.

Similarly he was distinguished by certain marked inner qualities. Harlequin exists in a mental world wherein concepts of morality have no being, and yet, despite such absence of morality, he displays no viciousness. On occasion, as in Scala's *Il marito*, he may blandly advise the heroine Isabella to be kind to all men, and once or twice he may be introduced as a pander, but somehow his words and actions have no flavour of evil in them. In contradistinction from many of his companions, too, he exhibits little malice. Another character who has been cheated or insulted will bear a grudge and seek means for securing revenge; only rarely does Harlequin behave in this way and when he does his actions arouse that sense of the unexpected which but adds life to his personality. Maybe a partial explanation of this quality may be traced to another aspect of his nature—his inability to think of more than one thing at a time or, rather, his refusal to consider the possible consequences of an immediate action. He gets an idea; it seems to him at the moment a good one; gaily he applies it, and, no matter what scrape it leads him into, he never gains from his experience: one minute later he will be merrily pursuing another thought, equally calculated to lead him into embarrassment. In *La figlia disubbediente* he pretends to

70

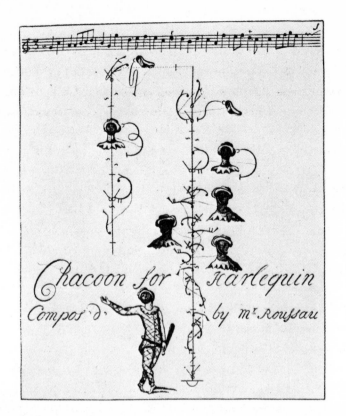

Chacoon for Harlequin
Compos'd by Mr Roussau

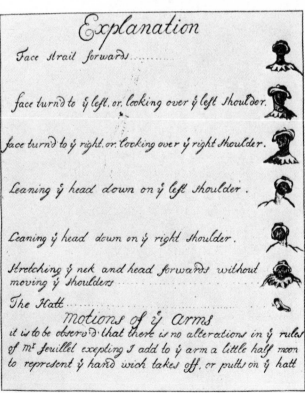

Explanation

Face strait forwards ....

face turn'd to ỹ left, or looking over ỹ left shoulder.

face turn'd to ỹ right, or looking over ỹ right shoulder.

Leaning ỹ head down on ỹ left shoulder.

Leaning ỹ head down on ỹ right shoulder.

Stretching ỹ nek and head forwards without moving ỹ shoulders ....

The Hatt ....

Motions of ỹ Arms

it is to be observ'd that there is no alterations in ỹ rules of Mr Feuillet exepting I add to ỹ arm a little half moon to represent ỹ hand wich takes off, or putts on ỹ hatt

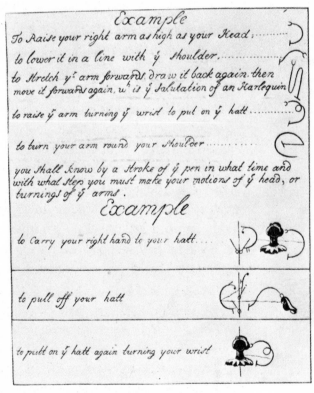

Example

To Raise your right arm as high as your Head ....

to lower it in a line with ỹ shoulder ....

to Stretch yr arm forwards, draw it back again, then move it forwards again, wh is ỹ Salutation of an Harlequin

to raise ỹ arm turning ỹ wrist to put on ỹ hatt ....

to turn your arm round your Shoulder ....

you shall know by a stroke of ỹ pen in what time and with what steps you must make your motions of ỹ head, or turnings of ỹ arms.

Example

to Carry your right hand to your hatt .....

to pull off your hatt

to pull on ỹ hatt again turning your wrist

45 HARLEQUIN'S HEAD AND ARM MOVEMENTS

be a poor soldier and begs for alms. Cinthio approaches; Harlequin raises his cap: 'Sir,' he says, 'Please help a poor dumb man.' Cinthio smiles: 'You are dumb then, my friend?' 'Oh yes, sir', replies Harlequin innocently, and on Cinthio's asking him how he can be dumb when he is able to reply to a questioner, he eagerly gives his explanation: 'But sir, if I were not to reply to you that would be rude; I am well brought up, I know how one should act.' In the very moment of saying this, however, he suddenly appreciates his error and quickly adds 'But you are right, sir; I made a mistake—I meant to say I am deaf.' 'Deaf!' cries Cinthio, 'That can't be.' 'Oh yes, I assure you, sir,' Harlequin answers, 'I cannot hear even a cannon going off.' 'But at any rate', says Cinthio, 'you understand what is being said to you, especially if somebody calls you to give you some money.' 'Most certainly, sir', is Harlequin's quick reply, and he goes on to claim that once more he had made a slight mistake; he really should have said he was blind.

This scene reveals another quality he possesses. Rarely does he initiate an intrigue, but he is adroit in wriggling out of an awkward situation. Although he may seem a fool, he displays a very special quickness of mind, and allied to that, there is evident in him a sense of fun. In the conversation with Cinthio, for example, he does two things at once: he tries to correct his errors and he delights in prolonging the amusing situation in which he finds himself involved. Another play shows him in despair because he thinks his Diamantina does not love him, and he announces that he will kill himself. Obligingly Diamantina hands him a sword and a rope; without a pause Harlequin luxuriates in a soliloquy. Looking sadly at the rope, 'My father's soul', he says, 'was poisoned by this drug and I am glad that it will release me also from life. I shall not be the first to finish my days in this way. Did not the Roman Lucrece', he continues, 'kill herself for Mark Antony, Cleopatra for Tarquin? Did not Aristotle die for Galen? It is fitting that I should hang myself without any hesitation.' At this he ties the rope to a window, puts the noose round his neck, and, holding it in his hand, pretends he is strangling himself. All at once, however, he stops, decides that this is a vulgar way to die and resolves to use a sword. He picks up the weapon, solemnly removes his cap and puts it on the ground in case he falls on his nose. 'Courage!' cries Diamantina, as Harlequin makes to stab himself. Then he pauses; the sword is still in the scabbard. Ever officious, Diamantina draws it for him, but now a new thought comes: 'Oh,' he says, 'how difficult it is to die! If I try to stab myself in front, I'm sure I shall get a terrible fright; and if I try to do it behind I risk cutting some nerve which will leave me paralysed all my life.' What is amusing in the scene is its complete absurdity, its fantasy, the pleasure of watching Harlequin struggle out of the position into which he has placed himself, while he solemnly delights in his own follies.*

Never is he at a loss. In one play he comes to Pantalone's house dressed as a physician, but he cannot resist the temptation to boast of all sorts of unconnected attainments. 'Apart from medicine', he declares, 'I am also deeply versed in astrology. For instance, I've discovered that "moon" is feminine and "sun" masculine. I can't tell you how many dissertations I have published on the twenty-six houses of the Zodiac.' 'When I went to school', remarks Pantalone caustically, 'I was taught that there were only twelve houses.' Harlequin's reply is immediate: 'Ah, you haven't taken into consideration the other houses built since that time.'

On a second occasion when he is once more disguised as a physician, he comes to Pantalone's house and receives a shock when suddenly he is introduced to the Doctor. 'Sirs,' he says, 'my patients are waiting for me', but pauses long enough to enquire what kind of doctor this is. 'A doctor of law', Pantalone tells him. 'Then you aren't a physician at all', gleefully remarks Harlequin to the Doctor. At once he struts forward to take centre stage. 'In that case', he assures the company, 'my patients can wait.' 'But,' the Doctor adds, 'I have studied medicine as well.' On hearing this, Harlequin decides to decamp. 'My patients *are* waiting for me. Goodbye, sirs!' And off he goes.

In another play he finds himself in a tomb, supposedly poisoned by a rival, alongside a supposedly dead Eularia. She wakens from the effects of a drug. Harlequin asks who she is, and is told 'I am a woman, alas! brought to this estate by a faithless lover on whom I doted too much'. 'And I', replies Harlequin, 'am a man poisoned by a madly jealous rival. Come over here,' he adds, 'although I am dead I feel I still have a taste for the ladies.'

His sense of fun explains the eagerness with which he seizes any opportunity of popping into disguise, but he can never carry through a disguise intrigue effectively because he never forgets himself and because he lets inappropriate words slip out, partly through a failure to consider fully what their effect may be and partly through his inability to prevent their bubbling up out of his sense of fun. In *Il medicino volante* he enters dressed as a physician; 'I do hope', he remarks on entering, 'that my patients don't die before I've made my round of visits.' Then he starts to examine Eularia. 'I feel sick,' she tells him, 'it's as though my stomach were full up.' 'I wish mine were', he replies. 'How is your appetite?' On her saying 'I don't feel hungry' he cannot resist his 'But I do'.

All these qualities go to build up this figure of fantasy and to give him the charm which has imprinted itself upon the popular imagination. He has been described as a chameleon assuming all colours,* and Marmontel effectively summarised the impression he makes: 'His character is a mixture of ignorance, simplicity, wit, awkwardness and grace. He is not so much a fully-developed man as a great child with glimmerings of rationality and intelligence, whose mistakes and clumsy actions have a certain piquancy. The true model of his performance is the suppleness, agility, grace of a kitten, with a rough exterior which adds to the delight of his action; his role is that of a patient servant, loyal, credulous, greedy, always amorous, always getting his master or himself into a scrape, who weeps and dries his tears with the ease of a child, whose grief is as amusing as his joy.'

'What do you think of him?' asks Pantalone in Goldoni's *The Servant of Two Masters*, 'Is he a rascal or a fool?'; to which the Dottore replies, 'A little of one, I think, a little bit of the other.'

Like Pantalone and the Dottore, Harlequin sometimes appeared under names other than his own. For Goldoni and Gozzi he often masqueraded as Truffaldino, a name recorded as early as 1620; Traccagnino's dress was identical with Harlequin's, and, to judge from an illustration of 1618, Bagattino, with his variants Bagazzo and Bagolino, belonged to the same tradition.* Slightly more puzzling is Trivellino, already established by 1620 and made famous later by Domenico Locatelli. Dressed like Harlequin, he seems to have been merely a wittier and more adroit version of the former, and the pair frequently appeared together in Paris at the close of the seventeenth century.

Possibly there were other aliases, other deviations, but Arlecchino survived them all. When Goldoni's *The Servant of Two Masters* is acted today, Harlequin flits over the stage and Truffaldino is forgotten.

SCAPINO AND BRIGHELLA

Riccoboni said that Scapino was Harlequin's companion; Goldoni named that companion Brighella. The fact is that hosts of servants, diversely styled, appeared with Harlequin on the boards, and of these a large number wore, or presented modifications of, one characteristic costume consisting of plain, striped or laced tight-fitting trousers or breeches and jacket. It is noteworthy, too, that whereas Harlequin only rarely displays any skill in music, many of these companions of his are shown in contemporary illustrations either engaged in singing or with guitars in their hands.

Thus in an illustration of 1618 Scapino holds a lute as he serenades Spinetta, while a string of diverse instruments, no doubt those he was accustomed to use, hangs from a tree by his side. Certainly the actor Francesco Gabrielli, who was one of the first to take this role, was famed throughout Italy for his musical skill, while later portraits of Scapino, guitar in hand, testify to the continuance of the tradition.

These portraits, however, show him in a dress which is markedly different from that which he wears in one of his earliest representations, a well-known engraving by Callot; and at first it might seem as though a mistake were being made in placing him in the category of servants clad in tight-fitting garments. Callot shows him in a baggy dress with a great peaked hat: this surely, we might say, must show him as originally he appeared on the stage. Before accepting such a decision, however, we must pause to consider just how far Callot's designs, here and elsewhere, may be taken as exact historical records.

Hardly any book on the commedia dell'arte refrains from reproducing engravings

74

Per la Varietà
degli Instrumenti
Musici di
SCAPINO

In Sonori concenti,
Ch'alternati à uicenda
Van rapendo le menti,
Chi fia che non comprend
Librata in uario suon uaria
Ch'ò p' in uariar' in Scena e bella
H. Prarrebole: Dedica

Il B. Intagliaua

46 SCAPINO TAKES CENTRE STAGE

from the charming *Balli di Sfessania*, and for doing so ample justification exists, both because of their artistic excellence and because of their vivacity. For the suggestion of atmosphere and gesture nothing can equal them; yet we may well enquire whether the characters represented by Callot are to be accepted, as commonly they are, as being faithful portraits of actors performing on the stage. In the first place, Callot's figures, despite the variety of names he has attached to them, show little individuality in costume; his zanni are mostly all alike, and his captains are uniformly dressed. Secondly, the backgrounds which the artist has sketched in suggest rather carnival displays than theatrical performances—and in this connection we have to bear in mind that the collection is entitled *Balli di Sfessania*, the Neapolitan dances. In the middle distance among some of the designs trestle stages are adroitly etched in but these seem to stand apart from the main persons delineated in the foreground and the distinction between the one and the other is increased by the fact that associated with these background stages appear figures—such as a patched Harlequin in tight-fitting costume—of a kind not represented elsewhere.*

All of this seems to imply that Callot's sketches should be regarded, as historical records, with very considerable reserve. It is possible that the artist did see Scapino on the stage dressed in the way he has drawn him; but even so, that would mean only

75

47 BRIGHELLA   48 BUFFETTO

that thus some Scapino was clad in Naples towards the beginning of the seventeenth
century. Since a good deal of evidence shows that the Neapolitans tended to level
the various clearly defined types under a few general forms, Callot's etching cannot be
accepted as indicating Scapino's proper appearance, even assuming that it is an actor
whom the artist has sought to delineate. Much more probably, the etching itself
was inspired, not by a theatrical character at all, but by a Scapino of the carnival—
and the same judgement appears proper concerning most of the diversely named
persons presented in this series of 'Neapolitan dances'.

At any rate, Scapino's characteristic uniform elsewhere consisted of white trousers
or breeches, jacket and cloak, all edged with green bands or striped.

In character Scapino appears to have been always an astute intriguer, a clever
inventor of plots and stratagems, and yet one who was never vicious. The actor
Francesco Gabrielli, who himself possessed a nature which made him beloved of his
companions, first set the musical model of this type, and his inspiration, followed by
others, made Scapino one of the Italian comedy's most appealing characters during
later years.

Brighella, so far as costume is concerned, can hardly be differentiated from this
Scapino. His name, although not necessarily in a theatrical connection, is recorded
at an early date, but probably the part was not fully developed until the time when
Carlo Cantù (1609–c. 1676) played it variously under the titles of Brighella and of

49 FLAUTINO   50 FINOCCHIO

Buffetto. Like Scapino, Buffetto–Brighella was a musician; his earliest portrait presents him with a guitar, other instruments lying at his feet. Music, however, has not charmed his soul; although the eighteenth century wrought a change in him for the better, his basic nature, revealed in his mask with its heavy nose and lips and with its slyly glancing eyes, is rough and brutal. Many of his typical sentiments are cynical—'Honour is like a snake,' he says, 'You catch it by the head and it escapes you by the tail.'* Typical is the advice he gives his master concerning a rival: 'Kill him' is the theme of all his counsels. As years went by he established himself as the purveyor of epigrammatic counsels or reflections, and perhaps his most characteristic interpreter was Atanasio Zannoni, author of the *Motti brighelleschi* of 1807, who was described by a contemporary as 'speaking with elegance, reasoning with good sense, one versed in the sciences and in himself something of a philosopher'.*

To attempt anything in the way of a complete record of the teeming diversity of these companions of Harlequin would be tedious and perhaps futile, but some brief indication is demanded of their general scope. The virtual identity of Brighella and Buffetto indicates one manner in which they were multiplied, by name rather than by essential nature: indeed, it is not only Buffetto who is Brighella; the latter can be discerned, with only slight modifications, in Fichetto, Finocchio and Flautino as well—names given to the same essential figures by various actors. Finocchio (interpreted by Pavolino Zanotti) in 1620 is described as a second Scapino; Flautino (acted

77

51 MEZZETTINO

by Giovanni Gherardi) varied the role by adding to the playing of musical instruments exhibitions of his skill in imitating these by his mouth.

Other performers sought to provide their own inventions, sometimes wrought out of a diversity of models. In 1683, for example, Angelo Costantini took the name of Mezzettino, which had already been in existence for many years, and applied it to a new figure, thus, according to a near-contemporary, 'creating out of his imagination a character half-adventurer, half a valet'.* This Mezzettino, whether wearing a costume with certain features reminiscent of Harlequin's attire or the vertically striped dress made memorable by Watteau, had his own moment of glory during Costantini's tempestuous lifetime. Costantini was a man of wit and vigour, one who had the ability to carry his part, as it were, into real life. Anecdotes concerning him abound and most have a kind of theatrical flavour. Like a scene from a play, for example, is the account of his dedicating a comedy to the Duc de Saint Agnan, a patron famed for his generosity. Expectantly Costantini presented himself at the ducal palace, where he found that before he could be ushered into the presence he was forced to promise a third of his gift-to-be to the gate-man, another third to the hall-porter and the remaining third to the valet. When eventually he was brought before the duke, he amazed that nobleman by asking, not for money, but for a hundred strokes of a cane; explaining his position, he requested that these be given to the servants to whom he had made his promises. For his part, the duke entered into the spirit of the scene, proving almost as good a comedian as the actor, rebuking his servants and giving a hundred louis d'or to Costantini's wife—so that Mezzettino might still have the money without breaking his word. From episodes such as this no less than from his performances on the stage the name of Mezzettino became famous in late seventeenth-century society.

Concerning the natures of most of the similar characters who come swarming upon the stage during these years little can be said. What, for instance, was the Sardellino who plays such a prominent part in one collection of scenarios or the Capellino who crops up frequently in several collections? The question cannot be answered, and there is no reason why they and many of their comrades should not be left in obscurity. Only three or four deserve, for various reasons, to be singled out and to stand as representative of the rest.

One picture serves at once to display two of them and to illustrate the wide differences which are to be found in this area. Here Beltrame and Trappolino appear together. Concerning the former we know that this part was made famous by the actor-author Niccolò Barbieri. His appearance here may be supplemented by reference to a print given on the title-page of that comedian's own work *La supplica* (1634), which more clearly reveals his coarse-featured, heavy-nosed and bearded mask—for mask it unquestionably is, although it has been erroneously taken as representing the actor's own features. Despite the fact that other information

79

52 TRAPPOLINO AND BELTRAME

53   TRASTULLO AND RICCIOLINA

does not exist, we may perhaps guess from his appearance that Beltrame was not unlike Brighella. The companion portrait, that of Trappolino, shows a figure entirely different, younger, dressed in more servant-like clothes of grey colour and a red hat, and with a suggestion of agility lacking in the other—all thoroughly appropriate for the intriguer who, under this name or under its variant Trappola, carried on a not inglorious career from the first part of the seventeenth century down to the middle of the eighteenth. Astute and active, full of quips and cranks, apt to move from self-confident chicanery to exhibitions of amusing folly, his part was praised by contemporaries and even a sonnet was penned on the contrast between his black and somewhat dismal mask and the laughter he purveyed.

Finally, because his dark costume resembles in shape that of Trappolino, we may pause for a moment with Trastullo. Here once more we encounter an instance where Callot is suspect. In one of his designs he has a character of this name in no wise distinguished from any other of his zanni, yet unquestionably the portrait of 1618 which shows him in his tight-fitting uniform is correct. Once more we can assume only that Callot saw fit to dress all his comic servants alike, or that he was depicting a non-theatrical figure, or else that the Neapolitan actors had abandoned all nice differences in their parts, levelling the whole group under the single clownish costume.

Apart from his appearance, which links him with Trappolino, this Trastullo, who was known as early as 1588* and who is clearly kept separate from Zanni in the Corsini scenarios, deserves his place here because of the way he is represented. The tightly costumed servants were introduced by the lute-playing Scapino: Trastullo appropriately ends the procession as, instrument in hand, he serenades his Ricciolina.

ZANNI, PULCINELLA AND PIERROT

In various scenarios, many, indeed most, of the servants so far discussed appear alongside a character called Zanni and are, therefore, distinct from him. Already reference has been made to this fact, but repetition is necessary as we turn to review the third group of serving-men. In considering them we must keep constantly in mind four things—first, that at the very beginning of the commedia dell'arte the typical servant was named either Zanni simply or else with a contracted form of the word 'zanni' attached to a second name, such as Zan Polo, or Zan Falopa, or Zan Selcizza, or Zan Capella, or Zan Panza di Pegora; secondly, that hardly any of the multitude of these double names recorded in the sixteenth or early seventeenth centuries correspond with those of the later individually designated servants, so that, for example, we look in vain for a Zan Arlecchino, a Zan Trappolino or a Zan Pedrolino; thirdly, that numbers of early prints clearly distinguish between the tightly dressed, patched Harlequin on the one hand and a loosely clad 'Zany Corneto' or simply 'Zany' on the other; and, fourthly, that in later years, although the generic

54 ZANNI
55 FRANCATRIPPA KNOCKING AT A DOOR
56 ZANNI, PANTALONE AND GRAZIANO

term 'zanni' was unquestionably applied to the race of stage servants in general, a single character called Zanni stood out in numerous plays as a person in his own right. Arlecchino may thus be a zanni in a general sense, but certainly he is not Zanni. It is possible that at the very start this Zanni was unaccompanied by any comic companion; certainly in the 1568 Bavarian show described by Massimo Troiano he stands alone. More probably, however, the earliest comedies included both a character called Zanni and another comic character who was given a special individual name. Of particular importance in this connection is the scenario of *La schiava* preserved at Modena, one of the most ancient of such texts; this presents 'Zane' as Pantalone's man, contrasting him with Burattino, Leandro's servant. What seems to have happened is that, while Zanni may have once ruled the comic stage unrivalled or with only lesser competitors, he soon came to share his glories with servants of a different kind, and, while his name was preserved as a generic term for the comic attendant, he himself was gradually forced to cede his place to the others.

Concerning his attire we possess ample evidence. His trousers are full and baggy, and equally loose is his open-necked blouse—together, they look somewhat like a pair of pyjamas; his hat commonly has a wide brim or else is peaked, thus distinguishing it from the round, often beret-like, caps worn by the other comic servants.

While his commonest role is that of a servant, occasionally he breaks away from such occupation to take the part of a bawd, a barber, a porter, a jailer, a ploughman, a gardener or (very rarely) an innkeeper. Throughout all of these he presents himself as a clown, a clown who is somewhat rough and uncouth. He delights in cheating others, but himself is easily cheated. The impression we receive is of a rude and unlettered creature, with perhaps a certain modicum of native wit, who, despite his activity and unlike Harlequin, displays no effervescent sense of fun and who differs from Harlequin, too, in bearing grudges. When, for example, he is tricked out of some money at the end of one act of a play, he never rests until in the next act he succeeds, often clumsily, in turning the tables on his tormentor.

Beyond this we find it hard to go. Harlequin and some of his companions possess such qualities as give them vital personalities; Zanni remains for the most part merely the clown, his role in each play being determined not so much by his nature as by the exigencies of the stage business. Despite the facts that he belonged to the Italian theatre from the very start and that his name was long remembered, he was, paradoxically, far less harmonised with the finer spirit of the commedia dell'arte than other comic servants, and perhaps it was not by chance that his name is not mentioned in Scala's basic collection.

What, however, assumes considerable importance is that various stage-characters grew out of this original Zanni type. Guazzetto seems to have been one of these, Stoppino another, Fritellino, the creation of the actor P. M. Cecchini, might be regarded as merely a livelier version of Zanni, and Francatrippa, even although he is distinguished from Zanni in the Corsini scenarios, has a costume almost identical. The Fossard album shows him alongside of Harlequin, and, while the latter could never be taken for anything but what he is, Francatrippa's attire displays not the slightest variation from that of the characters marked 'Zany' or 'Zany Corneto'. Elsewhere, his portraits are the same. In 1597 *L'Amfiparnaso* presents him in this wise; an early Italian print gives corroboration, as, for what it is worth, does a Callot sketch—all agreeing to demonstrate Nashe's mistake in speaking of 'Francatrip' Harlicken', as though these two persons were the same.*

Francatrippa and the rest, however, fade in significance when we turn from them to Pulcinella and Pierrot. In the enduring range of his career Pulcinella, Polichinelle or Punch, comes forward as Harlequin's chief rival: born certainly by the beginning of the seventeenth century, he gained one of his best interpreters in Antonio Petito (1822–1876); he has remained the principal person among the puppets; and his name and reputation in the nineteenth century was such that he was selected as the presiding genius of *Punch*.

The figure we recognise on the front cover of the well-known weekly, the figure once familiar on the puppet-stages set up by wandering showmen at street corners, differs, however, considerably from the true original Neapolitan Pulcinella. Among the commedia dell'arte figures Punch is almost unique in having two completely

57 PULCINELLA

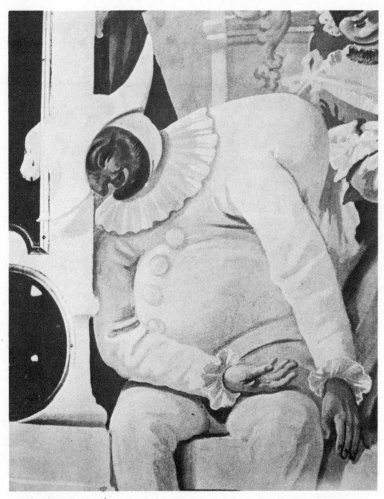

distinct costumes. In general, the other Italian characters either kept their original dress virtually unaltered from beginning to end or else modified their appearance gradually as the years went by. The strange thing about Punch is that he developed two contrasting uniforms. When an Englishman thinks of him he sees a hump-backed creature with a hanging belly, clad in trousers and jacket ornamented either by lacing or by strips of ribbon, and wearing a conical hat. His half-mask has a huge hooked nose, a low forehead and a large wart on the brow. With this image in our minds we immediately recognise Punch in the background of the picture which shows Angelo Costantini receiving Harlequin's costume at the Théâtre Italien in 1688, in Bonnart's print of 'Polichinelle', in Lambranzi's engraving of a male and female Punch, and in numerous other prints and drawings from the end of the seventeenth century onwards.

In Naples, on the other hand, these pictures would almost certainly not be recognised. There, Punch started by wearing the loose white dress of Zanni, and during his long career in that city he continued to appear in the Zanni costume, with only such slight modifications as the lengthening of the sleeves of his blouse and the heightening of his conical hat or cap. One of his first portraits represents him as an older man, without any conspicuous hump, and we can follow him thence through dozens of illustrations on to the paintings of G. D. Tiepolo. If we are concerned with Punch's part in the early seventeenth century and with its enduring fortunes in Naples, it is of such pictures we must think.

There is no doubt, of course, that Punch ranks with Harlequin among the most prominent and influential characters of the commedia dell'arte, yet stress must be laid on the fact that his position both in the plays themselves and in the popular mind differs entirely from that of his companion. First of all, like all the characters created in Naples, he makes his entries not in one set role or position but in dozens. His commonest business is that of a servant, but he is also at times a peasant, a baker, a slave-merchant, an innkeeper, a painter, even the head of a household and a lover. Clearly, with such variety there could be but little opportunity of presenting him consistently as an individual. The chief quality of his speech seems to have consisted in a kind of stupid wit or witty stupidity essentially gross and vulgar, which often expressed itself by crude similes wherein the finer emotions and things of the spirit were brought down to crass earth; the Neapolitan audiences were not interested in his character; rather they delighted in listening to the gross blunderings and crude comparisons uttered in a diversity of circumstances, and never worried although one day Pulcinella came forward as a cowardly credulous fool and the next as a bold, vicious and successful rogue. The result is that while Pulcinella might prove popular on stages where farcical merriment was the object, he could not survive in any theatre which had higher aims; in the Comédie Italienne he never established himself firmly, whereas on the booths set up at the Parisian fairs he became master of ceremonies.

In effect, Pulcinella was a characterless dummy which could be dressed up in any way a particular actor—or a particular public—desired. This explains why a Neapolitan can claim the Pulcinella of his stage as the very symbol of Naples' spirit, why a Frenchman can assert that Polichinelle is an expression of the Parisian populace, why *Punch* may be the title of an English periodical. A dramatic figure can never have individual personality if he is regarded as the representative of an entire people, and the identification of Punch with a whole community in itself testifies to the nature of his being.* Pantalone may be a Venetian and speak the dialect of his city, but he could never be claimed to represent Venice in its entirety; this claim could not be made precisely because he possesses an individuality of his own.

A third sign of the difference in principle between the creation of Pulcinella and that of the Tuscan characters may be found in the tendency to double, treble and quadruple his person. No painter would think of multiplying Harlequins on a single

87

59　A SCHOOL OF PULCINELLAS

canvas, but Pulcinella by the dozens is the common practice of Tiepolo and others—
a practice which can be traced back into the seventeenth century.* Whether such
droves of similarly clad, identical figures could have been actually found on the stage
or not does not matter; the significant fact is that Tiepolo with his artistic imagination feels Pulcinella in this way—not as a single recognisable entity but as a stock
type capable of extended reproduction. The difference between Harlequin and
Pulcinella comes closely akin to the distinction between a work of art wrought by
a master's hand and lifeless clay statuettes turned out mechanically by the score from
a single mould and tinted in various colours according to individual fancy.

The indeterminate nature of this Neapolitan figure receives emphasis when he is
compared with another character which, if we disregard the mask and the hat, often
bears a close likeness to him—the French Pierrot. The likeness itself is not surprising
since the latter either derived his being from the former or else stemmed from the
same source. The difference arises from the fact that, whereas Pulcinella has no real
basic 'character', Pierrot resembles Harlequin in that he is a developing personality,
each stage in this development remaining consistent within itself and all the stages
having a clear relationship to one another.

The story, an interesting one, starts in Italy. As early as 1576 a company was
known by the name of Pedrolino—which is, of course, the Italian equivalent of the
French Pierrot—and four years later the Duchess of Ferrara was taking delight in
their performances at her palace. This Pedrolino was a Giovanni Pellesini, whose
amazingly lengthy career stretched well into the century following; when, in 1613,

88

he acted in Paris, he was already 87 years of age. In the plays of the Scala collection the person of Pedrolino plays an active part, and, whether Pellesini was or was not the model, unquestionably the depiction of the character there must have been closely connected with his interpretation of the role.* He is a servant always, evidently one who has been attached to his master so long that he is trusted implicitly, and his actions in the comedies justify that trust. Although at times he indulges his sense of fun by cheating others merely for the sake of the joke, his intrigues usually are directed in the interests of his employer. As often as not the young lover secures his bride only through his 'tricks and clever stratagems'; the close of several plays finds 'all praising him' for his skill. In himself, he is fully aware of his abilities, and the phrase 'Leave it all to me' constantly forms itself on his lips when the plot gets into a tangle. Occasionally he overreaches himself, but not often; his errors give but the sauce of vitality to his clearly delineated personality.

From a woodcut of 1621 his earliest dress seems to have been close to that of Zanni, although not quite so exaggerated in its bagginess.* An interesting possibility, however, is suggested in one of the designs attached to the Corsini scenarios. This depicts a character called Bertolino in a costume which might well be taken for the later familiar attire of Pierrot, slack white trousers and blouse with a large ruff.

60   BERTOLINO ENNOBLED

89

Although Bertolino appears elsewhere mainly as an independent peasant, frequently a gardener, the kinship between his name and that of Pedrolino may well make us wonder whether Pierrot's characteristic dress may not have developed in Italy even before it became established at the Théâtre Italien in Paris.

For the next stage we turn to Molière, who in 1665 presented his *Le festin de pierre* with Pierrot in the cast. Some eight years later the Italian comedians brought out a kind of complement to this play and gave Pierrot's part to Giuseppe Giaratone. That actor's success was immediate; Pierrot became an established figure; the French authors who then were collaborating with the Italians soon made of him an important element in their plots. The new Pierrot was distinguished by several qualities; he was lazy, that is certain, and his laziness may have been responsible in part for the fact that, in contradistinction to his companions, he was largely a static figure. More significant is his combination of outspokenness and what may be styled his calculated stupidity; he mistakes absurdly, yet often his errors may be viewed as exhibitions of his common sense. He always sees the follies of his master, and to a certain extent his

61   PIERROT

62 HARLEQUIN, PIERROT, THE LOVERS AND THE DOTTORE

gross misinterpretations of orders given to him are indirect comments on the errors of others. In Regnard's *Le divorce* (1688), for example, he is the servant of the recently married and already worried M. Sotinet. The latter gives him certain orders and ends by enquiring 'You quite understand what I've told you?' 'Oh yes, sir,' replies Pierrot, 'You've told me not to let your wife into the house and to slam the door in her face.' M. Sotinet flies into a rage: 'You stupid fool! What I said was just the opposite. I told you not to let anyone in to see my wife and to slam the door on all callers.' 'But that's what I said, sir. Incidentally, you're jealous then?' 'That is not your business', his master informs him coldly, but Pierrot merely laughs. 'That's a good joke,' he says, 'Why the devil did you decide to get married at your age? Don't you know that an old husband is like a tree that can bear no more fruit and is good for nothing save to provide some shade?'

A very similar scene occurs in Losme de Montchesnay's *La critique de la cause des femmes* (1687), where he is the servant of a slightly younger but equally perplexed husband, Cinthio. The latter starts speaking to himself and deploring his lot: such a crowd of gallants flock round his wife, he reflects, that 'soon I shall be taken for

91

63   THE ITALIAN COMEDIANS

a —'. At this Pierrot interrupts: 'You've done fine, sir. You'll always be taken for
what you are.' 'What do you mean, you rascal?' cries Cinthio. 'Me?' enquires
Pierrot, 'Nothing, sir, I didn't say a thing.' 'What, you rogue? You didn't say
anything? Didn't you say I had done fine and would always be taken for what I
am?' Pierrot agrees: 'Yes, sir', and Cinthio asks: 'Well, then, you knave, what
am I?' Pierrot's reply is characteristic: 'Since you really want to know, you're a fool
for having married a seventeen-year-old filly, who finds every house better than
your own and who constantly drags a train of courtiers after her.'

Giaratone's costume for the part fundamentally resembles that made famous by
Watteau's artistry, although the refinement delineated there serves to carry Pierrot
into his third avatar. The commonsense downrightness becomes changed into sensi-
tivity, and the man who can so clearly discern the follies of others develops into a

still honest but gentler character, rather lonely in his visions. The famous Watteau painting which shows the members of the company surrounding Pierrot separates him from the others as though he were something likeable but strange. To the later romantics this new Pierrot strongly appealed; he was invested almost with an atmosphere of mysticism and became the central character in dramas such as Catulle Mendès' *Le docteur blanc* and Paul Margueritte's *Pierrot assassin de sa femme*.

These plays carry us far from the early commedia dell'arte, and we are carried equally far by the Pierrot brilliantly acted by Jean Gaspard Deburau at the Théâtre des Funambules in Paris in the early nineteenth century. Here he lost his power of speech, for Deburau excelled almost exclusively in mime, and, although he was given a characteristic series of attitudes, little attempt was made to present him consistently as a person. Rather, we might say, Pierrot's costume was assumed by Deburau as a convenient attire to clothe his own individual pantomimic skill. In effect, there was thus established the tradition which stretches down to the modern Pierrots of the trestle stages at seaside resorts.

64 PIERROT

Watteau.

93

No doubt the hold now possessed by Pierrot on the public imagination bases itself largely on these later developments, yet it is of importance to remember both that his growth may be traced regularly and steadily from the late sixteenth century and that each form he assumed until he became a creature of pantomime has been etched with clarity. Pierrot's original costume seems to have been akin to that of Zanni, and in the eighteenth century it was observed that it resembled that of Pulcinella, Zanni's Neapolitan variant. From the same Zanni character thus came two of the most prominent commedia dell'arte figures: Punch, with his vivid personality but indeterminate qualities; and Pierrot, clearly and accurately imagined—the honest and emotionally appealing creature who has become a symbol almost as powerful as the eternally bustling, constantly gay and irrepressible Arlecchino.

THE REST OF THE CAST

After having hacked our way through the jungle of comic serving-men, maybe there is a sense of relief when we turn to look at the less entangled areas inhabited by the other members of the commedia dell'arte troupe.

THE SERVETTA

First come the maid-servants, commonly called the 'serve', 'servette' or 'fantesche'. Just at the first glance, these may seem to be as diverse as their male companions, offering a rich array of individual names as variegated as those of the others. Armellinas, Corallinas, Olivettas and Spinettas flock in upon us, accompanied by numerous variants of similar kind, and we might well feel that these deserve separate attention.

Further scrutiny, however, indicates that all these creatures live in a comic world different from that of the zanni. In the first place, only a very few of their names became fully established: Franceschina was one of these during earlier years, Colombina and Smeraldina in later times became pervasive, and we can trace enduring traditions for Diamantina, Nespola and Ricciolina. Yet even these fail to reach distinct individualisation. It is amply apparent that the names themselves do not serve to designate personalities of the sort exemplified by Harlequin, Scapino, Brighella, Punch and Pierrot, but are merely dependent on the choice of actresses interpreting the one single part. No doubt one of these players performing, let us say, under the title of Rosetta produced an impression distinct from that of another actress who had selected the name of Suparella, but this does not mean that Rosetta was regarded by comedians or spectators as a character which in its own right was to be presented differently from that of the other.

A second observation is that, whereas the zanni normally come in pairs or trios, the servetta almost invariably acts alone: rare indeed are scenarios introducing two serving-maids. This, in turn, leads towards something even more fundamental. Active though the servetta usually shows herself, she does not form one of the focal

95

points in these comedies. A few later scenarios of Franco–Italian vintage may erratically elevate her to a dominant role, but normally she is a subservient figure.

The statement that the servetta presents herself as one single character, however, requires some slight comment and qualification. While undoubtedly expressing the truth, it should not be taken to imply that in comedies early and late this character was always delineated in the same manner. Even a slight familiarity with the commedia dell'arte's history makes evident the fact that the servetta of 1600 was both older and rougher than her younger, more refined counterpart of 1700. Sharp as the difference may be, on the other hand, the impression we receive is not one of two opposed personalities. Rather might we say that a comedy of 1600 which introduces Franceschina shows us a woman in early middle-age and that a comedy of 1700 which introduces a Colombina shows us a girl in her teens such as we could readily imagine growing into this Franceschina over the passage of years.

The general early trend in the presentation of Franceschina is symbolised in the fact that although an actress, Silvia Roncagli, was playing the part during the last quarter of the sixteenth century, the Franceschina of the great 'Gelosi' company in 1577 was certainly a man, Battista da Treviso, while in 1614 the Franceschina of the 'Uniti' was an actor, Ottavio Bernardini. Obviously the fact that these were female impersonations indicates that the role was treated in a rough comic manner and that the servetta was not intended to be of early youth. Such a conclusion receives confirmation both from iconographical evidence and from the scenarios. In sixteenth-century prints Franceschina is clad in a simple nurse-like uniform, with a long apron, a wide belt and a coif: she seems to be in her thirties or forties. In the comedies she appears frequently in scenes more than a trifle coarse, and it is quite clear that she is intended to be a woman with ample experience of the ways of the world. Throughout the Scala comedies her normal role is that of attendant upon one of the ladies, although she does come in once or twice as the keeper of a lodging-house or as the wife of a serving-man, sometimes seduced by Pantalone or Graziano. Light-hearted and loyal to her mistress, she frequently ends by joining hands with Harlequin or another. Hardly a comedy is without her and she takes a fair share in the intrigue, but this share is peripheral rather than central.

As the seventeenth century advanced, we begin to see her as she might have been in her adolescence—a young girl, often presented as the daughter of one among the men-servants or of an innkeeper, not as yet mature and, although daring, still inexperienced. At this age she reveals herself as sprightlier and perter, a girlish character whose merry wit easily defeats the efforts of older lovers to capture her heart: 'Old men are like trees', she declares gaily, 'When they can bear no more fruit, they're cut down for firewood.'* Youth alone makes its call to her.

This younger servetta dresses more daintily than the older Franceschina, and the daintiness becomes more pronounced after Caterina Biancolelli, at an early age,

65 FRANCESCHINA   66 ARLECCHINA

appeared at the Théâtre Italien as Colombina. Vivacious and buoyant, an incorrigible flirt, lively and animated, this Colombina is Watteau's heroine, and not only chance leads her to vary her name by appearing on occasion as Arlecchina. In spirit she draws close to the Harlequin of the late seventeenth and early eighteenth centuries; her adopting of his diversely coloured triangles and lozenges seems eminently appropriate.

THE CAPITANO

The other character who usually enters alone is the Capitano; for the most part the scenarios mark him out as being 'da sè', 'by himself', although he can be at times the son of Pantalone or Graziano and in so far associated with a family. He differs from the serving-maid, however, by his forming a focal point of his own within the fabric of each plot.

In one sense the Capitano is simply Bobadill writ large. Without a doubt much of the delight which contemporary audiences took in him derived from the very extravagance of his lengthy harangues. Francesco Andreini, who created the part of Capitano Spavento, knew what he was doing when he issued in 1607 his famous *Bravure*, fantastic discourses interrupted occasionally by the pertinent and impertinent questions or comments of his commonsense servant Trappola. Unquestionably, other actors profited therefrom, as they did also from *Le stupende forze, e bravure del Capitano Spezza Capo, et Sputa Saette* (Bologna, 1606) by Antonio Pardi, from the *Rodomuntadas castellanas* (Paris, 1607) and from G. C. Croce's *Vanto ridicoloso del Trematerra* (Bologna, 1619). The names by which he came upon the stage testify to the fantastic quality of his nature—he is Capitano Coccodrillo or Rinoceronte, Spezzaferro or Terremoto, Spavento da Vall'Inferna or Sangue e Fuoco.

Were the Capitano only this, however, he would today be of but slender interest to us, and his demise in commedia dell'arte performances might have come much earlier than in fact it did. We may grant that in his boasting resides a kind of grotesque magnificence—the magnificence of a man who, versed in all the famous records of conflicts mythological and historical, lives in a grandiose world of his own imagining, a creature whose visions are his only true reality. Like Browning's student he turns the pages of his Plutarch, dreams, 'Thus should I live, save or rule the world', and only with a wrench descends at times to the actual scenes around him. Yet even when we admit this, we feel we cannot long remain with any sense of pleasure either among the extravagances of his fantasy or among the many episodes in which he is sadly discomfited. The roaring of bombastic words must soon begin to pall and the sudden exhibitions of abject cowardice on the part of the man who had claimed to have pulled Jove's beard and out-Alexandered Alexander must cease to be amusing— even although occasionally the situation has a certain piquancy. The Capitano and Arlecchino enter, for example, and the former recounts his exploits, using many mighty-sounding words and bold gestures. Arlecchino listens in silence, and then, as the Capitano pauses for breath, he quietly remarks: 'Sir, in spite of all this, you'd better watch out for the police; they're going to arrest you.' The Capitano is terrified, asks what the charge may be and is told he will be accused of a falsehood. 'They say', Harlequin continues, 'that you have belied the proverb which declares that a shirt is nearer the skin than a jacket; I'm told you don't wear a shirt at all.' Hastily, the Capitano assures him that such had indeed formerly been his practice because, when he flew into a passion, his hair—'and I am hairy as Hercules', he adds—always stood on end and pierced his shirt so full of holes that it looked like a colander. 'However,' he goes on, 'for some time I have been able to moderate my passions, and so I wear a shirt now like everybody else.' The scene is ridiculously entertaining, but when repeated in varying forms it must inevitably lose its flavour—although, of course, we have always to remember that what may seem dull in the recounting possibly assumed true comic form when interpreted by a good actor. This 'hyperbolical part', full of impossibilities, could, according to Cecchini, be made truly

67   CAPITAN SPAVENTO

68 CAPITAN MATAMOROS

effective when lightly performed by a skilled and lively actor, smooth in gesture, with a good voice, dressed in bizarre and extravagant costume.*

Unquestionably this description of the Capitano—impoverished, cowardly, boasting, fantastic—is true to the way in which he commonly appears in the scenarios, and we can see him thus in many Callot designs where he stands with legs splayed out and back bent, hardly able to hold his sword, as he tries to retire from some ridiculous duel in which he has become involved. Yet, true though this may be, those many writers on the commedia dell'arte are in error who stop their account of him at this point. Ranged alongside the pictures of impossibly fantastic Captains are numerous others which display a handsome man, well set-up, neatly and elegantly dressed in military fashion, wearing or holding his sword in such a way as to suggest that he is thoroughly familiar with its use. Thus he stands forth in one of his earliest representations, that in the *Compositions de rhetorique* of 1601; thus appears 'Capitano Matamoros' in a late seventeenth-century print; except for long hair and moustache Capitan Spezza Ferre in France is not far different; and, most important of all, the portrait of the greatest of these Captains, Francesco Andreini, shows him as a dignified and indeed impressive figure.

Appearances, of course, are notoriously deceptive, and the pictures of such a kind might mean no more than that various actors achieved their effects by a contrast between their exaggerated speech and an outward seeming of distinction and nobility. Certainly we know Francesco Andreini's attire and we know the sort of speeches he delivered: the two are utterly at variance. A clue to something else, however, comes from a remark made by this very Andreini in the introduction to his volume of hyperbolical disquisitions: he explains how, early in his career, he deliberately applied himself to 'the part of the proud, ambitious and vaunting military man', calling himself Capitan Spavento da Vall'Inferna; and, he adds, 'I took such delight in this that I gave up performing my former chief role, that of the Lover'.* Precisely the same passage from Lover to Capitano was made by another actor, Francesco Antonazzoni, who left the character of Ortensio for that of the boasting officer. There seems, then, some kind of a connection between the two roles.

Perrucci remarks that 'all these vaunting captains can serve also as third or second lovers, but for the most part derided, cheated, laughed at and ridiculed by the ladies and the servants alike'.* When we turn to the Scala collection of scenarios, we find him frequently in such a role, endeavouring to win the affections of a Celia or Flaminia but, at the close of the action, deluded and left out in the cold. In situations of this kind he still shows himself as a ridiculous figure, arousing laughter and contempt; but it is important to observe that in numerous other comedies his role of lover differs considerably. At times he appears as Pantalone's son or as the bosom-friend of one of the sympathetic young lovers; here he not only acts as a suitor but wins his lady's affections. Thus, in one typical Scala play, he is the hero's friend and

FRANCESCO ANDREINI

succeeds in wooing his Flaminia into marriage; in another he is shown pursuing an actress but followed by a faithful girl who, devoted to him, has disguised herself as a page and whom he ultimately recognises and takes to his heart; in a third he is attacked and left for dead by the two young leading men, but eventually shows his worth, becomes their friend and marries the heroine.

This tradition continues in later collections of scenarios. He enters as the heroine's brother or as the second lover; he is a 'distinguished person' who wins a young and lovely bride; in one play, *La nave*, a tragi-comedy, he even acts as the noble

102

champion who, in a romantic plot, gains the hand of his queen. Here the Captain's dream of glory has been metamorphosed into actuality.

We must, therefore, be careful to see two sides to him—and they are two sides to the nature of one man and not two separate personalities. In fact, he is presented like Pantalone and not like Coviello. Just as Pantalone has his basic seriousness against which his follies are contrasted, just as he lives in the separate worlds of his well-regulated home and his stupid amatory adventures, so the Capitano is at one and the same time a military man who may fittingly be a friend to the hero or husband of a heroine and a dreamer who at times allows himself to become lost in an imaginary world of his own devising. Without doubt, the secret of his success in earlier times must have derived mainly from such a contrast, and perhaps his later disappearance from the stage may have largely been due to a gradual vulgarising of his part so that his basic 'seriousness' became submerged in clowneries.

This disappearance was gradual. Some individual companies retained him in their casts well into the eighteenth century, but by about 1630 his days of grandeur were gone and at the Théâtre Italien he utterly vanished. His importance, however, may be gauged from the fact that the gap thus left was appreciated by the players and that another derivative character was developed to take his place—for the second half of the seventeenth century was the time when Scaramouche soared up in the theatrical firmament.

Not that Scaramouche was born then—rather that he assumed new qualities to meet a particular need. Already in Callot's designs appears a Scaramuccia, dressed in somewhat untidy breeches and shirt, with a feather-ornamented beret on his head and a sword held awkwardly in his hand, giving the impression of a comic Captain; and under this name or under that of Scaramuzza he makes sporadic entry in divers early records. It was not, however, until Tiberio Fiorilli came on the scene that he was invested with real distinction and became a figure whose name developed into a by-word in seventeenth-century circles and whose interpreter found himself the centre of an elaborate myth. When in 1695 Angelo Costantini issued his *Vie de Scaramouche*, its pages were eagerly read by a French public prepared to accept its fantastic adventures as truth, and in numerous editions the volume carried the fame of Scaramouche far beyond the environs of the Parisian Théâtre Italien where Fiorilli won his greatest triumphs. At the same time prints of various kinds familiarised everyone—even those who were not regular theatre-goers—with his appearance. Hardly any character was better known than Scaramouche as Fiorilli dressed him—in a neat black uniform of breeches, jacket, cloak and beret, its sombre hue relieved only by a falling collar or a ruff.

Often these portrait-prints were graced with eulogistic verses. In one, the poet declared that Scaramouche 'was the master of Molière, and his own master was Nature'. When, in 1659, a rumour spread in Paris that Fiorilli had died during a

70 SCARAMUCCIA

71 GIANGURGOLO ON A TRESTLE STAGE

journey to Italy, the pamphleteer Loret hastily produced a set of lamenting verses, deploring the loss of the man who could exhibit such skill, the man who gave delight to all but especially to the intelligentsia, the man who was commonly styled 'the Prince of Wags and the Wag of Princes'.*

In these verses Loret spoke of Fiorilli's excellence in counterfeiting the sad and the merry, the foolish and the wise, adding the remark that these 'in brief were all different persons'; and perhaps these remarks point to the fact that Scaramouche was a character designed somewhat in the Neapolitan model, a bit of a Captain, a bit of a comic zanni, a stage-figure which permitted a brilliant performer such as Tiberio Fiorilli to make of it what he willed. And there is evidence that his brilliance expressed itself rather in action than in words: Fiorilli's greatest strength lay in his silent mimicry. In Gherardi's *Théâtre italien* the text of *Colombine avocat pour et contre* is suddenly interrupted by an account of what happened in a particular scene: 'Scaramouche enters, tidies up the room, takes his guitar, seats himself in a chair and starts to play while waiting for his master. Pascariel comes quietly behind him and beats out the measure above his shoulders—which terrifies Scaramouche greatly. In a

105

word, it is here that this incomparable Scaramouche, who is the ornament of the theatre and the model of the most illustrious actors of his time, who have learned from him the difficult art, so essential for persons of their kind, to stir the passions and to let these passions be aptly expressed on their faces—it is here, I say, that he convulsed the audience with laughter for a good quarter of an hour in a scene of terror during which he uttered not a sound. It must be acknowledged that this excellent actor possessed this marvellous talent to such a high degree of perfection

106

that, by the very simplicity and naturalness of his actions, he produced a greater effect than commonly can be achieved by skilled orators using the most persuasive charms of rhetoric. This is what caused one nobleman, who had seen him playing in Rome, to declare that "Scaramuccia does not speak, yet he says many fine things".'

One other allied character developed in Naples—the Calabrian Giangurgolo, but about him we do not know so much.* His portrait in the early eighteenth century, with its long-nosed mask, short trousers, red and white sleeves, conical hat and long sword, suggests an admixture of elements taken from the Captain and the zanni. Precisely when he came into being is not known, but the appearances he makes in various scenarios indicate that, like all his Neapolitan companions, he had no true personality. Usually he is a servant, a jailer or an innkeeper; that, however, does not prevent him from being on occasion a rival of the Capitano and even the head of a household. We shall not go far wrong in regarding him merely as a clown, although ultimately derived from the Capitano.

THE LOVERS

There must be a sense of wrench in passing from this degenerate and vulgar relic of the Capitano to the elegant Lovers. Generally there are four of these Lovers, usually called amorosi or innamorati, in each comedy, although not infrequently three pairs instead of two make their appearance; and, since the comedies invariably deal with the theme of love, in one sense they form collectively the core of the action. As often as not the plot begins with reference to them and it ends with a suitable series of marriages.

All this is true, yet fundamentally they are to be regarded much as Claudio and Hero in *Much Ado About Nothing*. Without doubt the fortunes of that couple form the basic theme of Shakespeare's story; at the same time, neither Claudio nor Hero has any great character interest, so that, when we call *Much Ado* to mind, we think immediately not of them but of the whole action of the play, its atmosphere and quality, and of persons such as Dogberry and Verges. Exactly so is it with the commedia dell'arte; the Lovers are in one sense dominant, in another they have only indirect significance.

Under various names they come forward before the public. Orazio, Silvio, Ortensio are favourites among the men, and among the women Isabella, Flaminia, Angelica, Eularia, but since each actor and actress selected his or her particular title the designations are legion. Like the names of the servetta, however, these rarely if ever indicate any special qualities associated with the parts, and as we look now at the commedia dell'arte scenarios we have an impression of just one innamorato and of one innamorata, however the characters may be called, infinitely repeated. In many ways such an impression, while justified by the texts, must be qualified by several considerations. Shakespeare's Claudio and Benedick are distinct personalities in *Much Ado*, but if we were to reduce that play to a scenario would we in fact perceive much difference between this pair or even between Hero and Beatrice? The answer obviously is that the sense we have here of separate individualities arises almost wholly from the words which Shakespeare has given to these characters. In performance the Orazios and Isabellas were provided with such words by the comedians, and we must believe that the personalities and styles of these comedians supplied for contemporary audiences the variety which, looking only at the scenarios, we feel is lacking. Each actor and actress had his or her own manner of playing, and the praise meted out to many of them in prose or verse serves to indicate how they impressed themselves individually upon the consciousness of contemporary spectators. Some descriptions of actors famous in this role might almost seem, not so much descriptions of individual players, but rather descriptions of a dramatic character. The Lover has an excellent voice, a supple body, a ready wit and unaffected charm; at a moment he can find a gracious quip which another person might throw away or render vulgar, but which from his lips issues with delicate point and tart vigour. Our thoughts here go to a character like Mercutio; and if we think of a companion actor whose skill lay more towards the romantically sentimental, we shall have an imaginative picture of contrasting figures not far different from those in Shakespeare's comedies.

The instructions provided for the interpretation of these roles are all in general terms and consequently such exercise of the imagination becomes essential if the force of the Lovers is to be appreciated. They had all to be fashionably dressed, elegant in their appointments; all of them—no matter whether they were the children of Venetian Pantalone or Bolognese Graziano—had to speak good Tuscan; and all were bidden to enrich their minds by wide reading in polite literature. Already reference has been made to the kind of dialogues which they might memorise and use on occasion; these demand some further comment. In perusing such dialogues, we must not assume that all the speech of the Lovers was in this style; many, indeed most, of their lines were certainly 'realistic' in the sense that they were the kind of things which young gallants and their mistresses would have used in ordinary conversation. Clearly, however, 'realistic' speech of this sort, if pursued throughout the length of a play, would have clashed in tone with the differently conceived words of the servants, of Pantalone, Graziano and the Capitano. The memorised dialogues, so highly mannered as to deserve the title of arias, were introduced deliberately to keep the Lovers in harmony with the comedy as a whole, serving to bring these elegant creatures, who otherwise would have remained apart, within the variegated fabric.

Although several records tell of actors who played as amorosi to an advanced age, our general impression of these persons is of extreme youth—youth whose irresponsibility and impetuosity explain and justify the tempestuous movement found in so many of the comedies. Sometimes this movement is relatively simple—two pairs of lovers opposed by parental obduracy and prepared to proceed to any length to

108

73 MARIO AND FLAVIA

74 FLORINDA

75 LEANDRO

satisfy their desires. More commonly there are complications, criss-cross affections, misunderstandings, outbursts of jealousy, the sweeping across of dark despairs. The love theme may be constant, but the variety in its presentation is infinite.

While it is true that the scenarios, in general, give only faint indication of differences amongst the Lovers, occasionally the action does suggest the individualisation of the Orazios and Ortensios, the Isabellas and Flaminias. Sometimes one of the pair of men finds friendship more powerful than passion; an Aurelio becomes enamoured of an Isabella but, realising that she is devoted to Orazio, nobly decides to abandon his own pretensions so that true love may triumph. Or else Orazio, in love with Isabella, and because of this the rival of his friend Ortensio, is racked by fears and doubts until he discovers that Isabella is really his sister. Sometimes, too, the hero has manifest faults; he can be a gambler, distressing his mistress by his passion for the saloon; or he can be a libertine, whose bride-to-be has the mortification of seeing him make love to every girl he meets; or, less reprehensibly, he is an incorrigible meddler, who continually upsets all his servant's efforts to aid him.*

On the whole, however, such clearly outlined traits are rare; most of the Lovers seem marked only by their love, and even then are often incapable of making plans designed to achieve their ends; all depend for their happiness on the ingenuity of their servants. A slight distinction, however, may be made here between the amorosi and the amorose. Not only do the latter often have the opportunity of varying their status, by appearing at one moment as marriageable daughters and at another as wives; they share that quality possessed by Shakespeare's maidens of being more energetic and passion-wrought than their male companions. Occasionally one of the men, like Orlando Furioso, will go mad for love, but the girls are always doing it, and their scenes of 'pazzia' were ever due for applause; even when they do not become lunatic in earnest, feigned madness is one of the most frequent tricks in which they indulge to gain their ends. Occasionally a faithful lover follows his mistress disguised as a pilgrim; the thought which inspires Rosalind, putting on doublet and hose, comes again and again to the amorose. The men wear swords but not often do they draw them; the girls, on the contrary, when they believe themselves thwarted, immediately rush off to snatch a phial of poison or a convenient dagger. Where the men generally try to conduct their affairs with at least a modicum of cultured decorum, their mistresses permit no veneer of civilisation to control the impetuosity of their loves and hates.

CAVICCHIO, LAURA AND OTHERS

With these pairs of lovers the main focal characters of the commedia dell'arte reach their end; but we must not forget that, when occasion demanded, these plays had resources beyond the staple ten or dozen characters consisting usually of the two 'vecchi', the two serving-men, the captain, the servetta and the pairs of lovers.

77 DORALICE RUNS MAD

78 COCOLI

Although, as has been noted, actors generally kept to single parts, many players must have been able, when called upon, to interpret characters other than their principal roles. Rarely, if ever, was there doubling within the scope of a single play, but of comedians who could take more than one part in different plays there are numerous records.

Sometimes the presence of characters other than those which formed the basic group was made desirable in order to provide what might be styled local colour. Thus, for example, when the supposed location of a particular comedy was taken out of the city into rustic surroundings, an old peasant called Cavicchio was all ready to suggest the atmosphere of the countryside. Other characters, too, might on occasion serve a similar purpose. In Scala's *Il vecchio geloso* part of the spirit of rusticity is created by the gardener called Burattino, who carefully tries to tutor his daughter how to till the ground and plant seedlings. Burattino, however, does not always play such a role, and indeed the description given of him by Garzoni in 1585, his portraits as presented in two Bertelli prints and in one of the Corsini drawings, together with his listing as a servant in several scenarios, might well lead us to consider him some kind of zanni; yet the facts that he seems often to be an older man and that he is not infrequently presented in an independent position—gardener, country steward, innkeeper—must make us believe that his was a 'character part' which might be adjusted to suit the requirements of particular plots, and that the air of the countryside commonly was associated with him.

A character redolent of city streets rather than of the country is the bravo, the seventeenth-century representative of the modern gunman, who can be hired on occasion to protect an individual or a house. Niccoletto in one of Scala's comedies represents the type in general, although sometimes the bravo enters without a name or else gives a chance for one of the serving-men to effect a disguise and play still another trick.* Some comedies call for panders, slave-merchants and other kindred types, but here for the most part the zanni are called into service and under their own names assume different vocations, as we have seen them acting the parts of inn-keepers and jailers. One unique illustration presents in 'Chocholi'—evidently intended for Cocoli—the only known indication of a really ancient commedia dell'-arte character, in long gown and skull cap, bent in body, slippered and with spectacles in gnarled hand. With this exception, it would appear that, apart from occasions when Pantalone was caricatured, the Italian actors avoided such repre-sentations of extreme age.*

Among the women two types of a kindred kind may be discerned. One, variously styled Laura and Lavora, although she seems to have escaped the atten-tions of the historians of the commedia dell'arte, plays a small role from Scala's scenarios onwards. Apparently she was a middle-aged woman who entered either as a widow or as the wife of Pantalone, Graziano, Coviello or Tartaglia. No picture

8-2

of her has come down to us, and perhaps none is needed; she may be thought of as being played by one or other of the amorose who had become rather old to interpret the young heroine. Her counterpart among the servette was the Florentine Pasquella, who might present herself as the wife of Cola, Burattino or Cavicchio, but whose chief position was that of an elderly servant nurse. Apart from these, other variant roles, such as that of the courtesan, were seemingly taken by the amorose under their own names; Flavia, Celia, Rosalba and Cinzia thus all enter for the nonce as ladies of frail virtue.

Thus the cast comes to an end. There were, of course, many classes and professions unrepresented in this kind of comedy, but on the whole the commedia dell'arte succeeded in embracing fantastically most of the potentially comic life of its age—age was balanced with youth, ingenuity with folly. In turning now to consider the plays in which these characters appeared we may well take as our cue the words ascribed to P. J. Martello, an author who is commonly thought of as an exponent of tragic passion and as the standard-bearer of the literary classic style in drama. 'What melancholic soul', he asks, 'could maintain its gloom on seeing the Dottore nervously curling and uncurling the huge brim of his enormous hat, all dented and crushed by the restless movement of his hands?' He goes on to describe this Graziano delivering lengthy harangues entirely off the point, expressed in his rough Bolognese dialect which sounds so comic to Italian ears—Pantalone, with an owl-like mask, uttering his Venetian saws and sentences, arousing laughter when he deceives himself into thinking he is in his first youth again—Finocchio, with his rude Bergamo speech, in costume black and green with a flat beret on his head and a mask which makes him look like a squirrel, boldly indulging in the most brazen of stratagems and, when he is in danger of reprisal, snatching at any straw in an endeavour to escape—Arlecchino, with a black monkey-like mask, in tight motley dress, never sure whether he should stand motionless in one contorted pose or dash frantically over the stage, at one moment gesticulating violently, at the next remaining apathetically immobile, mingling folly with audacity, indulging in cries, exclamations, somersaults—the pert servetta, light and crafty, voluble and saucy—the impossible Coviello, Giangurgolo and Pulcinella—the Lovers, comic because of their affectations. All of these, Martello declares, arouse delight; and he closes his account, this author of an *Alceste* and an *Ifigenia in Tauride*, with a trenchant declaration: 'I must confess that I would give Sophocles' *Œdipus* and Plautus' *Amphitryon* for one of these incredible plays performed by good actors.'* And even the greater Goethe was in agreement: speaking of the troupe with which Gozzi was associated, he averred that 'the effect produced by these people was extraordinary'.*

116

THE COMIC SCENE

Behind all these characters, from Pantalone to Orazio, hovers the spirit of laughter, and only within the bounds of comedy's dramatic form could they expect to move freely, effectively and harmoniously. To this dramatic form, therefore, attention must almost exclusively be directed. At the same time, before the scope of the comic realm comes under review, a curious fact must be noted—that, although this Italian stage is and was familiarly thought of in terms of merriment, its actors frequently mingled their amusing performances with others of vastly divergent tones.

TRAGEDIES AND PASTORALS

In the Scala folio we proceed for the first forty scenarios through a territory of romantic delight or farcical intrigue. Then, suddenly, with *La forsennata prencipessa* an abrupt descent carries us into a gruesome tragic land whose horrifying terrors remind us of such Elizabethan dramas as *Tancred and Gismund* or *Titus Andronicus*. Stygian darkness envelops the action, broken only by startling flashes of lurid light. A Moorish prince elopes with a Portuese princess and takes refuge in the court of the King of Fez. There, wild passions consume the characters, the second act opening appropriately with the ominous display of a moon stained blood-red. The princess arouses lustful emotions in the breast of the king; the king's daughter, who loves her page, is pursued by the prince; the princess' brother arrives determined to wreak vengeance. As the action advances, the princess runs fervently mad in white satin and casts herself from a rock; the Moorish prince's severed head is brought on stage; the page's heart, torn from his body, is given to the king's daughter, who promptly places it in a cup of poison and quaffs the brew; the king commits suicide, and, for good measure, the Moorish prince's father, who has come to seek his son, perishes in combat. The whole production is disastrous, both in the ancient and in the modern signification of that word.

Following this dismal tragedy, Scala goes on to grace us with other dramatic experiments in varying styles. *Gli avvenimenti*, appropriately called an 'Opera mista', or 'mixed work', has one act comic, one tragic and one pastoral, something like the Elizabethan *Three Plays in One*. For the next piece, *L'Alvida*, the designation 'Opera regia', or 'regal work', applies to a vastly complex story of fantastic adventure, replete with combats and alarms, and introducing a wonder-working Magician, a most intelligent Lion and a sapiently sympathetic Bear. The next drama, *Rosalba incantatrice*, is labelled an 'Opera heroica', followed by an 'Opera reale', or 'royal work', entitled *L'innocente Persiana*, and the same designation appears attached to still a further dramatic variant, *Dell'Orseida*. The Elizabethans produced many two-part plays, but Shakespeare's *King Henry VI* is almost unique in its tripartite structure; *Dell'Orseida* follows its example by spreading its action over no less than three separate dramas. The last pair of plays in the folio are a pastoral, *L'arbore incantato*, and another 'regal work' called *La fortuna di Foresta, prencipessa di Moscovia*, which carries us to a Cracow setting and brings in a medley of Russian and Polish characters involved in adventures tragic or tragi-comic.

In the Scala collection such plays form merely a fifth of the total, but as the seventeenth century advanced pieces of this kind markedly increased. Even although most of the extant manuscript scenarios are comic, sufficient records exist to indicate that, principally under the impact of Spanish drama, the 'regal' productions became more frequent, imposing a tragi-comic impress on the stage and substituting for the earlier spirit an atmosphere of love and honour. Sometimes the plots tended towards the introduction of impossible and fantastic adventure, with magicians by the dozen controlling the action, with droves of spirits drifting in and out, and with numerous personifications—Death, Love, Reason, Pity, Hope, Desperation, Error and Time— appearing at appropriate moments in the plots. Often the extravagant adventures take place in a pastoral or 'Arcadian' setting, producing stories not dissimilar from that of *The Tempest*, dallying with the loves of shepherds and shepherdesses, and enveloping them with an aura of magical wonder. More commonly the spirit reflects that of Lope de Vega's and Calderón's dramas, seriously setting forth characters in the grip of violen tpassions and constantly battling between the force of their affections and the code of honour.

In the plays of pastoral flavour, perhaps the Italian actors were not wholly unfitted to capture effectively the scenes of Arcadian fantasy. The very concept of pastoralism emanates from ideas and not from facts, and it can never be anything save artificial and imaginative. Although such plays did not offer opportunities for the displaying of the same parts in diverse situations but instead brought forward groups of differently named shepherds and shepherdesses, the atmosphere of artificiality surrounding the Lovers in comedy could readily enable an Orazio and an Isabella to masquerade as a Sireno and a Clori—or, like Rosalind and Celia in *As You Like It*, associate under their own names with the denizens of Arcadia. Similarly, the spirit of magical wonder which enwraps nearly all these pastorals was not entirely out of

79 A PASTORAL SCENE

harmony with that which informed the comedies. We may, therefore, find justification for the inclusion of these works within the Italians' repertory and, at the same time, appreciate the contemporary esteem in which they were held.

Since almost the only sure direct contact between Shakespeare and the commedia dell'arte comes within this realm, at least some of the pastoral scenarios are reasonably well known, and consequently no need arises for any detailed description of their contents. Sufficient be it to say that from the time when Ferdinando Neri published his *Scenari delle maschere in Arcadia* (1913), most Shakespearian students have been prepared to recognise that one of the impulses which led Shakespeare to pen *The Tempest* derived from this source. Just as soon as we turn to such a piece as *Arcadia incantata* and find there 'a tempestuous sea, with a shipwreck', meet a Magician who rules this land through the assistance of spirits and read its opening scene in which Pollicinella, dripping wet, struggles ashore to tell us of the loss of the ship's company, and in which Coviello, at the other end of the stage, repeats his actions and words—the pair behaving exactly in the manner of Stephano and Trinculo—it is virtually impossible not to believe that Shakespeare had witnessed the performance of an improvised pastoral of this kind. And this belief receives ample confirmation as we trace other connections, the food offered by spirits to the famished mariners and its

119

sudden snatching away, the Magician's effort to right old wrongs and his voluntary abandonment of his art. Here is a world of enchantment which the Italian comedians could appropriately exploit.

The story, however, is far different when we examine the 'regal works' and those connected with them. As a general rule, dramas of these kinds display two distinct groups of stage persons—the 'serious' figures, sometimes pastoral and sometimes aristocratic, and the comic 'masks'. Pantalone and Graziano will appear as court counsellors, Olivetta as a maid attendant upon a princess, Buffetto as a servant or jester, Bertolino as a jailer. In effect, the arrangement does not deviate overmuch from that in several of Shakespeare's romantic comedies; we are reminded here of the contrast between the courtly quartets and the comic persons in *Love's Labour's Lost*, or, in *The Tempest*, of that between the ducal parties and the clowns. Yet there is a mighty difference. Hardly any of the commedia dell'arte pieces of this sort display any endeavour to secure an integrated and harmonious whole; the two groups of serious and comic characters are permitted to remain separate, poles apart.

As an example may be taken an interesting scenario which treats the Elizabeth–Essex affair in romantically conventional manner—'The Honourable Loves of the Queen of England, with the Death of the Count of Essex' (or 'Sessa', as the original title presents his name).* Essex has long loved Lucinda, but, after returning from a successful military expedition to Bohemia and after having romantically saved his queen from a would-be assassin, he attracts the attention of Elizabeth; in a fury of jealous rage, Lucinda determines to murder the queen, who, for her part, falls into a torment of despairing hate when Essex informs her that Lucinda has been his mistress for many years. As a result, although the noble count thwarts yet another attempt on Elizabeth's life, he is sent to execution, and the drama closes with an allegorical show of Love and Death. Into the midst of this sad story come the ridiculous antics of Buffetto, Essex' servant, Bertolino, Elizabeth's gardener, Coviello, servant to a French prince, Pantalone and Graziano, counsellors. The two worlds—the world of love, honour and tragic passion, and the world of merriment—simply cannot harmonise.

Despite the popularity of such inchoate dramas, it seems manifestly obvious that they were unfitted by their very nature for adequate presentation in the commedia dell'arte style. For the comic scenes, of course, the improvising method can be effective, but its power must inevitably be severely restricted when tragically conceived situations and passions call for expression. Quite apart from this, the nature of the 'regal works' necessarily involved a complete departure from the characteristic principle operating to create the special qualities manifest in the comic plays. Certainly Pantalone, Graziano, Buffetto, Bertolino and the rest, when transferred into the tragi-comic realm, could proceed without too great difficulty along familiar paths: even in such a piece as *La regina d'Inghilterra* the fervours of Elizabeth and

81 AN ORIENTAL SCENE

Essex did not prevent Bertolino and his companions from indulging in their comic business. The only thing wrong here is their removal from the environment proper to their beings into another milieu strange and at times antagonistic.

But when we consider the other characters something far more serious emerges. This may be illustrated from some of the Casanatense scenarios, which had obviously been adapted for use by a company in which the actors who played the Lovers bore the stage-names of Mario, Aurelio, Angela and Leonora. Now, if we turn to the play called *Avocato criminale*, we find that four of the chief characters are Roberto, Rosildo, a Princess and Teodora: in the manuscript whoever was responsible for the production has set down the stage-names of those actors who were to play these parts—so that Mario assumes the role of Roberto, Aurelio that of Rosildo, Angela that of the Princess and Leonora that of Teodora. Clearly, however, such procedure destroys the very basis of the commedia dell'arte's characteristic, and indeed unique, style in the presentation of dramatic figures. Instead of seeing a Mario or an Angelo brought in again and again within a series of plays, each interpretation adding to the creation of a cumulative personality, the audience here has simply a set of performances in which different, and differently named, roles are assigned to members of an acting group. In fact, we turn from what gave the commedia dell'arte its strength and individual flavour to a domain where its improvisation could not prove truly effective and where individual dramatists, working in association with actors accustomed to memorise the lines of written plays, would have been likely to create an impression more harmonious and more potent.

While, therefore, the tragi-comedies and the 'regal works' were freely introduced into seventeenth-century repertories, we may well decide that this aspect of the commedia dell'arte's activity, possessing at best merely a flimsy historical interest, can be set aside. It will be necessary to return to these plays when we seek to determine the causes of that theatre's decline, but of intrinsic interest they can offer little or nothing. The source of the improvised comedy's strength lies exclusively within the field of comedy, and discussion of the various conventions and methods employed by the Italian players may be restricted to that dramatic form.

PREPARING THE COMEDY

Unlike the meagre records of the Elizabethan stage, information concerning the preparations made for the performances of the Italian comedies is so ample that with even a slight exercise of the imagination we may easily re-create the circumstances attending the presentation of a new piece.

When the actors played indoors either in a rented hall or in a theatre of their own, the setting was both simple and, allowing for a few modifications demanded by particular plots, standard. The 'comic scene' was, in fact, as fixed and immutable as Serlio's familiar design, consisting simply of three or four 'case' or houses, each fitted

82 A COMIC SCENE

with practicable doors and windows, placed as though they were part of a city street
or square. The actors, gathered to rehearse a new comedy, knew from their experience
two things. They knew that the action would be closely associated with these houses,
which would offer them opportunities for much comic business in opening and
shutting the windows, pushing their way through the doors and utilising the edges
of the houses themselves for the purposes of concealed eavesdropping. It would be a
most eccentric comedy which did not present at least a few situations during whose
course the peering head of Harlequin or Pedrolino was shown to the audience
at one of the corners. The actors also knew that the physical houses of the setting
were sure to be intimately connected with their own positions in the comedy about
to be performed. With but few exceptions, each manuscript scenario started with
a list of the characters arranged in what may be called household groups, either
divided by ruled lines across the page or distinguished by the headings of 'Prima
casa', 'Seconda casa', 'Terza casa'. Pantalone's household might consist of a son
and a man-servant, Graziano's of a daughter and a maid, and to each one of the
'case' would certainly be assigned. So simple was the scenic arrangement that,
if on tour the players had to perform without such a setting, a painted back-cloth
could easily serve this need; Pedrolino might peer round its side and, if necessary,

123

a Franceschina could feign to be at a window by merely sticking her head over the top.

The comedians, then, are assembled, each familiarly expert in his established role, each accustomed to act in a team, each conscious of the traditional conventions of his stage. What they do not know, however, is the assignment of the houses for this particular play, the general scope of the plot and the arrangement of their scenes. Hence for the commedia dell'arte a director—'corago', 'concertatore' or 'guida'— was obligatory, and as a general rule the leading actor carried out the duties of the post.* First of all, he points out which house belongs to or is associated with each character, since, says Perrucci, 'every actor must know his own house; it would be ridiculous and absurd if a man were to knock at and go in by the door of somebody else's house instead of the door to the house belonging to him'. Next, the director reads aloud a very short 'Argomento', a brief outline of the chief past events leading up to the beginning of the play. The actors are aware that this Argument demands their close attention, since assuredly from time to time in the course of the comedy they will have to refer to previous events described therein. They are also aware that the Argument will be made available to them for later consultation, no doubt tacked to a wall in the wings. Thus, if the play to be performed is *La fortuna di Flavio*, the actor taking the part of Orazio will find that in the second act the Capitano asks him who he is: the instruction in the scenario reads: 'Orazio, keeping his eyes on Flaminia, narrates his life-story in detail as it appears in the Argument'. Or, if the play is *Isabella astrologa*, Orazio will discover that he has to come in as a Turkish slave, concealing his identity. An allusion is made to past events which affects him deeply: asked why he is so sad, he explains that he once had a friend called Orazio, 'who many times told him all the story of his miseries'; and the scenario adds, 'narrating all the events outlined in the Argument'. Similarly, at the very close of the play, Isabella, Orazio's beloved, is bidden to recount the story of the past, 'telling as a kind of epilogue everything that is written in the Argument to the comedy'.

Such instructions may seem undramatic, but, apart from the fact that all dramas must allude to episodes outside the stage action, the introduction of narrative material of this kind does not vary overmuch from similar practice in Shakespeare's works. The narrative which comes at the close of *Romeo and Juliet*, the explanations which are necessary in *Twelfth Night*, the record of earlier events introduced into *Measure for Measure*—these and others operate on the same principle. In Shakespeare's plays, of course, the author provided his own words; the composer of a scenario could do no more than pen his brief résumé, referring his actors to that.

Having thus read the Argument, the director now proceeds to go through the plot, indicating what each player will have to say, suggesting appropriate business and, in particular, making sure that business and dialogue will be properly har-

124

monised. 'This is no light task', remarks an eighteenth-century author. 'On the director depends the whole integration of the performance, and if the leading actor lacks the necessary theatrical experience, that will result in a corresponding lack of integration in the production, and the play will thus suffer greatly.'* In those days, be it observed, long stage experience was deemed essential for the man who undertook this task; there was none of the modern willingness to hand over a comedy to the tender mercies of any young and uninitiated tyro.

When the leading actor finishes his remarks, all that remains for the actors is to go away by themselves in order to meditate on what they will say and do when the time of performance arrives. Of rehearsals, in the present-day sense of the term, there seem to have been none.

TITLES AND ACTS

The time of performance arrives, and the spectators are gathered on their benches. Before the play begins, they listen to a prologue, almost always spoken by one of the comedians in character, with words not related to the drama which is to follow but rather designed amusingly to be an exhibition of Pantalone's, Graziano's or Franceschina's qualities.

83   THE DOTTORE SPEAKS THE PROLOGUE

From the title of the play the audience may form some general conception, if not of its plot, at least of its quality. For the majority of written dramas produced during the Renaissance period, comedies tended to have either impersonal and often pro-verbial titles, such as *A Humorous Day's Mirth*, *Much Ado About Nothing* and *Bartholomew Fair*, or else titles which laid emphasis on the generic type quality of a prominent character, such as *The Blind Beggar of Alexandria*, *The Humorous Lieu-tenant* and *The Woman Hater*. Tragedy, on the other hand, generally pre-empted the right to use personal titles, labelling its offerings by the names of its heroes. Frequently, these heroes were historical figures, a Julius Caesar or an Antony, and even when they were invented, like Othello, the title stress upon their names tended to emphasise the living, individual nature of their beings. We might say, therefore, that the usual procedure in written comedy was to underline the general and in written tragedy to emphasise the specific.

To a certain extent, the improvised comedies followed the line of the literary. Among the Scala scenarios, for instance, there are a few, such as *La mancata fede*, which refer in broad terms to the theme, a few, such as *Lo specchio* and *Il ritratto*, which allude to an object prominently utilised in the plot, a few, such as *Il cavadente*, which call attention to some amusing incident, and several, such as *Il marito* and *Il vecchio geloso*, which recall titles of *The Humorous Lieutenant* type. What deserves notice, however, is that a fair proportion of the comedies follow the practice not of written comedy but of tragedy in using as titles the names of particular characters. *La fortunata Isabella* and *La pazzia d'Isabella*, *La fortuna di Flavio* and *Le disgratie di Flavio*, *Il Capitano* and *Il Dottor disperato*, are only a few culled from the Scala col-lection. There seems justification for suggesting that here we have contributory evidence concerning the way these characters made their impact on the public; they were like living personalities whose stories were put forth upon the stage: Flavio and Isabella were thus not merely types presented for the nonce as the types in literary comedy usually were: rather were they akin to tragic characters, persons endowed with an enduring individual life.

It was not only in the early plays that titling procedure of this kind abounded, although later the trend began to take a changed direction. In the Scala comedies none of the comic servants is elevated to title rank, but when we move on in time to other collections we encounter *Il Zanni astuto*, *Zanni barbiero*, *Sardellino invisibile* and the like; and this emphasis continues to increase until scores of plays concentrate upon a Pulcinella or an Arlecchino. Furthermore, signs of degeneration are manifest in the tendency to focus not so much on the character in question as on the disguises he might be bidden to assume, so that comedies are brought forward under such forms as *Arlecchino finto gentilhuomo* or *Arlequin feint magicien*, reaching even to cumbersome absurdities like *Arlequin feint vendeur de chansons, caisse d'oranges, lanterne et sage-femme*.

126

Of one further thing these spectators, assembled to see a new comedy, can be reasonably certain—that the play will be in three acts. Had they been attending the performance of a literary drama they would have had to sit through five acts, but in this the professional comedians almost always broke away from an academic tradition firmly established both in theory and in practice. Precisely why they did so cannot be determined with absolute assurance, but we may guess that the three-act division had something to do with improvisation. In all probability the players found it easier to memorise their appearances within a range of three major sections than they would have done had they been confronted with a more complex arrangement. Whatever the cause, there was thus definitely fixed a clear distinction between the regular academic written plays and these comedies of professional manufacture. About one thing in this connection we must be clear. In later times farces were commonly distinguished from comedies by the number of their acts, and it is easy to fall into the trap of assuming that the Italian actors adopted the three-act form precisely because they regarded their plays as farces. Such an argument, however, reverses the relationship. Undoubtedly, the fact that as the commedia dell'arte proceeded on its career clownish material tended to predominate strongly influenced the content and form of late seventeenth-century farce; but another fact is equally certain, that at the beginning most of the Italian improvised plays were constructed in comic and not farcical terms.

KINDS OF COMEDY

While the expectant audience can, of course, not know in detail what episodes will be offered for their delectation in the new play for which they are waiting, they must feel certain that it will fall into one of three general categories. These categories have already been summarily exemplified in the specimen plays from which we started, but now some further and more detailed comment has to be devoted to them.

The first category may be styled the cuckolding comedy, and of this *Il vecchio geloso* provided an illustration. In several respects, however, *Il vecchio geloso* cannot be regarded as thoroughly typical. Its central theme shows an elderly husband cheated of his young wife by a handsome gallant. Without doubt this theme reappears from time to time in other plays, but stress must be laid on the fact that it is not of very frequent occurrence. Only sporadically does Pantalone appear with a wife, and he is as apt to be the one who cuckolds or who tries to cuckold some other husband as a man who is himself cuckolded. True, in his undignified intrigues he is likely to fall into ridiculous misadventures, but often he shows himself able to put the horns on some husband's head.

A second thing may be observed here. Although the cuckolding theme occurs fairly frequently, it generally does not form a single central element as in *Il vecchio geloso*, and in most plays wherein cuckolding appears as the main theme it tends to be enlarged, to concentrate not on one man but on several. Here, a piece called

Li tre becchi from the Corsini collection may be selected as an example. Instead of introducing one husband whose sole thought is to guard his wife, this comedy brings forward three husbands, two of whom engage in illicit intrigues. Pantalone has an affair with Franceschina, Zanni's wife, Coviello has a similar affair with Flaminia, Pantalone's wife, while a gallant called Leandro seduces Cinzia, the wife of Coviello. In each of these intrigues the lover, in order to gain access to his mistress and to escape her husband's eyes, indulges in a trick: Coviello gets himself delivered to Flaminia's house concealed in a crate supposed to contain lemons; disguised as a lame beggar Leandro visits Cinzia; Pantalone first eludes Zanni's attention through a trick of Franceschina's and later emulates Falstaff by allowing himself to be carried away from her house in a buck-basket. The scenario works up to an hilarious scene at the close of the second act when all three husbands, each thinking his own household safe, laugh at the cheats imposed on the others, until gradually the truth dawns on them and they all start shouting 'cuckold' at one another.

Several historians of the commedia dell'arte have inclined to suggest that such rough cuckolding pieces formed a large part of this theatre's repertory, but such a suggestion stresses only one aspect and has the effect of falsifying the whole. Cuckolding intrigues are frequent, certainly: usually, however, they are incidental rather than central, minor themes set within a major comic story. Even in *Il vecchio geloso*, where the core of the plot is the attempt of the young lover to capture Pantalone's wife, the rural atmosphere with its musical accompaniment attracts most of our attention and establishes the special quality of the play. In fact this comedy, in its structure, closely resembles *Twelfth Night*, wherein the cheating of Malvolio is modified and mollified by the musical, romantic world in which it is placed.

By far the majority of the plays which introduce the cuckolding theme introduce so many other plot elements that the theme itself becomes merely a subordinate diversion. Scala's *La fortunata Isabella* offers a thoroughly typical illustration. Graziano here pursues and seduces Franceschina, wife of a neighbouring innkeeper, Pedrolino; but this episode fades in importance because the main interest of the comedy concentrates upon the complications involving Isabella, who has followed

9   84   PANTALONE CHEATED BY HARLEQUIN   NWH

85 PANTALONE CHEATED BY HARLEQUIN

her errant lover, the Capitano, in disguise, as well as the complex amatory adventures of Graziano's two sons, Orazio and Flavio. The whole comedy might well be regarded as a compendium of those many elements which went to make up the fabric of the commedia dell'arte. Excellently constructed, it introduces and successfully pursues a variety of motives and episodes—the girl who leaves her home in search of her lost lover, her surprising change of heart, the love affairs of the young men, the merry jesting of a rogue who creates disturbance in others' minds only to find himself gulled at the end. Within this framework Graziano's escapade takes only a secondary position, and the cuckolding theme, apart from the fact that it is cuckolding by and not of the 'vecchi', forms merely one slight thread in a larger and variegated pattern.

Indeed, so subordinate is this element in the plot that *La fortunata Isabella* might have been taken as representative of the second category of comedies, those concentrating upon the confusions and misunderstandings of lovers. Of this kind let us take Scala's *La sposa*. The comedy opens with the strains of happy music: prepara-

---

❧ *La Sposa* ❦

PANTALONE, a Venetian merchant
FLAMINIA, his daughter,
    betrothed to Orazio but
    in love with Capitano Spavento
PEDROLINO, his servant, in love with
    Franceschina (really his sister)
FRANCESCHINA, his maid-servant,
    in love with Arlecchino

CAPITANO SPAVENTO,
    in love with Flaminia

ISABELLA, his sister,
    in love with Orazio
ARLECCHINO, his servant,
    in love with Franceschina

GRAZIANO, Pantalone's friend
ORAZIO, his son, betrothed to
    Flaminia but in love with Isabella

BURATTINO, father of Pedrolino and
    Franceschina

---

tions are being made for a double marriage, that of Graziano's son Orazio to Pantalone's daughter Flaminia, and that of Pantalone's two domestics Pedrolino and Franceschina. Trouble, however, soon arises. The Capitano arrives in haste, accompanied by his sister Isabella and his servant Arlecchino—a trio intent upon breaking up the weddings: the Capitano loves Flaminia, Arlecchino is devoted to Franceschina, and Isabella so dotes on Orazio that she declares she will rather kill his bride-to-be than let him go. Episode follows exciting episode: Isabella, dressing as a man, terrifies Flaminia by her threats, Arlecchino fights a comic duel with Pedrolino, Pantalone flies into a rage when he finds his plans upset, the Capitano elopes with Flaminia, Isabella snatches her Orazio, while Arlecchino is united to Franceschina, following the discovery that in reality Pedrolino is her brother.

Of such style were scores among these comedies, exploiting jealousies and despairs, fervent declarations of love and reprobations, parental worries and the ecstatic demands of youth, all complicated by the frequent discoveries of relationships unknown to the characters themselves and suddenly revealed in order to bring the plots to a happy conclusion. Perhaps one other illustration may be adduced, not from the Scala collection but from a manuscript in the Biblioteca Nazionale in Rome; and, since no example has so far been given of the actual handling of individual scenes, the plot of this play, *Flaminio disperato*, may be presented episode by episode rather than in brief summary. Flaminio and Cinzia are the children of Anselmo, whose servant is Spazza; Merlino Pulpettone (the Dottore) has a daughter Isabella and a maid-servant Ricciolina; Capitan Sprofonda has a servant Coviello.

Flaminio Disperato

ANSELMO, an elderly merchant,
    in love with Isabella
FLAMINIO, his son,
    in love with Isabella
CINZIA, his daughter,
    in love with Capitan Sprofonda
SPAZZA, his servant,
    in love with Ricciolina

MERLINO PULPETTONE,
    Anselmo's friend

ISABELLA, in love with Flaminio
RICCIOLINA, his maid-servant,
    in love with Spazza

CAPITANO SPROFONDA, at first in love
    with Isabella, later with Cinzia
COVIELLO, his servant, in love with
    Ricciolina

The first act shows the Capitano and Coviello just arrived at Osimo after a bad trip from Bologna; the Captain has come here because he loves Isabella. They go out and Anselmo enters in great distress, partly because his son Flaminio has long been absent abroad, partly because he too has fallen in love with Isabella. In the third scene Spazza reveals to Ricciolina his master's doting on this girl. Then Coviello comes in declaring that he is dying of hunger; the Captain 'discourses of the beauties of the city of Osimo and indulges in boasting about himself', whereupon Coviello begs him 'for this once to call a halt because he is dying of hunger'. The Captain knocks at the Doctor's door but is forced to decamp. When this pair has left the stage, the errant Flaminio comes in dressed as a stranger and lets us know that he also loves Isabella. Immediately after this, Ricciolina starts her tricks, advising Anselmo to disguise himself as a clog-maker, and giving the same advice to the Captain.

Thus the first act introduces most of the characters, poses the problems to be solved and suggests the beginning of an intrigue. So far, however, we have not met Cinzia, so she starts the first scene of the second act, paralleling Anselmo's appearance by expressing grief because of her brother's absence and because of the fact that she has fallen in love with a certain Captain. No sooner has she gone in than Anselmo enters crying 'Clogs for sale!' 'Clogs for sale!' is the Captain's cry too; and the pair quarrel violently, actually coming to blows when Ricciolina calls from a window, saying she wants some clogs, and they both simultaneously try to push their way into the house. The third scene shows Flaminio recognised by Spazza, who agrees to aid him, and this is followed by an episode wherein Cinzia pathetically makes love to the Captain and is rejected. Finally, the act closes with a fresh element—a violent quarrel between Spazza and Coviello over Ricciolina.

In the third act we find Flaminio in despair because he has not been able to see Isabella; the Captain, angered by that lady's obduracy, turns his affections to Cinzia; while Spazza, faithful to his young master, succeeds in persuading Merlino to give his daughter to Flaminio. Without knowing of this, Flaminio, still in his 'stranger's' attire, listens in desperation as his father Anselmo formally requests Merlino to allow him to marry Isabella, but before anything can be done about this the Captain is discovered while seeking a clandestine meeting with Cinzia. Although Anselmo promptly bursts out in wrathful passion, Merlino contrives to pacify him, pointing out that the Captain is a 'persona commoda' who will prove a worthy son-in-law. Accordingly, the comedy closes, as most comedies do, on the meeting of lovers, Isabella with her Flaminio, Cinzia with her Capitano and Ricciolina with her Spazza.

The bare recital of the several episodes, of course, leaves us far from an appreciation of what this play would appear in action; yet the scenario indicates quite clearly that Scala was by no means alone in his skilful weaving of a comic pattern. Easily and harmoniously the story unfolds itself, and the balanced contrasts and repetitions are thoroughly in accord with the general treatment of the plot. Just sufficient comic business, just sufficient disguising, is permitted to enter in, without drawing the essentially comic spirit into the mood of farce.

Very often such themes were enwrapped in the atmosphere of romance, and plays of this kind, in which strange adventures meet with situations whose interest rests in the unfolding of intrigue, may be regarded as composing the third comic category. Naturally, it will be understood that because of the very nature of the subject-matter, variations within this sphere are numerous, and several examples must be selected to indicate its scope.

Some, indeed most, deal largely with children who, after having been snatched away by Turkish pirates, return as slaves to be recognised by their parents. The very early scenario of *La schiava* is of this kind. Here it is Pantalone's daughter Hortensia who has been lost and the grieving father appears on the point of setting off by ship in search of her. His departure, however, is delayed by a series of fortunate accidents. Zane, who is really Pantalone's servant, appears in the guise of a Turk, leading in a girl slave—and, of course, in this world of the felicitously unexpected we experience no surprise in finding that she is the long-lost daughter. It would not, however, be appropriate if she were to be immediately restored to her father, so she is sold to Burattino (who pretends to be an agent for the merchant Graziano) and handed over, like another Marina, to a courtesan. But if her situation is akin to Marina's, she has a Lysimachus to aid her in the person of Leandro. Confusion after confusion results. Zane tells Leandro of the sale, then, confronted by Pantalone, declares that Hortensia is dead, and finally, in association with Burattino, decides it may be better to decamp. Poor Hortensia's fate hangs in the balance, but naturally all ends well; Leandro finds her and she is reunited with her father.

Sometimes the 'vecchi' and not the children have spent part of their lives in slavery. In *Le disgrazie e fortune di Pandolfo* we thus are introduced at the start to a man called Anselmo who, after having spent ten years as a slave, has returned to Italy and lives there under the name of Pandolfo. Since this play well illustrates both the romantic atmosphere brought into many of these comedies and the way in which various focal points of interest are wrought into their structure, its story may be summarised not as a whole but according to its sections. The first concerns Pandolfo, who eventually discovers a long-lost son in Ottavio, a daughter in Lucinda and a wife in Gostanza. Thus a central romantic core is provided, resembling that in *The Comedy of Errors, Pericles* or *The Winter's Tale*. The second focal point concentrates on the lovers. Ottavio and Lucinda, not realising that they are brother and sister, are devoted to each other; Ardelia fervently seeks Ottavio's hand, and for her

Valerio, who had ceded his interest in Lucinda to his friend, has an unrequited passion. Much of the action concerns the fortunes of the quartet, but their affairs are bound up with those of Pandolfo not only by the final discovery that the first pair are his children, but also, and more actively, by the fact that, seeking a new wife, he aims at marrying Lucinda. At one moment in the play, indeed, Ottavio and Valerio attack him with an intent to murder—and it is interesting to observe that single-handed he drives them off, 'remaining victorious'. By the combination of these two sections, therefore, we have elements involving romance, reciprocated and un-reciprocated passion, jealousy and friendship. In addition, a third section concerns Cola, Pandolfo's servant, Pasquella, Lucinda's adopted mother, and Stoppino, the servant of Ottavio and Valerio. Pasquella wishes to marry off her 'daughter' to Pandolfo; Stoppino seeks to aid Ottavio; while Cola finds himself in hopeless confusion, since on the one hand he wants to ingratiate himself with Pasquella by assisting her to effect this marriage and, on the other, he has hopes that, if Pandolfo remains single, he may become his heir. In the end all the various threads are brought together; Pandolfo rejoices in discovering that his Gostanza still lives; Ottavio and Valerio embrace as brother and sister; Lucinda agrees to marry Valerio and Ardelia's devotion to Ottavio finds its reward.

INTRIGUE DEVICES

All these plays give over a large amount of their action to the fortunes of lovers, and it is obvious that the audiences both delighted in watching intricate variations played on familiar themes and were prepared to accept the repetition of certain common conventions. The amatory passions, particularly on the girls' part, were ungovernable and violent. Already we have seen how an Isabella, believing herself neglected, is apt to run raving mad; if she remains sane, as often as not her thoughts turn to bodkins and phials of poison. Even the young men, who are usually more restrained, can decide that the easiest way of attaining their object is to murder their rivals. On the other hand, a Lucinda who discovers that her Ottavio is really her brother can promptly turn to give her hand to a Valerio and Valerio, for his part, can without an apparent qualm cede his Ardelia to another. After all the lunatic displays in Scala's *La finta pazza*, Orazio, who has run mad for the love of Isabella, suddenly cedes her to his brother and agrees to marry Flaminia. In play after play changes are rung on fervent ardours and easy changes in affection, on almost hysterical transports and facile renunciations. We are close here to the spirit of *Measure for Measure* and *The Two Gentlemen of Verona*.

Nor is it only within this sphere of love that the commedia dell'arte depended on the constant employment of devices which in themselves held not the slightest flavour of novelty. Only very occasionally among the scenarios do we find any elements that are new. *La bellissima commedia in tre persone* remains absolutely unique in structure by

135

introducing only three characters—Cola, Valerio and Lucinda; once or twice the composer of a scenario invents or borrows some hitherto unexploited situation, as does the author of *Non può essere* for the rather interesting opening scene which shows the meeting of an 'academy' whereat Violante is elected president, various persons recite sonnets of their composition and a riddle-problem is debated; sometimes a single character finds novel development, as, for instance, the presentation of the rich Clarice in *L'amante interesato* who proudly flaunts until her money vanishes. But in the main the situation sand devices, like the characters, are repeated in ever-changing forms over and over again. The audience sits intent, not upon having the gloss of novelty flashed before it, but upon experiencing the deeper delight which rests in the sight of familiar things freshly and skilfully handled, the kind of delight inherent in Shakespeare's comedies.

Peculiarly, the commonest of the devices used in the commedia dell'arte are identically the same as those popular on the Elizabethan stage. The characters are continually resorting to disguises; even in Scala's plays, where this trick does not appear inordinately, many plots, such as that of *Il finto Tofano*, would fall to pieces were costume transformations omitted; and later scenarios become just such a mass of disguise deception as Chapman's *The Blind Beggar of Alexandria*.

The introduction of a girl dressed as a man forms, of course, a special application of this; and Rosalinds and Violas are as common on this stage as on Shakespeare's—the only difference being that here they are real girls, not boy-actors performing the difficult task of pretending to be girls pretending to be men. Isabella in Scala's *La gelosa Isabella* dresses in male attire and is taken for her twin brother Fabrizio, and in *Li tappeti alessandrini* goes through a considerable part of the play in similar garb. In *La vedova costante* two girls dress as soldiers and attach themselves to the brigades to which their lovers belong, and in *L'onorata fuga di Lucinda* a lovesick maid, deserted by her sweetheart, draws her sword upon that faithless gentleman.

Frequently the employment of twins adds to the merriment and the intrigue. As in *Twelfth Night* these twins are often brother and sister, the latter masquerading in man's dress; an instance of this has been given already from *La gelosa Isabella*. Often they are twin sisters, as in *Due Flaminie simili*. Hardly any single commedia dell'arte character does not have one scenario or more in which he or she is thus doubled, the most frequent contrivance being the introduction of one twin living at home and the sudden appearance of the other unexpectedly arrived from abroad. Thus in the *Due simili* Virginio finds his affairs complicated by the entry of another Virginio, distinguished from him in the scenario by being called 'Virginio the stranger'. Orazio has a kindred double in *Baron Todesco*, and, as its title indicates, there are two Captains in *Li duo Capitani simili*; Pantalone has an identical brother in *Li duo vecchi gemelli*. The composer of *Zanni incredibile* agrees with Shakespeare in drawing amusing dramatic material out of the presence of a pair of twin masters and a pair

86 THE TWIN TRAPPOLINOS

of twin servants, while a fellow author, in *Li sei simili*, carries the joke still further by
juggling not with one but with three pairs.

One further common device deserves notice, a device which, although never
made use of by Shakespeare, was familiar to Elizabethan audiences as to Italian.
The commedia dell'arte players loved night scenes of the kind which figure so
freely, for example, in Porter's *The Two Angry Women of Abingdon*. In considering
their dramatic force and appeal one thing must be kept constantly in mind—that all
of these were performed, whether on the Elizabethan or on the Italian stages, under
the full illumination of daylight or the light of candles. Thus the entire effect was
created partly perhaps by verbal allusions to the supposed darkness, partly by the
bringing in of lanterns but mainly by the feigning of the players. In the scenarios
sometimes there is merely a marginal notation of 'Night' or 'Dawn', a symbol to
be elaborated by the actors, but often this receives expansion in the texts, with
instructions that some character or other shall enter 'pretending it is night'; on such
occasions, as Perrucci tells us, the actors were accustomed 'to grope about, to bump
into each other, to make grimaces, to climb up ladders and to indulge in a variety of
silent actions'.* What has to be appreciated is, first, that the effect created was purely
an imaginative one and, second, that a special dramatic appeal existed in the contrast

137

87 A NIGHT SCENE

between the feigned darkness which was supposed to enwrap the actors and the real illumination which allowed the spectators to view every smallest movement. In effect, a species of magic was being wrought by which these spectators were being granted the power of penetrating the folds of the night.

Before passing on to consider a few examples a further comment needs to be made. In many of these plays the sign marking the fall of darkness will suddenly appear in the very midst of an act, and, after a period of groping, light will supposedly come again; or else there will be a scene in which one character promises to meet another when, in an hour's time, darkness has descended, and immediately after the comedians move on to their pretence of night. There is thus both condensation of time and an almost complete rejection of any formal clinging to reality.

No very great exercise of the imagination is required in order to reconstruct the impression created or the effectiveness of these scenes. One play begins with a servant, lantern in hand, sleepily waiting for his master to return from a gambling den. In another the action starts with the opening of a window at which we see Isabella peering into the darkness, wondering why Orazio is so late; Pantalone and Graziano, a trifle tipsy, cautiously feel their way home from the inn where they had been having supper; servants enter with torches; the Capitano struts in preceded by Arlecchino

88 L'AMOUR AU THÉÂTRE ITALIEN

bearing a lantern; other windows open to reveal Pedrolino and Franceschina, candles held aloft, straining their eyes downward. In still another comedy Orazio serenades Isabella; his rival Ottavio challenges him to fight and Orazio is left for dead; Brighella feels his way on to the stage, stumbles over the body and comically displays his terror; Isabella, candle in hand, weeps over her lover's supposed corpse, while Orazio's servant Gradellino 'trips over the body, rises, thinks it is his master's corpse but in order to make sure gets a light, sees the blood, is terrified of being accused and runs off'. No sooner has he departed, however, than Orazio, who has only been wounded, 'starts to rise, calls to Gradellino, and, when no one comes, slowly struggles out by holding on to the wall'.*

Dozens of plays contain similar scenes; in many property lists there is a call for what appears in one scenario as 'lanterne bellissime assai'—fine lanterns a-plenty. The impressions fixed on the minds of the spectators receive characteristic display in a famous painting by Watteau. When he depicted a love scene at the Théâtre Français his characters are set in full sunshine, but when he showed 'L'Amour au

139

Théâtre Italien', his canvas portrays a scene of darkness, fitfully illuminated by flickering flames. Watteau here is not engaged in representing the reality of such performances; what his artist's vision has revealed is the imaginative image wrought by the players' skill.

Love indeed is the theme, youthful love and not the love of married domesticity. In another famous picture, 'L'embarquement pour Cythère', Watteau, although he infused into his canvas a refinement of his own, reflected that element of idealisation which is inherent both in the Elizabethan comedy of romance and in many among the commedia dell'arte plays. Watteau's art finds inspiration in a nostalgic vision of what the Italian players had put on the stage, and when a modern producer sets *Love's Labour's Lost* or *As You Like It* in a Watteau environment, he unconsciously testifies to the kinship between the atmosphere of these plays and that of the improvised comedies.

This spirit of love, even when it is accompanied by scenes of clownish merriment or by other scenes of vulgar content, mirrors a dream rather than a reality; and this means that certain elements of actual existence must be excluded. Since its atmosphere, despite the households headed by Pantalone and Graziano, distinctly avoids the domestic, we may readily understand why, in particular, mothers and children should have but a minimal part to play in these scenes.

In Shakespeare's comedies mothers are almost completely rejected. The long-lost wife who turns up at the end of *The Comedy of Errors* can barely be esteemed a dramatic role, so slight is her share in the action, and from the time when he wrote this farcical piece up to the period of the 'dark' comedies and the semi-tragic dramatic romances Shakespeare has no mother to give us. Only within the framework of plots with serious implications can the Countess of Rousillon, Dionyza and Thaisa, Cymbeline's Queen and Hermione breathe and take their being. In the early Italian scenarios the practice is similar. A long-lost wife may turn up at the close of the action, but of mothers involved in the plots there are very few to be found. Even in such a piece as *Le disgrazie e fortune di Pandolfo* noteworthy is the fact that the young marriageable Lucinda appears under the care not of her real parent but of an adopted mother; when, as in *Il creduto morto*, a widow heads a household, she takes very little part in the intrigue. Only sporadically in later scenarios do we encounter a termagant Lucrezia, a freedom-loving Flavia, an actively participant Claudia, a protective Lavora. Possibly part of the reason motivating the usual exclusion of such figures is that all the characters in the best commedia dell'arte plays are carefully chosen and fashioned to further the general comic pattern and that there was less opportunity for extracting laughter from Pantalone's wife than from Pantalone himself; but the main reason lies deeper still. The mother who is ambitious for her daughter or the mother who guides and guards her child may be proper to more realistic drama, the kind adumbrated in Jacobean 'citizen comedy' and cultivated from the eighteenth century onwards, but the presence of mothers would prove discordant and encumbering in the world of love-intrigue which both Shakespeare and the authors of the Italian scenarios exploit. Neither could Hero's story develop as it distressingly does in *Much Ado about Nothing* nor could Beatrice exhibit herself with such freedom had their mothers a part to play in the action. In these plots the girls need to be free; their own emotions, although fervent, harmonise with the wider comic pattern; were a mother's sentiments to intrude, that comic pattern might well be shattered and confused. And so for the most part the Isabellas and Flaminias, the Celias and the Lavinias exist in an independent world of their own.

Still more interesting is the exclusion of small children. One thing is certain: comedy which includes children inevitably must have an atmosphere different from comedy which has none. Mothers suggest the past and children the future; they are both therefore proper to the realistic social play. But when dramatists aim at creating an ideal world, at arresting and holding time within a moment's vision, both the past and the future must be forgotten. Such comedy need not have a romantic framework; we find it as clearly marked in the Restoration comedy of manners, with its scenes of Hyde Park and the Mall, as in Shakespeare's Italianate fantasies. Only when we watch this kind of comedy giving place to eighteenth-century forms do little prattlers, rigorously kept from our vision in *Twelfth Night* and *The Way of the World*, begin to toddle across the stage. For Shakespeare's comedy of romance and for Congreve's comedy of manners alike the introduction of children would have been discrepant; theirs are plays of courtship; what happens thereafter has no significance. If we start to wonder how Bassanio and Portia, Lorenzo and Jessica will get on when the dawn's rays dissipate the enchanted shadows of the Belmont garden, we shall be false to the mood which Shakespeare seeks by his magic to conjure up before us. The outspoken Benedick's declaration that the world must be peopled remains almost the sole allusion in Shakespeare's mature comedies to the familiar result of marriage; again, only in the semi-tragic atmosphere of *Pericles* and *The Winter's Tale* can a babe be born or a little Mamillius intrude.

At first glance, it might seem that the presence of at least a few children in the commedia dell'arte offers a contradiction, but closer scrutiny indicates how the improvised comedies fall into line. In the Scala scenarios small children are absent, and when on two occasions we find a babe introduced we realise that in these plays there is evident a movement similar to that from Shakespeare's romantic comedies to the dramatic romances. At the close of *Li finti servi* Pedrolino enters 'with a baby in swaddling clothes, they all kiss it and so ends the comedy', and in *Isabella astrologa*, amid an action involving pirates and threatened execution, the Turkish slave Rabbaya appears 'with her little son in her arms'. We are in a world here similar to that of *The Winter's Tale*, but otherwise the Scala comedies eschew such situations.

Occasionally in some farcical plays both early and late what may be called bunches

*A Dieu mon Roy, & Reine, & mes Amis
Pour vous obeyr ie m'en vay à Paris.*

of children can be brought in for the laugh's sake. Thus, for example, an early print shows us Harlequin with a crowd of little Harlequins, some at his feet, some in a basket on his back, and in the Neapolitan *Disgratie di Pollicinella* Rosetta pretends to be Punch's wife who, having been deserted, follows him with six children and a half; a stage direction tells us that 'here six little boys come out dressed like Punch, saying they are his children and calling him "Papa, papa" and crying "Bread, bread".' This is a joke: yet it gives a clue to an interpretation of the rare scenes wherein children are seriously introduced. These scenes come only in later plays which, as it were, move out of the true ambience of the commedia dell'arte and into that of incipient sentimentalism. Thus in *L'amico infido* Adriana has a little boy, but the situation is pathetic because her lover Fabrizio cannot support her and she is forced to beg for bread—exactly as the little Punches do, but now with serious purpose. Similarly, *Il Dottor bacchettone* introduces a Corallina, with her little son, as a wretched woman cheated by a hypocrite, while in *La bellissima commedia di tre*

142

90 HARLEQUIN BRINGS THE CHILDREN HOME TO THEIR REAL FATHER

persone another child appears in the midst of an almost melodramatic scene wherein a ragingly jealous Valerio threatens to kill it while the mother runs after him, crying 'Give me back my child!' The picture created by these scenes accords with observations concerning the general development of comedy: although occasionally children may be introduced, particularly in bunches, for farcical merriment, comedy as a whole avoids the use of these characters except when it tends towards the semi-tragic or sentimental-realistic style.

Rosetta, in *Le disgratie di Pollicinella*, pretends to come in with six and a half children—and this reminds us that throughout the whole of the commedia dell'arte's career references to pregnancy are frequent. Like madness, if the girls are not actually in that condition, they are always ready to simulate being so in order to help their intrigues; and there are comedies, such as *Le tre gravide*, where allusions to pregnancy enter into the very titles of the plays. What has to be noted here, however, is that pregnancy in these comedies bears, so to say, no implications. When we hear that Lucinda, Aurelia and Colombina are all staying in their rooms because

143

they are 'gravide', the comic impression aroused is similar to what would have been experienced had we been informed that they were suffering no more than an awkward but mild attack of measles or mumps; and when we are told that Orazio, Ottavio and Zanni were responsible for the girls' indisposition, it is as though the men had had an attack of mumps or measles themselves and had unfortunately and involuntarily infected their sweethearts. We could put this in another way and suggest that pregnancy is treated simply as a comic fact existing solely at the present moment of the action and that in no wise does it carry our thoughts into any realm of future consequences.

THE COMIC TRICKS

So far, in concentrating upon the plots of the scenarios and upon conventional situations introduced into these plots, practically all attention has necessarily been devoted to romantic and other elements which, although certainly tinged with the comic spirit, are not inherently laughable in themselves. But the theatre of the commedia dell'arte was basically a theatre of laughter, and, in order to gain a true picture of its essential being, consideration must be given to episodes deliberately designed for this purpose alone.

Quite frequently, such episodes stand apart from the plots themselves—forming small oases of business which either break up the telling of the main stories or else form hilarious conclusions to each act. Occasionally they are short, involving only one actor; but often they provide little actions of their own within the fabric of the larger design, and as such they can develop into almost separate 'intermezzi' which divide the acts one from another. Audiences and actors evidently delighted in closing the first two sections of each play with some scene of bustle and excitement, and the Duke of Guise was not wrong when, in drawing a distinction between Spanish and Italian performers, he declared that whereas the former liked to close their acts with dances, the latter commonly ended theirs with knockabout incidents.*

In assessing these incidents we must, of course, again remember two things—first, that their effect inevitably depended on the players' skill, and secondly that we lack entirely the words which, in the original performances, graced and invigorated scenes of which the scenarios give but the barest indication. Furthermore, we must recognise that in this exploitation of laughable incident the Italian comedians, remaining true to their general design, sought rather to introduce infinite variations of a few chosen devices than to bring in constant novelty.

Two of the most important of these devices may be described as repetition and thievery. Both are paralleled in Shakespeare's comedies; we need think only of the tricking of the Clown by Autolycus in *The Winter's Tale* and, in *Love's Labour's Lost*, of the scene when Berowne, secretly in love, eavesdrops upon the King's ecstatic devotion to his lady, followed by Longaville's similar expression of senti-

144

ments and by Dumain's. If we were to reduce these episodes to mere description—saying simply 'Here Autolycus pretends to have been robbed and cheats the Clown of his money' or 'Berowne, with a paper, confesses his love, and retires; the King, with a paper, does the same; Longaville, with a paper, does the same; Dumain, with a paper, does the same; Longaville accuses Dumain; the King accuses Longaville; Berowne accuses the King'—they would seem dull and lifeless; it is Shakespeare's lines which give them vitality. In looking at the very similar scenes in the Italian comedies, therefore, we have to set our imaginations actively at work in order to convert the skeletons, which are all the scenarios offer us, into living flesh and blood.

Granted that the imaginative process enables us to reconstruct the actors' skill in movement and in speech, we can come to realise both the kinship between many of the Italian scenes and Shakespeare's, and the effect they must once have created. Let us take an example, expanding slightly upon the bare description given us in the scenario. Pandolfo hands over a gold collar to Zanni for safe keeping, bidding him guard it carefully. Pulcinella, watching from the side of a house, determines to get it, hastily slips on a devil's disguise, roars at Zanni and snatches the collar as the latter rushes away in abject terror. Pulcinella, however, has not been alone in his eavesdropping, for Cola has secretly spied on this piece of chicanery; in turn, he puts himself into a shroud, confronts Pulcinella with awesome ghostly movements and sepulchral tones, and triumphantly seizes the collar. And there is still more to come. Pandolfo and Ubaldo have also witnessed the trickery, hurriedly put on gendarme dress, threaten to arrest Cola and let him go only when he surrenders his booty.*

In divers ways the repetition trick receives its twists and turns. One scene shows us Pantalone arrived outside the door to his own house, which stands next to Graziano's. In amazement he sees one after another of the characters coming out from his residence and going into his neighbour's; each one greets him with a bow, but not a word is spoken. At the end Pantalone, bemused, remains alone on the stage; for a few seconds he stays motionless, and then, in absolute silence, he bows to the audience and departs.* There is no difficulty in re-creating the humour of this scene as interpreted by clever comedians; nor is there difficulty in recognising how the basic mould could, by the introduction of sounds and of words, be made to yield a multiformity of effects. Two further examples will serve. In *Flavio tradito*, Pedrolino, who has been trying to help his master, finds that one of his tricks goes wrong, and he receives a violent scolding. Struck dumb by his master's ingratitude, he remains motionless and silent in the middle of the stage, and so continues while, one after another, several characters address him; to their questions he answers not a word; he does not even by a sign acknowledge their presence. At last the Captain, irritated by his refusal to move or speak, starts to beat him—when suddenly, without the faintest warning, Pedrolino, as if he had awakened from a long trance, utters a wild yell which sends those around him into a panic, and then calmly walks off.

The second example, showing the same trick diversified with words, comes from *La fortunata Isabella*. Pantalone has been engaged in trying to find a husband for his daughter Flaminia, but the affair has become complicated because a number of characters are each intent on getting her wedded to someone else. Since she herself has set her heart on a young suitor of her own choice, Pantalone starts to upbraid her—whereupon Harlequin checks him: 'You can shout as much as you like', he remarks, 'It will be as I say'—and departs. At once Burattino interjects: 'Don't you believe him; it will be as I say'—and he, too, goes off. The young suitor now addresses Pantalone: 'You'll be out of luck if you don't do what I want'—and he stalks away. At the end, the young girl herself comes forward: 'My dear father,' she says quickly, 'I am quite sure you will do exactly what *I* want', and she leaves her father, stupefied by this battery of words, alone on the stage.

The trick of repetition, of course, was by no means confined to the one device illustrated by these episodes. Sometimes it was exploited fairly simply, as when Burattino comes in with a luscious basket of fruit. Two thieves spot their quarry, greet him and place themselves one on each side. The first begins to charm his ears by saying that he has just come from the far-off country of Cockayne, a land full of strangest marvels; and, while he is talking, of course his accomplice gobbles up part of the contents of the basket. Then, when he has had enough, he in turn attracts the gaping Burattino's eager attention by remarking that in this wonderful country any persons who want to work are punished by law; and, as he dilates on the theme, naturally the first thief empties the basket. The couple politely bid Burattino farewell and he stands for a short time thinking over all the extraordinary things he has been told; finally he looks down at his basket, in amazement sees it has been emptied, slowly comes to a realisation of the trick which has been played upon him and bursts into tears.*

Sometimes the exploitation was more elaborate. In *Il pedante*, the Captain bids his servant Arlecchino present a dish of macaroni to Pedrolino. Dutifully the task is carried out, but Pedrolino, instead of expressing pleasure, weeps copiously as he takes the dish. 'What's the matter?' enquires Arlecchino. 'My wife's just had an accident', blubbers Pedrolino, and, while he says this, he takes out a spoon and starts to eat, still crying bitterly. Partly infected by the tears, partly anxious to share in the repast, Arlecchino also starts to weep, also takes out a spoon, and the pair sit down on the ground with the plate between them. While they are thus engaged, Burattino enters, likewise starts to cry and likewise sits down to join the lachrymose party. When the plate has been cleared, Pedrolino, in the most miserable manner, requests Arlecchino to present his best thanks to the Captain; wiping his eyes with his hand-kerchief, Burattino follows suit; while Arlecchino, left alone, crying wretchedly and licking the plate with his tongue, wanders off the stage.

In all of these episodes one thing is apparent. The comic business derives not from

naturalistically conceived situations but from the creation of stylised actions. They are thus thoroughly in accord with the patent formalism of the central plots, and in their own way they parallel the mathematical arrangement of these plots. Furthermore, they are most commonly based on a folly or stupefaction so exaggerated as to leave the world of actuality far behind. In one comedy Pantalone and Graziano are questioning Harlequin, and, as he is going off, he remarks over his shoulder, 'Do what you will, you'll still be a cuckold'. The comic effect of the situation depends on their reaction; in silence they look at each other for a time and then both say at once, 'Was he talking to you or to me?' Or else Cola, engaged to murder a certain character, fires his gun, sees his victim walk away unharmed and stamps with rage on realising he had forgotten to put the bullet in. Or else the foolish Pulcinella

92 ZANNI TRIES HIS HAND AT MURDER

engages Coviello to stand behind him when he has an interview with his lady-love, so that he may prompt him; Coviello, agreeing, whispers a lot of nonsense which the absurd lover gravely repeats word for word.*

These characteristics of the typical comic business require to be borne in mind when we consider the bawdiness and apparent cruelty which unquestionably were freely introduced into the commedia dell'arte. We need not endeavour to refute the judgement of that early Jeremy Collier, Domenico Ottonelli, who, in his *Della Christiana moderatione del theatro* (1646), declared that often 'the Zannis, Coviellos, Pantalones, Grazianos and the like seek to extract laughter from the obscene'.* Even in the Scala plays evidence enough offers itself to prove his case: the later plays provide still more ample material, while numerous prints, obviously seeking to make popular appeal, leave no doubt concerning the vulgar gestures sometimes employed by the comedians.

All of this can readily be admitted, yet there is a triple defence. The commedia dell'arte may be blunt in its references to the facts of life, but rarely is it suggestive. The actors aim at arousing laughter, not sniggers, and about their performances is a spirit of frank animalism. If we contrast, in imagination, the elegantly clad and socially cultured gentlemen and ladies of Restoration comedy with the crouching

148

animal-like postures of Harlequin and Pantalone shown in numerous prints and china figures, and if, further, we look at the same kind of speeches put into the mouths of these characters, we realise that the impressions created in the two forms of comedy were entirely different. The Restoration dramatists clearly knew they were being naughty; the writers of the Italian scenarios were vulgarly frank. Another comparison might be made between these plays and certain modern bedroom farces, and no doubt we should give the preference not to the sniggering, snickering suggestiveness of the one but to the bluntness—even if at times it lacks cultured refinement—of the other.

Apart from this, we must take fully into consideration the milieu in which such episodes occur. In the bedroom farces a surface realism prevails and, although the stories may be impossibly exaggerated, a general impression of actuality has been aimed at by the playwrights. In the Italian comedy, on the other hand, the mathematical and musical patterning, the fantastic adventures, the admixture of masked and unmasked actors, all combine to draw us from the real world into a world of the imagination—so that what might have been thoroughly distasteful with a comedy naturalistically presented can here be accepted within the framework of the palpably fictitious. The constant utilisation of firmly established situations also contributes towards this end. The writers of the scenarios are rarely intent on introducing novelties; they aim rather at devising variations of effects already well known; and the very familiarity of the vulgar episodes attracts attention away from their subject-matter to the skill with which they are integrated into the plots and particularly to the skill with which they are interpreted.

Such histrionic skill forms the chief element to be considered in viewing this subject. A recent commentator on the commedia dell'arte, in discussing the agility by means of which Thomassin, as Harlequin, was able, in a scene of terror, to turn a back-somersault without spilling a drop from the wine-glass in his hand, has acutely observed that 'fear, which makes men clumsy, has here transmogrified awkwardness into an exhibition of consummate skill'.* And such a judgement applies with equal force to the episodes we are now considering. What may appear rather repulsive in the barren description must have provided opportunities for creating hilarious scenes in which the spectators' attention was directed away from the bawdiness itself to the dexterity of the players.

Much the same may be said concerning certain scenes which, particularly from the modern point of view, may appear unpalatable because of their unsentimental approach. Already in the seventeenth century Perrucci offered his defence of these. Noting that often the amusing situations made use of 'natural defects', such as caricatures of noses, peaked faces, baldness, lameness, he remarks that 'these defects, counterfeited by the use of masks and by the actors' skill, although in real life they would be pitiful and apt to arouse commiseration, become in the world of fiction simply laughable. Thus we find it most amusing to see a Zanni with tiny little eyes, dark face, bushy eyebrows and awkward movements, or a Pulcinella rude in person with a long hooked nose, unkempt, stupid and foolish in all his gestures; thus, too, we find it amusing to view the Zanni's patched costume and Pulcinella's sackcloth garments.'*

REALISM AND ANTI-REALISM

This, of course, leads us directly to an examination of the basic question: What kind of comedy was this that the Italian actors offered to their public? The examples of typical plots have given some indication of the general style and range of the productions, demonstrating the two fundamental components—the main plots with their conscious patterning and frequent romantic flavour, and the comic episodes which, although sometimes integrated within these plots, often remained independent 'turns'. Both components are of almost equal significance, and a distorted view of the commedia dell'arte will result either from over-emphasis upon the stories or from over-emphasis upon the comic episodes.

The question now arises concerning the central purpose which gave these performances their being. Historical criticism has of late tended to stress the social basis of many art forms, particularly the art of the theatre; and the commedia dell'arte has not escaped. Recent studies have underlined the facts that Pantalone represents the Venetian merchant, Graziano the Bolognese academician, Zanni the Bergamask peasant who has come to the city seeking work: the social milieu of the characters has received careful scrutiny and elucidatory comment. From this the passage is easy to an interpretation of these figures as objects of satire and hence of the comedy in which they appear as satirical comedy. 'Bourgeois historians' who fail to agree that 'the spirit of the comedy of masks was its social-critical satire'* are castigated by the extremists within this school of thought.

Such views require to be regarded with caution. At the very start, it may be said with absolute confidence that of social satire the true commedia dell'arte shows not the slightest trace. When sentimentalism began to daub its dreary colours upon the kaleidoscopic canvas of the earlier plays, we may very occasionally find scenarios, such as the Neapolitan *Ricco epulone* and *Ruberto del diavolo*, wherein a rich libertine flaunts his way upon earth, disdaining or grinding the poor, and wherein duly moral tableaux-endings show his soul bitterly lamenting in Hell; but apart from such dismal pieces we encounter no signs of any ulterior satiric purpose. One can well imagine what excellent comic business Harlequin might have devised had he been informed that he was 'the expression of the active protest against the force of the feudal-Catholic reaction'.*

This idea we may, then, reject outright. Concerning the other, less doctrinaire, stress upon the social origins of the commedia dell'arte, we can at once admit that of course Pantalone is a Venetian merchant, Graziano a Bolognese doctor and Zanni a native of Bergamo; but this still leaves the essential questions open—why were these characters chosen, how were they treated and what was the essential nature of the comedy in which they played their parts?

For the first question an immediate definitive and conclusive answer seems clear. These characters, confessedly taken from actuality, were selected for their comic potentialities and not with any social-political objective. Pantalone does not figure in almost every play because of a desire on the part of the actors to ridicule Venetian mercantilism; he is a central figure because, in association with other characters, he can arouse merriment and stimulate delight.

This first question, however, cannot be fully answered until we consider the second. Those who propound the idea of a satiric comedy argue that these Italian plays were basically realistic. For such an interpretation some slight apparent evidence might indeed be brought forward. Perrucci's advice that too many rhymed couplets should not be used because these were unrealistic could be cited, together with his following remark that couplets of this kind might be permitted for the Lovers because young men and girls in love tend towards the poetic. Since, however, his instructions elsewhere make free employment of artificial devices, it soon becomes clear that in this instance he is doing no more than reiterating his standard principle—a firm holding to moderation. He realises that the commedia dell'arte can, in the hands of poor or careless players, tend towards exaggeration and excess; thus in this instance he does not by any means condemn the introduction of these unrealistic couplets, he merely warns that they should be kept within reason. It has been noted above that some contemporaries, in speaking of the Italian comedians, commented upon the 'truth' and 'verisimilitude' afforded by the improvising method; but once more we cannot take such remarks at face value. When the comments are examined carefully, it becomes evident that the writers were contrasting in their minds the effect produced by the commedia dell'arte performances with the effect produced by the more formal gestures and delivery associated with the literary drama; furthermore, the tone of their remarks makes clear that they were thinking, not of realism, but rather of liveliness. When Desboulmiers says that improvisation 'gives the scene a naturalness and truth which the very best authors rarely attain', or when we read elsewhere that the comedies give an impression of 'vividity and truth',* no doubt can remain that it is the liveliness consequent upon the exercise of improvisation to which they refer. Quite obviously, 'realism', in the modern sense of the term, stands far removed from these dramas.

In their plots they make no effort to keep to the easily credible. 'Stravaganti successi'—extravagant events—as they are styled in Scala's *Il fido amico*, provide much of the story content of the comedies and frequently these veer from the improbable into the realm of impossibility. One commonly recurring episode is by itself sufficient to demonstrate how far the performances moved from actuality. In *Il vecchio geloso* we have already encountered the situation involving a young wife, an older husband and a young lover: the gallant wants to marry the girl, and, at the close of the play, the husband, convinced and shamed by his arguments, simply hands her over.* No question of divorce arises, and we are led to assume that her husband's acquiescence leaves the wife absolutely free to wed her lover. In the actual life of the seventeenth and eighteenth centuries matrimonial tangles were hardly managed so easily; the world of the comedy is not a reflection of ordinary existence, rather is it a youthful gallant's Utopian dream. We are no more here within the area of actuality than we are when we listen to the trial scene of Shakespeare's *Merchant of Venice*.

In any case, judgements which refer to 'naturalness' and 'verisimilitude' are amply balanced by numerous others in which the commedia dell'arte is bluntly dismissed because of its artificiality. Saint-Évremond declares that the Italian players, instead of exhibiting pleasant love-scenes, offered only affected discourses; instead of presenting authentic comic characters, they brought forward merely buffoons who, however excellently they might be displayed, always remained buffoons.* And a recent writer on this theatre uncompromisingly asserts: 'What the commedia dell'arte ignored completely was real life. The comic scene, which was based on the masks, with its types in which artificiality prevailed over truth, the grotesque over the comic, caricatures over satire, could not give the impression of life as it is.'*

Unquestionably such an interpretation comes much nearer the mark than the other: it makes full allowance for the artificial designing so apparent in most of the scenarios. Yet it, too, errs by veering towards the opposite extreme. Even if we admit that numerous performances both early and late must have been vulgar, absurd in their extravagance and marred by the efforts of incompetent comedians to snatch laughs at all costs, there still remain many scenarios which, despite the deliberate patterning of their plots and situations, utilise material culled from the actual life of the time. The idea of satire and the idea of social realism, as we have seen, may summarily be put aside, but equally we may reject the idea of performances utterly removed from the existence of the time in which they were conceived and exhibited.

One of the latest studies of the commedia dell'arte seems to propose a more valid answer to our question. This suggests that the actors, instead of saying to the audience 'What we are about to show you is a tissue of impossibilities', declare rather 'This is your city; here are people such as you might encounter in its streets; here, in fact, is something akin to actuality. But just see how these people can be transfigured and made to live in a strange world, the world of comedy.'* Such an interpretation comes close to the truth, but perhaps even here something is missing. When the spectators see before them the eccentrically clad Harlequin, when they look upon his mask and the masks of his companions, they cannot think that these are persons such as they would meet in their daily lives; and it is precisely the presence of these masks which gives the commedia dell'arte its individual quality.

Here once more a comparison with Shakespeare's comedies may prove fruitful. In essence both he and the Italian actors aimed at, and usually succeeded in achieving, the same object; where they differed was in the approach which they made towards their ultimate goal. In his romantic comedies Shakespeare generally starts by imagining a milieu which, although strange to his audiences, is not too strange. For *Twelfth Night* he may venture far into Illyria, but Italy—and, be it noted, contemporary Italy—suits his purpose best. Few among the spectators could themselves have seen Padua or Venice, but all knew that Italy existed, many must have had the opportunity of talking to travellers who had thence returned, some might even have been familiar with Italians resident in England. This Italy is, then, a far-off country in contemplation of which the imagination may have some scope to range; but Shakespeare is careful to restrict and control the wanderings of fantasy. In a sense he may be said to present the denizens of this land 'realistically'. Other contemporary dramatists might impose an artificial pattern upon Italian characters, treating them as fictional persons whose moral codes and inordinate passions could bear little relationship to those of London's citizens; Shakespeare presented to view dramatic figures who, despite the romantic ambience consequent upon their living in this far-off land, were such as might be immediately acceptable, with features akin to those familiar in London's court and city. Indeed, he went even further and introduced among his cultured aristocrats comic characters whose behaviour was patently English.

By these means Shakespeare thus reached to a comic spectacle which can be described neither as 'realistic' nor as 'anti-realistic'. Claudio, Don Pedro, Hero, Benedick, Beatrice—all these could find their parallels in English society, and certainly with Dogberry and Verges we move far from thoughts of a distant Messina. Yet Messina is the place where these characters live, and in Messina, remote and strange, the adventures of the plot can proceed easily without our asking any of the awkward practical questions which might have come to our minds had the setting been London or Oxford. So, in *Twelfth Night* we can follow without doubting the story of Viola's masquerade and, at the same time, still harmonise that masquerade with the follies of the obviously English Sir Toby and Sir Andrew.

Now let us contrast this with the method employed in the commedia dell'arte. In these plays the settings are also Padua or Messina or Venice, but clearly these cities arouse in the Italian audience no such imaginative impressions as they do among London's audiences. These locations for them are real; they are known; they may even be the very cities in which the comedies are being performed. Consequently the Italian comedians, aiming at the creation of a theatrical mood virtually the same as that aimed at by Shakespeare, cannot follow his procedure by the presentation of characters invested with the appearance of reality. Dogberry and Verges, Sir Toby and Sir Andrew, would not serve their needs. Hence the use of masks, hence the employment of eccentric costumes. In some modern productions of *Much Ado about Nothing* Dogberry has been transformed into a grotesque caricature, clad in extraordinary raiment and with a face so bedaubed with paint as to seem mask-like; but such procedure inevitably destroys the trembling balance of Shakespeare's comic scenes. Dogberry and Verges are real just because they live in Illyria. In exactly the same way, although as it were in reverse, Arlecchino and Brighella must be unreal in conception and interpretation just because they move and have their being in a Venice or Rome familiar to the spectators. Both Shakespeare and Flaminio Scala thus may be said to have their gaze set upon the same objective—an objective which stands distinct from realism on the one hand and anti-realism on the other. To assert either that the commedia dell'arte aims at reflecting the actual life of the time or that it seeks to escape from that life is false; its quality depends on a subtle harmonising of the two.

While, then, the setting of the action in Shakespeare's comedies is more distanced than that in Scala's, compensation is provided by the fact that Scala's characters are more distanced than Shakespeare's. Just how much this implied and involved receives interesting illustration in the play of *Il ritratto*. This brings on stage, among the regular commedia dell'arte characters, an actress Vittoria, and at once we realise that she has been conceived in a style different from that of the others. The explanation seems to be that, in moving from the Pantalone–Arlecchino world into the world almost of the play-within-the-play, Scala seeks to make a distinction. If the Pantalone–Arlecchino characters had been realistically delineated, then clearly Vittoria could have been shown in an artificial manner; but they are not, and consequently the author of the scenario, paradoxically, and exceptionally, permits the real to intrude in his depiction of the actress. That this is indeed to be regarded as an exception becomes obvious when we note the unexpected and almost unique description of her appearance and sentiments. She enters at the beginning of the second act, 'richly dressed, with gold chains, pearl bracelets, diamonds and rubies glittering on her fingers, accompanied by Piombino, to whom she praises the city of Parma, the duke and all his court, telling of the numerous courtesies which every day she receives from the gentlemen there'. Later, at the beginning of the third act, she appears again with Piombino, and their dialogue tells 'how, having dined at the house of a gentleman in love with her, they have received valuable gifts; they refer, in the course of their talk, to presents given to comedians, to many of the chief cities in Italy, where she has been showered with many gifts, and, finally, to her tricking, and laughing at, these lovers who offer her such presents. Piombino exhorts her not to fall in love with any of them but rather to concentrate upon gathering money which may comfort her when she gets old.'

It would be hard to find elsewhere among the scenarios anything quite so specific or so close to actuality, and an episode towards the close of the comedy still further underlines the method by which Vittoria has been depicted. A band of gentlemen and bravoes rush in, swords drawn, seeking Vittoria; they see her with Pantalone and Graziano, thrust this pair aside and carry her off. The scene is so vivid that one wonders if this actress in *Il ritratto* is not a portrait drawn from the life. Whether or not there exists any justification for such a suggestion, certainly she has been drawn in dimensions different from those of the other characters. Her features are realistically delineated. Particularly worthy of note is Piombino's advice that she should gather money to comfort her old age. When we look at the other women in the play, Isabella for instance, we never think of them except in terms of their present existence; Isabella, like the figures on the Grecian urn, has been seized in an eternal and immutable youth, and the thought of what she may become never enters our minds. This, of course, does not mean that she is less vital than Vittoria—it means simply that she lives in another world. Vittoria has individuality; so has Isabella; but their individualities are artistically conceived on different planes.

One further comment may be made concerning this subject of the commedia dell'arte's spirit and method. Perhaps it is wrong to lay too much emphasis upon what has been styled the 'plastique du théâtre', as though the sole value of the Italian comedy lay within the restricted area of theatrical exhibitionism.* Unquestionably Shakespeare wrote his comedies for stage performance; unquestionably they were cast in eminently theatrical moulds; yet equally evident is the fact that, while his comedies are exquisitely conceived as the basis for theatrical 'shows', they incorporate within themselves a vision which carries us beyond the theatre. It is true that the scenarios are more restrictedly 'theatrical' than *Twelfth Night* or *Much Ado about Nothing*, yet in the best of them is enshrined a vision which may at least be related to Shakespeare's. Had they not possessed this, we may well believe that, whatever the skill of the performers, the commedia dell'arte would not have laid its deep impress on the imaginations of succeeding generations. Those artists from Watteau on to Cézanne and Derain who have turned to the Italian comedy for subjects were attracted not by the adroitness of particular players, not merely by the strange costumes exhibited upon the stage, but by the basic vision consecrated in the comedies these players interpreted.

COLOUR, MUSIC AND DANCE

This, of course, is not to deny that the commedia dell'arte owed a large part of its popularity to the way in which it offered to the public a display of what may be called pure theatre. Action, words, colours, music were all here combined into a single appealing whole. Sometimes, when we look at black-and-white photographic reproductions of the actors or scenes, we are apt to forget the impression which must

93 SONG AND DANCE

have been made by the bright hues of the costumes apportioned to the several
characters and by the way these were marshalled on the stage. The Elizabethan
theatre must also have presented to the eye a rich array of colourful costumes, richer
than those commonly seen in real life, but we find little evidence there of an attempt
towards formalisation. Consequently the effect created must have been measurably
different from that in any of the Italian productions—with Pantalone in contrasting
black and red, Graziano in black and white, Brighella in white and green, Arlecchino
kaleidoscopic in patches, triangles or lozenges.*

And harmonising with the colour there was music. *Il vecchio geloso*, exploiting
the instrumental and vocal entertainments at Pantalone's villa, was by no means
unique. Already attention has been drawn to the fact that numerous illustrations of
commedia dell'arte characters depict them with guitars or other instruments in their
hands, and numerous records, such as those relating to Gherardi's Flautino, lay
special stress upon the musical skill of individual actors. Particularly interesting in
this connection is the *Infermità, testamento, e morte di Francesco Gabrielli detto Scapino*,
published at Verona in 1638. These verses tell how all Scapino's companions, hearing
of his illness, gather at his bedside and ask him to make his will; after assigning
legacies to some of them, he proceeds to leave his violin to Cremona, his bass viol
to Piacenza, his viol to Milan, his guitar to Venice, his harp to Naples, his bonaccord
to Rome, his trombones to Genoa, his mandolin to Perugia, his theorbo to Bologna,
his lute to Ferrara, and 'all the other instruments' to Florence. No doubt Gabrielli

156

94 FRITELLINO

95 PULCINELLA

96 SCARAMUCCIA

was especially gifted in this way, but he had many companions who thus added to the gaiety and variety of these performances. As a result, a definite link exists between the commedia dell'arte and the early comic opera. In 1597 appeared Orazio Vecchi's *L'Amfiparnaso*, a 'comedia harmonica' which, as it were, puts into musical form the typical plot of an improvised comedy, while numerous popular publications present Pantalone and his companions not speaking, but singing their lines, often in dialogue and often in duets, trios or quartets.*

With music, naturally, comes dance. Several scenarios give indication of such divertisements, but formal indication of this kind was, in reality, not needed. Among the hundreds of prints depicting characters and scenes in the Italian comedies, many show the actors in dance positions, and we may well imagine how often the actors varied and intensified their ordinary actions and words in this manner. We need not be surprised to find a 'chacoon' for Harlequin, or the series of comic dances offered to us in Lambranzi's *Nuova e curiosa scuola de balli theatrali* (Nuremberg, 1716). There were numerous courtly dances for the Lovers, but what attracted the public most were the sarabands executed by Scaramuccia or Harlequin 'in contorted manner and particularly with false and laughable steps'. It was just such a dance which caused the death of the great Domenico Biancolelli: in the part of Harlequin he executed a parody of a new court-ballet movement, and, seeing that the king took particular delight in this, he continued until he was worn out; on leaving the stage, covered with sweat, he caught a chill which within a few days brought him to his grave.

All these elements of dance, song, colour, instrumental music added to the dynamic quality of the performances, and it is dynamism we think of first when we consider the commedia dell'arte. Its inner force lies here. Yet we must not isolate the acrobatic, terpsichorean and other elements and concentrate on them alone, as though these shows depended entirely upon physical skill. The commedia dell'arte had a soul as well as a body, and it was its soul, the continual aspiration towards expressing a certain kind of comic spirit, that gave it the power to carry on its career throughout so many long generations.

TRIUMPH AND DECLINE

Most of the examples already cited have been taken either from Scala's early collection of plays or from other scenarios which appear to belong to the first commedia dell'arte tradition. At the same time, in the discussion of the characters indication has been given of the way in which the Italian improvising theatre gradually assumed new forms and even changed its main direction as it proceeded on its career through the seventeenth and eighteenth centuries. Obviously, therefore, some account must now be given of its general fortunes during these years and of the conditions which led it on from its originally established style towards the 'fiabe' of Gozzi and the 'parodies' of the Parisian Théâtre Italien.

Many records have been preserved concerning the activities of at least the more important theatrical companies, so that often we may trace their itineraries month by month, from town to town; but, apart from the fact that historical studies of this kind are already available, it would clearly not be in keeping with the plan of the present study to introduce detailed material on this subject. What we are concerned with is the central spirit of the commedia dell'arte, and consequently the tracing of itineraries and the exposition of detailed facts related to the various companies lie outside our immediate scope. The general activity and not the particular must be that on which we set our gaze.

At the same time, one special feature of the commedia dell'arte makes any account of its historical development abnormally complicated. When we are concerned with most national theatres, our attention will properly be placed on stage activities within each country. Thus a history of the 'Elizabethan' playhouse will consist fundamentally, first, of an examination of the stages from the erection of The Theatre in 1576 on to the banning of theatrical performances in 1642, and secondly of the various troupes operating during that period. The facts that an individual actor such as William Kemp travelled abroad, even crossing the Alps into Italy, and that little groups of 'englische Comödianten' toured abroad are interesting but strictly peripheral. These facts have a distinct bearing upon the development of theatrical activities in the countries within which the English actors performed, but we cannot discern any change in histrionic style within England itself consequent upon the players' experience abroad. So, in later periods, the visit of an English company to Paris in 1828 exerted considerable influence upon rising French romanticism, but it did not alter in any respect the progress of the English theatre; the visit of the Saxe-Meiningen company to London in 1881 made a considerable impress upon productions in that metropolis, but it altered not a whit the methods of the German players.

The commedia dell'arte stands apart and distinct; indeed, we have to think, not merely of one single, restricted line of development, but of three interconnected outgrowths. First, and of course primal in significance, is the rise and continued career of this comic style within Italy itself—a career which extends from the second half of the sixteenth century on to the close of the eighteenth century and beyond. From the very start, however, various groups of Italian comedians toured abroad and very shortly some of them settled down in other lands, there developing stage methods, calculated to appeal to foreign audiences, which were different from those practised by their companions performing in Italy itself. So successful were they, indeed, that at certain times one may well consider the focus of the commedia dell'arte as being in Paris rather than in Venice or Florence. Yet in Paris, or elsewhere, the commedia dell'arte remained always basically Italian and, as a result, there was always a coming and going northwards and southwards across the Alps; and this meant that much of what developed in performances abroad was brought back to Italy and inevitably exercised an influence even on those actors who had not indulged in performing outside their own country. Thus we have to think, not of one thing, but of three—the commedia within Italy, the commedia as it changed shape abroad and the commedia which, although remaining true in the main to native traditions, was influenced by forces from outside.

These forces must be carefully considered with particular reference both to the theatrical conditions operative in the several European countries to which the commedia dell'arte penetrated and to the differing ways in which the various audiences could appreciate what the Italians had to bring them. Thus, the French and Spanish tongues, being Romance languages, clearly permitted the publics of Paris and Madrid to follow at least a little more of the Italian dialogue than could be understood by the publics of London, Dresden, Warsaw or Petersburg; and, further, the kinship between, say, French and Italian made the thought of substituting dialogue in the former tongue for dialogue in the latter an easy and natural one. In 1734 Aaron Hill, after seeing some performances by a Parisian company, declared that, for his part, he 'could not see why Harlequin should not speak English as well as French'*—but his words were ironical: the giving of French dialogue to the Italian players had been a fairly simple process; to dream of transforming it into English seemed a chimera and an absurdity.

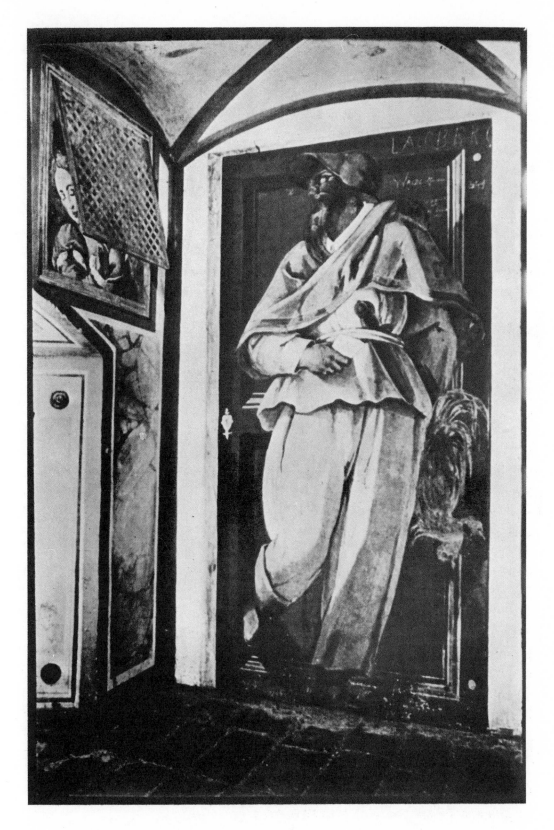

97 ZANNI

Apart from this question of language, there is the question of the several native theatres. In the sixteenth century the commedia dell'arte came to Spain just as Lope de Vega was preparing to launch out on his golden career; to England it came at a time when the way was being prepared for Shakespeare or when already he had established himself; to the Germanic countries, and later to the Slavonic, it penetrated during periods when hardly anything of a native drama existed and when social and other conditions prohibited the immediate rise of popular theatres in these lands. We can readily guess that the welcome given to the Italian players would inevitably be different, that their influence in such countries would take a variant course and that any influence imposed upon the commedia dell'arte would assume a dissimilar form from corresponding developments consequent upon its transportation to France. To the other countries the Italians journeyed as strangers; in Paris they found a court closely allied to Italian courts and a theatre which had been developing on lines similar to those in Tuscany. No surprise, therefore, need be felt on watching the gradual establishment and long-continuing career of a Parisian Théâtre Italien— a playhouse destined to exert as great an influence, throughout the course of many decades, as the house of Molière.

All of these diverse developments we must trace, and in tracing them we have to look for evidence which may assist us in answering several specific questions.

The first of these concerns the quality of the performances themselves. One school of thought tends to assert that the true, and the only great, expression of comic vigour in the improvised theatre came in the early plays belonging to the period about 1580 to 1620. Those who hold this view are prepared to admit the worth of the Neapolitan contributions, but after that they see nothing save slow, inevitable decline. In opposition, another school races to the contrary extreme and insists that the 'new blood' brought strength to a languishing form, giving it the power to carry on an active existence which otherwise it could never have done. Since, in general, discussion of the commedia dell'arte has tended to veer thus towards extreme opinions—often arousing a strange acrimony in debate—it may be suggested that consideration should be given to the possibility that truth lies somewhere between these two nodal points. The problem is a complex one, so complex, indeed, that simple, categorical solutions seem unlikely to explain and expose all its varied facets.

Something of the same suggestion may be offered concerning an associated question. One group of commentators declares that the improvised comedy drew its pristine strength from its 'popular' character and sees the main cause of its degeneration in its passing from the people to the princes. Another group, equally emphatic, lays stress upon its early encouragement by Renaissance courts and deplores its vulgarisation when it had to appeal to popular audiences. Very easily each proponent can select evidence to fit his own views, but again quite clearly the truth may be determined only by viewing the entire range of records without preconceived opinions, and once more it seems probable that the truth will be found in a middle position.

A third matter of interest arises not out of a question but out of a fact. There is no doubt that the commedia dell'arte, after persisting for so many generations, virtually vanished in the nineteenth century. What, then, were the causes of its disappearance? Was some one central force responsible, or did a variety of impulses, from within and without, contribute towards its ultimate decay? Any answer we may offer to this query must be based, first, upon the facts themselves and, secondly, upon our essential attitude both towards the commedia dell'arte itself and towards the fundamentals of theatrical art.

THE EARLY COMPANIES

The very first glimpse we have of an Italian professional company appears in a contract among eight actors, drawn up on 25 February 1545 at Padua, but unfortunately it does not tell us much. Probably the comedians improvised their parts, but we cannot tell; the chief of the troupe, Maffeo dei Re, was called 'Zanini', one actor went by the name of Zuane da Treviso, another had the nom de théâtre of 'Moschino'; these suggest type characters, but 'Moschino' does not appear to be elsewhere known, so that there is no possibility of saying precisely how this company's plays may have been related to regular commedia dell'arte productions.*

By the mid-years of the century, however, we certainly know that Pantalone and Zanni were delighting audiences in Rome, and from this time on there are numerous documents which give information concerning both companies and individual performers. With many of these there is no need to linger; but a pause must be made over two records from the year 1568. The first concerns the production of an Italian play at the Bavarian court, doubly celebrated by a descriptive account written by Massimo Troiano and by the frescoes on the walls of Trausnitz Castle. This was an amateur performance organised by several Italians in the service of Duke William, and its very amateur status gives it distinction—since nothing could more emphatically demonstrate how firmly established the professional comedy had become by that time. The Bavarian show could not have come into being had there not been a strong and familiar foundation on which its episodes and characters could be built.

The second record is still more significant, reporting the first known performance of that troupe, the Gelosi, which was universally accepted by all contemporaries as the most distinguished acting organisation of its time. With its name based on the motto 'Virtù, fama ed honor ne fer gelosi', it set a model which others sought to copy, and, under the later direction of Francesco and Isabella Andreini, became famous throughout Europe. An association of a purely professional kind, it seems to have won fame both among popular audiences and among more courtly spec-

tators; we can trace its wanderings from city to city, where public performances delighted the citizenry, and we have also ample glimpses of the way in which princes sought eagerly for its participation in their court festivities. When Henri III was on his way back from his rather unsuccessful escapade in Poland, one of his first thoughts was of the Gelosi, and excited arrangements were made for meeting his majesty's wishes. On that occasion Tommaso Porcacchi, penning a pamphlet on the king's journey, spoke of 'the rare quality of this troupe in the performance of tragedies, comedies and other theatrical pieces' and proceeded to give particular praise to Simone da Bologna, a Zanni whose wit and clever inventions were unique, to Giulio Pasquati, a brilliant Pantalone, to Rinaldo Petignoni, the Lover who went by the name of Fortunio and who was then leader of the company.

It need hardly be said that the Gelosi changed their personnel as the years passed by. Francesco Andreini himself (who was born about 1548), after spending several years as a slave in Barbary, did not join the company until after 1576, when, first as Lover and later as Capitan Spavento da Vall'Inferna, he gradually came to take control of its fortunes. In his *Bravure* (1607) he called to mind particularly the Graziano (Lodovico da Bologna), the Pantalone (Giulio Pasquati), the Zanni (Simone da Bologna), the Francatrippa (Gabrielle da Bologna), the Lovers (Orazio da Padova and Adriano Valerini), the Zanobio and Piombino (Girolamo Salimbeni), the pair of amorose (Isabella, Francesco's wife, and Prudentia da Verona) and the Franceschina (Silvia Roncagli). These, however, by no means always correspond with names mentioned in other documents, and we must suppose a continual series of alterations in the company—individual performers such as Vittoria (Vittoria Piissimi) and Pedrolino (Giovanni Pellesini) joining it for a spell, leaving and then returning. We must also recognise that on more than one occasion it certainly formed an amalgamation with one or another of the rival acting troupes which sprang up in this period.

For our purposes neither the details of its composition nor the complete record of its journeyings is of importance: all we are concerned with is its reputation from the

seventies of the sixteenth century until in the summer of 1604 Isabella died in child-birth on the journey from Paris to Italy and her husband, grief-stricken, retired from the stage and allowed the Gelosi to be disbanded.

Although no evidence exists to associate Scala's scenarios with Andreini's company, the kinship between their dramatis personae and the parts recorded as belonging to the Gelosi warrant at least the assertion that the plays this troupe produced must have been similar in style to Scala's. In both, the commedia dell'arte confronts us in its Tuscan form, before the incursion of new Neapolitan types. The praise accorded to it likewise gives us assurance for assuming that the Gelosi performances established models for the interpretation of Pantalone, Graziano and the rest which proved the foundation for later interpretations of these parts. It is not too much to say that here we are considering the most important and the most influential of all the many various companies of Italian players.

So far as we can tell, it did not belong to any particular prince but was conducted as a professional association engaged in presenting public performances in various Italian towns. We first hear of it in Milan, and from that time onwards its actors are to be traced in Genoa, Ferrara, Venice, Florence and elsewhere. At the same time, despite its position as a 'free' company, its members were obviously befriended by the heads of states, in particular by the Duke of Mantua, and sponsorship from such sources must have played an important role in its activities. The earliest extant letter of Isabella Andreini, dated 14 January 1587, is addressed to the duke, extols him as a god on earth and offers heartfelt thanks for his having taken her daughter Lavinia into Mantuan service; in April of the same year she pens a note to the duchess, and, nearly ten years later, she half-jokingly begs the duke to reinstate her in his favour, which had apparently been a trifle impaired by his having listened to some gossip purveyed to him by an ill-wisher.* When, in 1604, the Gelosi left Paris, it was to the Duchess of Mantua that the French Queen wrote a letter expressing the delight she had taken in Isabella's performances.

This last letter reminds us that it was not only in Italy that the Gelosi presented their wares. Already in 1571, only three years after their first documentary mention, they were in Paris, where the English Ambassador, Lord Buckhurst, saw them and praised their skill: 'for good mirth and handling thereof', he declared, they 'deserved singular comendacion'.* As we have seen, Henri III anxiously called for them at Venice in 1574, and in 1577 they were back in France where, after giving some performances at court, they rented the Hôtel de Bourbon; although they charged four sols for admission, a serious-minded commentator complained that they drew audiences larger than the combined congregations of the four most famous preachers in Paris. At the beginning of the following century, in 1603, the Gelosi returned once more to France, again playing at court and again giving public performances, this time at the Hôtel de Bourgogne. It was on the homeward journey from this expedition that Isabella died, and the company sadly ended a career which amply brought it the fame and honour promised in its proud motto.

PERFORMANCES IN FRANCE, SPAIN AND ENGLAND

During the thirty-six years of its activity numerous other troupes were formed, and, as has been indicated, occasionally members of these rival organisations associated themselves with the Gelosi. Some, such as the Desiosi, which is first heard of at Pisa in 1581, when Montaigne took pleasure in their performances and chatted with the actresses back-stage, and which seems finally to have vanished at Cremona in 1599, were professional companies unattached to any particular court and, so far as we know, did not travel beyond Italy's confines. Others, however, appear to have originated and carried on their work under somewhat different circumstances, while still others were active in spreading the reputation of the commedia dell'arte abroad. Of the second type the Uniti and Confidenti may be taken as characteristic. The former first emerges from obscurity in 1578, at Ferrara, the latter at Cremona, Pavia and Milan in 1574. Certainly in 1583 these two were at least temporarily amalgamated and equally certainly both were closely connected with the Gonzagas of Mantua. The active and personal interest taken by these princes in theatrical affairs finds good illustration in the attempts made by Duke Vincenzo in 1583 to persuade Francesco Andreini to reconstitute a Mantuan company.*

Precisely in what way high patronage of this kind affected the comedians' economics and freedom of action we cannot tell. Certainly it did not prevent them from engaging in itineraries and the presentation of plays in public; at the same time, it obviously associated them closely with courtly audiences, and we must presume that the quality of their performances was calculated to appeal both in the civic hall and in the princely palace.

More important are the records which tell of the dissemination of the Italian comedy abroad. By no means were the Gelosi either the only players to make such journeys or the most influential in their impact upon foreign spectators. In 1571, for example, Paris saw not only the shows given by this company but also those of another group under a Zan Ganassa, identified as Alberto Naseli, and almost all our information concerning this actor refers to his activities outside Italy. He was in Paris again in 1572, when the Earl of Lincoln attended a 'pastyme showed him' by the 'Italian players', while various documents testify to his presence in Spain from 1574 until at least 1582.* Ganassa actually built a theatre for himself in the Corral de la Pacheca in Madrid—an indication of the warm welcome given by Spanish audiences to the Italians at that period; their continuing interest in the commedia dell'arte warranted Tristano and Drusiano Martinelli, acting as 'Los Confidentes Italianos', to follow Ganassa's footsteps about the year 1587 and to remain in Madrid until 1588.

Both Drusiano and Tristano Martinelli are of particular significance to us. The former, 'one Drousiano, an Italian, a commediante, and his companye', was certainly in London in 1578, two years after the building of The Theatre, the first commedia dell'arte player visiting England of whom we know the name. Already in 1546 there had been 'certen Spanyards & Italyans who dawnsyd antycks & played dyvrse other feets' who performed before the Mayor of Norwich and his associates; the Mayor of Nottingham in 1573 likewise watched 'serteyne pastymes' given by an Italian troupe. A royal audience graced this company at Windsor the following year, and from the list of properties they required it seems they presented a pastoral: shepherds' hooks, lambskins, arrows for nymphs all were demanded. 'The unchaste, shameless and unnaturall tomblinges of the Italian Woemen', thought one puritanically inclined contemporary, offended 'God & honestie', but what Queen Elizabeth thought unfortunately we cannot tell.*

It would not seem, however, that English audiences in general took great delight in their shows. Italian was for the majority an unknown tongue and the Elizabethans were passionately devoted to words. These words, in ever richer melodies, were being purveyed to them by poets, so that the exhibitions of skill presented by companies from abroad could not thoroughly attract them. The very fact that Drusiano and his companions were described as 'tumblers' provides in itself a clear indication that for English audiences only the actions were meaningful—and, as we have seen, such actions formed only one part of the commedia dell'arte's characteristic quality. It is possible that closer scrutiny of contemporary records may reveal the presence of other Italians from time to time in London or the provinces, but nothing at present is known of any such theatrical visitors after 1578 until, in August 1602, a 'Flaminio Curtesse' was made an official award 'for his Chardges and paynes of himselfe and certen other Italian Comedians who were comended hither out of Fraunce and sithence there coming have shewed one of there playes or Interludes here at the Court on the xxixth day of this moneth at night'. The charges amounted to £6. 13s. 4d. and the Queen gave a special reward of 66 shillings and 8 pence, raising the total to £10.*

EARLY SEVENTEENTH-CENTURY COMPANIES

Drusiano Martinelli's brother Tristano was a much more important figure, and both his activities and his personality provide a link for the transition from the sixteenth to the seventeenth century.

When he went to Paris in 1600, Tristano Martinelli was a member of a newly formed company, the Accesi—still another of the troupes sponsored by the Duke of Mantua. Later he joined the Fedeli, returning to France with them in 1613–14 and in 1621–2. Before dealing with these groups it may be well to consider the significance of his own position. In 1601 he published a pamphlet entitled *Compositions de rhétorique*, and this establishes him as the first actor known certainly to have taken the part of Arlecchino, besides providing us with the earliest datable representation of that character. Even beyond its factual information, however, the *Compositions* has prime value. Its object was, by prose oration and verse pleas, to extract the gift of a gold collar from the royal treasury, and its style shows the actor Martinelli carrying his part with him out of the theatre and addressing the French monarch in tones of familiar levity. These two tendencies are reflected in most of the several extant letters which he addressed at various times to reigning princes, and some of their notes to him prove that the liberties he took were not regarded as impertinent. To the Grand Duke Ferdinando de' Medici he writes in jocular style and does not hesitate to subscribe himself 'almost a brother' of that mighty lord. Familiarly he discusses with the Duke of Mantua petty quarrels among members of the theatrical company: one epistle is addressed to the Duke as 'Most cousinly coz and our dearest gossip' ('Cosinissimo cosin e compadre nostro carissimo'). He stands on no formal terms with Cardinal Gonzaga, calling him 'Compare gallo della gresta rossa'—'gossip cock of the scarlet crest'. He even ventures further with

Segnor Dotour.   IlSegnor Leandro.   Pantalon.

Meillere Pantalon, cheminons fans parler,   Or fus l'efpee au poing, reiettons toute peur: Ce génin Harlequin me penfe trauailler,
Pour les prédre en furfaut d'vn genereux courage,   Môtrons à ces mutins que nous fômes gédarmes   Ie le veux étriper, puis fes boiaux bailler,   v.
Ie les veux tuer tous, ne faictes que faller,   Affrontons brauement nos ennemis fans cœur,   Aux maftins & limiers, pour feruir de curer.
Nous en aurons affez pour tout noftre chernage.   Nous fçauôs, long téps a, le manimêt des armes.

101   A COMIC FIGHT

the same pun on 'gallo' (cock or Gaul) when, after writing to the Queen of
France as 'the Queen my gossip', he refers to her as 'Comadre Gallina Regina
di Galli', which may be taken either as 'Gossip Hen, Queen of the Roost' or
'Gaulish Gossip, Queen of the Gauls'. 'Your most Christian Gossip', he signs
himself. Even allowing for the greater licence permitted in Renaissance courts,
the acceptance by royalty of such indecorous inscriptions may seem just a trifle
strange. But royalty did accept them; even a Queen expressed pleasure in being
asked to act as godmother for a child which Harlequin had informed her his wife
was about to bear.

The fact was, of course, that Martinelli was not merely the first recorded
Harlequin, he was also the first actor known to carry his stage character into his
ordinary life and to demand an esteem greater than that granted to his companions. What that meant in stage performances can readily be imagined—the
breaking of the composite, integrated pattern by the excessive scope given to an
individual player; and what it meant for harmony within the troupe to which such
a player belonged receives full documentation in diverse letters of complaint which

170

Harlequin.   Zany Corneto.   Il Segnor Pantalon.

O la belle chanfon, Pantalon chantons bien, | Accordons nous tous trois, ſi bien & proprement | Courage(mes amis)ie chante le deſſus,
Si voulez eſgayer voſtre maiſtreſſe belle, | Que puiſſions l'endormir au doux ſon de ma lire, | De ce plaiſant trio, compoſé pour madame,
C'eſt le moyen certain pour en fin ioüir d'elle, | Encor que comme vous ie n'ayé apris à lire, | La douceur de ma voix luy penetrera l'ame:
Qu'eſtre muſeau de chien, dy-ie muſicien. | Ie ne laiſſeray pas de ioüer brauement. | Mes paſſages ne ſont ni tortus ni boſſus.   j.

102   A COMIC SERENADE

have come down to us. When a king, Henri IV, descends to make a special request for Harlequin's presence and when a queen, Marie de' Medici, has to tempt him to come by writing to him that she has a rich present all ready which she wishes personally to put in his hands, there need be no wonder that Harlequin's head should become a trifle swollen.*

To see the effect of this we must now turn to consider briefly the two companies with which Martinelli was associated—the Accesi and the Fedeli—together with one other which continued to play a distinguished part during the first decades of the seventeenth century, the Confidenti. Of these, the first is of least import; at times it even lost its identity by a fusion with the Fedeli, and on one occasion it seems to have assumed independent being only because quarrels and rivalries caused some players to secede from a united company. Sponsored, as has been seen, by the Duke of Mantua, its most constant member was Pier Maria Cecchini, inventor of the part of Fritellino; from 1605 his wife Orsola, who may have been the daughter of Flaminio Scala and who acted as Flaminia, also played a central, and often disturbing, role in its affairs. Records of their activities, both in Italy and abroad, extend as far as the year 1623.

171

The other company, the Fedeli, was of far greater significance. Indeed, established about 1601 under the aegis of the Duke of Mantua by Giovan Battista Andreini, son of Francesco and Isabella, it may be said to have assumed the mantle of the disbanded Gelosi. Andreini himself, acting as Lelio, was its director, and with him were closely associated both his first wife, Virginia Ramponi, who acted as Florinda, and, after 1628, his second wife Virginia Rotari, who acted as Lidia. Unquestionably it attracted, during its long career up to 1652, many of the most accomplished players of its time.

For the third company, the Confidenti, a troupe which, although it bore a time-honoured name, must be regarded as distinct from the Confidenti of the sixteenth century, there were also a central guiding actor and an interested patron. Its director from at least 1611 was Flaminio Scala, and its patron was Don Giovanni de' Medici. Possibly Scala did not act much himself, and if so we are confronted, not with a group of actors of whom one was the chief, but with an association of performers playing under the aegis of a man whose sole business was to guide them and take general care of their stage arrangements. Thus Flaminio Scala may well have the distinction of being the first professional 'producer' in the history of the stage. In 1615 the company was praised as one of the best of its time, and we are told that it included then two servants, Scapino (Francesco Gabbrielli) and Mezzettino (Ottavio Onorati), two innamorate, Lavinia (Marina Antonazzoni) and Valeria (Valeria Austoni); two maid-servants, Nespola (the wife of Marcello di Secchi) and Spinetta (the wife of Domenico Bruni); two Lovers, Fulvio (Domenico Bruni) and Ortensio (Francesco Antonazzoni); Pantalone (Marcantonio Romagnesi); Beltrammo (Niccolò Barbieri); a Capitano; and an 'Italianate Frenchman', Claudione.* No Graziano is mentioned in this list, but the interesting information is provided for us that Fulvio sometimes took the Doctor's part as well as his own, and that other members of the troupe were able, when occasion demanded, to act more than a single role.

In considering these three troupes, we encounter several matters of interest. While we could wish for still further information, their affairs are fairly fully documented, and the first thing that attracts our attention is the series of interminable and complex squabbles which racked their unity. Already at Paris in 1601, among the Accesi, a bitter quarrel raged between Martinelli and Cecchini—and here we must return to that development in the histrionic world of which the former was a symbol. No doubt there were rivalries and enmities within the ranks of the Gelosi, but nothing from that age can compare with what we now find among the Accesi and the Fedeli; and obviously the fundamental cause rests in the appearance of actors and actresses intent rather upon the exploitation of their own personalities than upon working as members of a team. It is true that in 1608 Giovanni de' Medici praised Cecchini for his maintaining the unity and harmony of the scenarios, but many notices indicate that he was as bad as Martinelli in flaunting his own personality.* Nor was it only Harlequin and Fritellino who thus clashed. Among the Fedeli a bitter war was carried on by Flaminia, Cecchini's wife, and Florinda, wife of Andreini. Swearing and dire threats were commonplace; each prominent player thought he or she was of more worth to the company than any other and angrily demanded a larger share in the proceeds; rival gangs arose within the body of the troupes, and illicit love affairs added to the confusion. Perhaps such developments are inevitable in any theatrical company in any age, but the dismal series of complaints and rebuttals, of vicious accusations and spiteful threats, makes us wonder at times how any performances ever effectively reached the boards.

Nor were the Confidenti, in spite of their having Flamino Scala as director, in any better a position. Valeria and Lavinia were always ready to tear out each other's eyes; success for one in any particular play was sure to fan the flames of rage in the breast of her companion. The men were almost equally at fault, and the enmities here, as among the Accesi and Fedeli, were intensified by criss-cross love affairs among the players. Letters of complaint were constantly being sent to Don Giovanni. In 1620 that harassed nobleman penned a lengthy epistle which perhaps better than anything throws into relief both the troubled state of the Confidenti and his own difficulties as its patron. He described almost 'all of them' as being 'in a rebellious state, hardly able to hold their company together, as is the common way with actors'. Then he proceeds: 'I let them fry in their own grease, as they say; but then came Lent and their soup grew watery; one by one they started to bombard my ears, all crying out for "unity, unity". Then the whole band of them arrived— not just once, but four separate times—declaring that positively they did not wish to break up the company. I told them and told them again that I did not want to get involved in this matter, but I said I would let them know what course might seem to me advisable both in their interests and my own. Back they came again, humbly praying me not to abandon them, saying they were fully resolved not to do anything which might break up the company, that they were most ready to obey any commands I might give them.'* Don Giovanni then goes on to tell his correspondent that the actors firmly expressed the intention, if the company were disbanded, of giving up the stage and engaging in other occupations, no matter how menial. 'On your life', he asks, 'can you tell me how I could say, "You must go," "You will remain," "You must give up your chief role and take one not so important"—and so persuade men who live in liberty and in association to accept my orders and proposals? What Christian charity would I have extended to these poor men and their families? What act of courtesy or gratitude would I have shown to those who for seven successive years have obeyed my wishes, if I had ruined and sent them to disaster, as they believe they will be if the company is split up? Sir, I am poor—yes, but I have a sense of honour, and I confess that I am soft-hearted, that I cannot do hurt to those who honour me. You know that the world is ruled by beliefs; these poor men think that disunion means ruin, and, for the reasons which I have given you, I simply have not been able to find words for inaugurating that disunion, not to speak of persuading them to it. So I have informed them that I will help them.'

Don Giovanni emerges from all of this with distinction, but his letter clearly reveals a disturbing atmosphere within the companies. Despite his pity for these 'poor men', he knows full well that 'the Lelios, the Florindas, the Flaminias, the Fritellinos and the Arlecchinos' are men and women 'most avid and ambitious of power and domination'.

This excessive exploitation of individual personalities finds reflection in the introduction of new, or at least of newly named, character parts. Cecchini himself does not remain content with one of the established roles but has to invent his Fritellino; Lorenzo Nettuni caps this with his Fichetto, Niccolò Barbieri with his Beltrame; the Lovers assume fresh designations, and the maid-servants desert the old Franceschina in favour of Ricciolina, Nespola and Spinetta.

At the same time, the Neapolitan influence becomes apparent. Already in 1575 five players in Naples drew up a contract for giving professional performances, and probably this was only one group among many. The inhabitants of the south seized with avidity on the improvised comedy, bringing to it an abandoned vitality and inventing new characters. The appearance of Cola among the Accesi and Fedeli serves as an indication of the way in which such Neapolitan types, conceived differently from those of the north, began to intrude into the Tuscan scenarios—adding to the expansionist trend consequent upon the invention by individual players of characters suitable for the exploitation of their own individual personalities.

Paradoxically, during this period when signs of disintegration became amply apparent within the commedia dell'arte, a determined and sometimes rather humourless effort began to be made by some of the comedians to defend and, if need be, to reform their art. They realised that all was not well with the stage and that its shortcomings were occasioning attacks at the whole practice of playing. Such attacks had already started in the sixteenth century; even during the time of the Gelosi, St. Carlo Borromeo had tirelessly assailed the immodesty of the actors. But the onsets did not become really serious until the seventeenth century witnessed a whole series of denunciations by more or less learned ecclesiastics which culminated in G. D. Ottonelli's *Della Christiana moderatione del theatro* in 1646.* These works, bristling, like Prynne's *Histriomastix*, with authority from the Fathers of the Church, are perhaps not of any vital importance, but their appearance, associated with certain doubts concerning the course which the commedia dell'arte was taking, resulted in the preparation by the comedians themselves of several serious compilations in which rebuttal of ecclesiastical arguments mingled with warnings directed towards those who were bringing the theatre into disgrace. G. B. Andreini occupied himself with the theme in prose and verse, lauding early actors of pious fame and

presenting half a score of sonnets 'praising theatres and their virtuous exponents'.*
Among these lyrics appears a 'prayer that bad actors should be inspired constantly
to pursue their art virtuously' and another sonnet dealing with the familiar theme
that life is like a play. In kindred spirit, Andreini's irritating colleague Fritellino
published in 1614 his *Discorsi intorno alle comedie*, starting with the usual reference to
St Thomas and the Fathers and proceeding to a reasoned defence of at least the more
'virtuous' among the comedians, while Beltrame, Niccolò Barbieri, who was also
involved in the internecine feuds, issued in 1628 his *Discorso famigliare*, in which he
pleaded that a distinction should be made between good and bad players and urged
the comedians themselves to follow the way of virtue.

The contrast thus apparent between practice and precept, together with the
obviously anxious seriousness with which these actor-authors viewed the state of
their art, provides a kind of pointer towards the future. Despite the pleas which are
made in defence of comedy, we sense an underlying awareness of errors and a desire
for improvement. Thus was the foundation for later 'reform' being laid.

THE ESTABLISHMENT OF THE FIRST THÉÂTRE ITALIEN

During this half-century, the Italian actors made more and still more visits abroad.
In 1614 Fritellino took the Accesi to Linz and Vienna, returning home jauntily with
the patent of ennoblement of which he was so proud. There had been wandering
companies visiting these regions before, and quite possibly the 'Julio' recorded at
Vienna in 1570 was the famous Pantalone, Giulio Pasquati, but the performances
given by the Accesi appear to have been the earliest important 'season' of improvised comedy at the Bavarian and Imperial courts. Obviously, from the honour
he accorded to Cecchini, the Emperor Matthias enjoyed the performances, but there
is little sign that the commedia dell'arte made any material impress upon the native
German and Austrian stages. No doubt the clownish type of Hanswurst owed
something to the Italians, but the connection is so slight that nothing very much can
be made of the indebtedness of the German clown to any particular Italian character.
The truth is, of course, that at this time the Teutonic countries were racked by wars,
and the possibility of the development of a popular stage remained still far distant.
Even the later visit of G. B. Andreini in 1628 to Prague and Vienna left no more
permanent impress.

The true home of the commedia dell'arte outside of Italy was France. To Paris
the Accesi went in 1607–8, where they acted both at court and in the Hôtel de
Bourgogne. A few years later, the Fedeli made a visit which extended from
September 1613 to July 1614, with performances before royalty and at the same public
theatres. Clearly, they found a lively welcome there, since they soon returned for
another season from January 1621 to March 1622. Even such a stay was not sufficient
to satisfy the demand, and within a few months the king was eagerly asking for a

Ce docteur est remply de si grande seiance
qu'il luy fault arracher tous les motz de ses doigtz

Pantalon et Zany le sont a sa semblance
Dont ilz ont a tirer si fort comme tu vois

I · Honeruogt excudit

103   PANTALONE, THE DOTTORE AND ZANNI

repeat, a request which resulted in still another trip in 1623. G. B. Andreini was
their leader then, and twenty years later this actor returned once more to Paris; on
this occasion he seems to have remained for several years.

By this time we are rapidly approaching a new era when, instead of witnessing
occasional performances given by visiting players, Parisian spectators were to have
an Italian theatre of their own. Another troupe had been there from 1639 to 1641,
and this was followed in 1644–5 by a company which created an even greater stir—
not surprisingly, since it apparently included the famous Trivellino and future
Arlecchino, Domenico Biancolelli (Dominique) as well as the still more famous
Scaramuccia, Tiberio Fiorilli. From 1645 to 1661 the coming and going between
Italy and France was constant; then at last the Italians settled down to give regular
performances in Paris.

During these years the Comédie Italienne was established. The first move came
when, in 1658, Molière shared the Petit Bourbon with the commedia dell'arte
players. When that theatre was demolished in 1660, a similar sharing arrangement
was pursued at the Palais Royal, and finally in 1680 the Italians secured a playhouse
of their own, the old Hôtel de Bourgogne, now named the Théâtre Italien, where
they stayed until in 1697 several indiscreet comments in one of their plays aroused the
wrath of Madame de Maintenon, the king's mistress, and weepingly they were forced
by royal command to depart.

The establishment of the commedia dell'arte in Paris wrought in it mighty changes. In the old days the actors had arrived as visitors, given their pieces and returned to Italy; they clearly needed to give no thought to ways in which they might adapt their performances to the demands of audiences different from those with which they were already familiar. When, however, they had to maintain a permanent theatre, when they came into close association with French actors who themselves were inheritors of a long tradition and when several of them, including Tiberio Fiorilli and Dominique, abandoned their native country to become naturalised Frenchmen, conditions were such that modification of the older styles in production and acting became inevitable.

Fundamentally, the force which operated with greatest power to effect this modification was the fact that the Italians now had to consider an audience the members of which spoke a language akin to, yet different from, their own. Some among the public could no doubt follow a little of the dialogue, but very few indeed could have appreciated its subtleties, and presumably none could understand the dialects employed. Whereas in Italy the comedians could count on a fairly constant attendance of spectators familiar with the plays and deriving pleasure from the different ways in which the actors improvised their scenes, they now had to consider means of attracting the public by other methods. Thus, they turned to utilise scenes and machines. It is true that the employment of scenic spectacle and effects was by no means unknown in commedia dell'arte performances in Italy. Already in Scala's *La forsennata prencipessa* such visual aids were called for, and among later scenarios many of the tragi-comic kind depended very largely on stage devices. In the property list of the Neapolitan *Barliario*, to take but one example, the requirements included a cloud machine to carry Angiolina to the skies, a subterranean cave, a dragon which could rise from the ground and then fly off with Dario on its back, a device by which the same character might be transformed into a fountain and back again, a grotto with a large stone on top which could fall and block the cave's entrance, a flying-machine for Pulcinella, another for the allegorical figure of Reason, a trick fire designed to consume a quantity of books, and an apparatus to simulate the cutting off of a head.

All of this is very distressing, but we must remember that in Italy devices of this kind were reserved for the tragic, semi-tragic and pastoral plays; comedy continued as before content with its simple arrangements of 'houses'. What happened in France was that the actors, introduced to the scenic wonders created in Paris by Giacomo Torelli and the two Vigaranis, Gaspare and Carlo, seized upon tricks of this kind as the central elements in new scenarios. In 1694 Evaristo Gherardi, the exponent of Harlequin, published a volume of plays presented at the Comédie Italienne, and, despite the complaints of his comrades, proceeded several years later to increase its contents, publishing the whole in six volumes. Each play in the 1700

Les Intrigues d'Arlequin

collection is adorned with a frontispiece, and these indicate how largely the Italians had come to depend on scenes and machines. Here are Chinese pagodas and sorceresses' caverns, here are royal palaces and Pluto's court, here Harlequin ascends in the chariot of the sun, Pasquariel mounts a winged horse. Classical mythology is tortured to provide fantastic and frequently absurd themes for the display of visual effects. Titles such as *Arlequin Empereur de la Lune*, *Arlequin Jason* and *Arlequin Chevalier du Soleil* clearly point out the direction which was being taken.

178

The emphasis in these titles upon Harlequin points also to the intensification of the trend which we have already noted towards emphasis on single players. An appreciation of the harmonised team-work reflected in the earlier commedia dell'arte demanded a knowledge of Italian which the French public did not have; that public was much more likely to take delight in exhibitions of virtuoso playing on the part of individual comedians. Tiberio Fiorilli as Scaramouche, Dominique as Arlecchino, were more important in themselves than as members of a company, and as a result

the delicate balance which is to be sensed in Scala's scenarios tended to vanish. This meant, in effect, that Harlequin and Pantalone slowly changed their essential dramatic entities; instead of being characters with an existence of their own, interpreted by divers actors, the actors assumed prominence and, as it were, merely dressed up in Pantalone's and Harlequin's clothes. The feeling for continuity in the stage person had gone or was going.

Fiorilli's performances demonstrated something else. His Scaramouche was played without a mask, and from this period on we hear more and more how this comedian and that, usually at the particular desire of the public, abandoned their traditional facial coverings and showed their own features on the stage. Specifically we are told, for example, that in the early eighteenth century Giovanni Bissoni as Scapino was compelled by audience demand to abandon his mask because 'in France spectators like to see various emotions exhibited on the actors' faces'.* It need hardly be said that thus the characteristic and central structure of the original commedia dell'arte was being shattered; its very lifeblood was being sapped away.

Equally disastrous was the paradoxical but perfectly natural double trend in the dramatic form itself. Since the language spoken by the Italians was a foreign one, quite understandably many of the star actors increased the measure of pantomime in their performances; since words were largely meaningless, they sought to appeal by means of movement, and from this they proceeded to interlard their plays with much more song, dance and acrobatics than had been usual in the past. Once more, in a different way, the balance was being disturbed. Alongside of this trend came another of a contrary kind. Instead of resorting to silent pantomime, some of the players began to intermix French sentences with their Italian dialogue, and very soon this led to the preparing of texts which included both improvised scenes and other

107 HARLEQUIN SITS FOR HIS PORTRAIT

181

scenes in French specially written by Parisian authors. It was but a step from such plays to others penned largely in French but adapted for production at the Comédie Italienne. Thus the dramas printed in Gherardi's collection are totally unlike the older scenarios. 'These comedies', Gherardi explains, referring to the contents of his volumes, 'are not the kind of Italian pieces I spoke of in my introduction when I said that such pieces "could not be printed because they cannot be separated from the stage actions" and that "the Italians perform without learning anything by heart". The comedies presented here are those played by the company when, in order to conform to the taste and intelligence of the majority of the spectators, it was compelled to get more French than Italian into its plays—comedies which the authors call French plays accommodated to the Théâtre Italien.'*

How this worked out is clearly to be seen in the Gherardi texts. One specimen will serve for many. In the first scene of the second act of *La thèse des dames* (1695) Mezzetin enters singing a French song and follows this with a soliloquy in the same tongue; in scene ii Colombine greets him in anger and there is a written French dialogue for the pair; similar dialogue is provided for scenes iii (Angelique and Colombine) and iv (Colombine, Angelique, Octave and Scaramouche). Then we come to scene v, which appears thus in the text:*

OCTAVE, SCARAMOUCHE

OCTAVE. Ah, mon cher Scaramouche, que j'ay de joye de ce raccommodement! (*Octave dit à Scaramouche qu'il voudroit bien donner la colation à Angelique dans les Thuilleries, & qu'il voudroit le faire d'une manière galante pour la surprendre agréablement. Il prie Scaramouche d'y rêver, & s'en va.*)

And, when Octave has gone, the next scene is entirely in the style of a scenario: 'Harlequin enters grumbling, recounts a pleasant story of a mishap. Scaramouche tells him what they have to do, and the two of them walk round the stage, each thinking out what might be planned for the dinner; from time to time one turns to the other, saying "I've got it" and then, immediately after, "No, that wouldn't be so good". At last Scaramouche starts a rambling discourse as he walks, making Harlequin shift his gaze from one side of the stage to the other, and finally goes out without reaching any conclusion. Harlequin exits, saying "Oh, that can't help being a success".'

In addition to this mingling of written French dialogue and of scenes marked for improvisation, these plays sometimes introduced situations in which French written dialogue was mixed with Italian. Thus, in *La fille de bon sens*, Pierrot talks to the Doctor. In French he asks for his master's old gown; when he gets it, he says, 'I'll be a Doctor as well as you'. '*Barone,*' replies the Doctor, '*tu credi d'esser Dottore per averne il vestito?*' 'Why not?' Pierrot enquires in French, 'There are dozens today who don't pay any greater attention to ceremony. I know fifty people in Paris, especially those practising medicine like yourself, who have no more of the Doctor in them than the costume and a good figure.' Whereupon the Doctor answers in mixed form: '*Tu credi dunque, matto che sei*, that you need only be a Doctor's valet in order to become a Doctor yourself? *Come se la dottrina?*'* And so on. Clearly this takes us very far from the commedia dell'arte we know in Scala's scenarios.

With this double development—of excessive pantomimic movement and of written dialogue in French or in mixed forms—another dual tendency demands notice. On the one hand, extravagant action was intensified and impossibilities were indulged in for their own sake. In the earlier Italian comedy disguising was a frequent device, but it was kept within bounds until the Neapolitan actors came to exploit its possibilities; now, the employment of absurd disguise went much further than even the Neapolitans permitted, and it often assumed a different orientation. For the most part, disguise in these earlier scenarios had been a convenient device for the carrying on of the plots; when confronted by a difficulty, Harlequin or Pulcinella immediately thought of dressing up for the purpose of hoodwinking some other character. In such a play as *Ésope* (1691), however, Harlequin does not dress up as Aesop, he is Aesop, just as in *Arlequin Phaeton* (1692) he is Phaeton, Octave is Apollo and Mezzetin Momus. We must admit that in the tragi-comedies and pastorals of earlier times something of the same procedure was followed; yet there was a difference. This may best be explained by saying that in such Italian scenarios certain of the actors were called upon to take special parts outside the comic range, whereas in the Italo-French plays it was the characters who were thrust into different roles. In a typical early pastoral or tragi-comedy Pantalone and Graziano, Arlecchino and Pedrolino, enter in their own persons—the former pair commonly serving as counsellors and the latter playing their usual servant parts. Alongside them will be the magicians, the kings and the princes demanded by the plots, but in the performance of these roles, no attempt is made to impose characters proper to the comic world upon them. In *Ésope* and *Arlequin Phaeton*, Harlequin does not come in as a servant to one of the central persons; instead, he is presented, in his familiar multicoloured costume half-covered by a gown or a regal cloak, as being one of these central persons. A crude concept of parody is here at work, and the spirit of these plays comes measurably close to the vulgar burlesques which later littered the nineteenth-century English stage. Apparently the joke pleased certain audiences in the past, but it has now lost its savour, it is crude and it is alien to the spirit which had animated the commedia dell'arte in the past.

While this trend is marked in dozens of plays, another, utterly opposed, makes its appearance. The French authors who supplied the Théâtre Italien with texts delighted to make use of the opportunity offered them for the introduction of satirical scenes and realistic topics. That volume of Gherardi's collection which includes *Ésope* and

183

Arlequin Phaeton opens with Regnard's *Les filles errantes* (1690), full of social comment, and the even more emphatic *La coquette* (1691). This, in turn, encouraged the Italians to make topical sallies of their own. As has been seen, no signs of satire are to be traced in the early commedia dell'arte; its introduction here in the Comédie Italienne is a new development, inspired no doubt partly by changing social conditions, but induced mainly by the appearance of virtuoso stars who thought that all they did and said would be accepted, and by a desire to spice the shows with lively matter. Repeatedly the company was warned to be careful; they disregarded the warnings and the closing of their playhouse in 1697 was the direct result.

From this time on the tendency to comment on social affairs or to indulge in literary parody becomes a feature of the Italian comedy in its own home and abroad. Even when Goethe visited a debased 'theatre of Pulcinella' during his Italian tour, he found that topicalities abounded, so that the show became 'a sort of living newspaper'.*

THE NEW THÉÂTRE ITALIEN

For nearly twenty years Paris remained without a Théâtre Italien, yet what the actors had achieved during the final decades of the seventeenth century refused to be banished by royal command. When the Italians sadly packed up their costumes and departed, the theatres of the fairs joyfully seized upon Harlequin and his tricks, developing these in a manner suited to their own styles. Acrobatics, low comic business, music, dance and song all were exploited; French actors assumed the characteristic roles, and for such dialogue as appeared in the plays French was substituted for Italian. Although some native dramatists, such as Alain-René Lesage and Alexis Piron, applied themselves to composing pieces for the performers at the fairs, the main trend was towards a rough form of comic opera and towards panto-mimic effects. From all accounts, vitality, verve, humour could be found on these stages; they were exceedingly popular; but the commedia dell'arte was here being drawn further and further away from its original atmosphere. It now was breathing a new and less wholesome air.

Meanwhile, those who had known the Théâtre Italien before 1697 constantly pleaded for a return of the Italian players, and in 1716 at last their efforts were successful. The Duke of Orléans asked, or was persuaded to ask, the assistance of the Duke of Parma in re-establishing a company in Paris, and as a result Luigi Riccoboni, known as Lelio, arrived in 1716 with a troupe of carefully selected comedians. Besides Riccoboni himself and his wife, Elena Balletti (Flaminia), there were the latter's brother Giuseppe (Mario), Giovanni Bissoni (Scapino), the adroit Tommaso Visentini (Arlecchino), Pietro Alborghetti (Pantalone), Francesco Materazzi (Dottore), Giacomo Rauzini (Scaramouche), Zanetta Benozzi (Silvia), Margarita Rusca (Violetta) and Ursula Astori, described simply as a 'singer'.

108 LELIO AND HARLEQUIN

The company was a fine one, and its first performances were eagerly awaited. Many Frenchmen, like Watteau, had long been dreaming nostalgically of the Italian nights, and no playhouse could ever have been opened to greater expectancy. At first, Riccoboni found everything according to his wishes, but soon it became clear that his path was not to prove an easy one. Serious-minded, he tried his best to present a balanced repertory of scenarios, but the audiences of 1716, partly because they had become accustomed to the performances at the fairs, were different from those of the past; the Italians did not attract as they should have done; and the receipts fell steadily lower and lower. In an effort to stimulate flagging interest, the director decided to engage P. F. Biancolelli, the son of the famous Dominique. This man, then aged thirty-six, seemed well fitted to draw the public into the playhouse. After having acted as Harlequin in the itinerant company of Giuseppe Tortoriti, he had settled down to a career in the theatres of the fairs, where his reputation was great. Born in France, he spoke the language of that country as a native and conse-quently was able to introduce when need arose dialogue of a kind which the audience could understand. There were, of course, practical problems to be solved in intro-ducing him to the company, since already Riccoboni had with him the skilled Visentini; but these were solved by giving Biancolelli the part of Pierrot for his début. With his advent, the takings rose, but after a short time once more they started to decline. One device after another Riccoboni tried, but in the end he came to realise that what the public most missed was dialogue in a language they could follow and plays adapted to the spirit of the times. Gradually, as in the days before 1697, French crept in. In one play, Visentini as Harlequin stepped up to the foot-lights. 'Sirs,' he said, 'I want to tell you a *piccola* fable which I read this morning— for sometimes I like to *divenire* a scholar. But *la dirò* in Italian; and those who *intenderanno* it *esplicheranno* it to those who don't understand.' The story itself, designed to illustrate the difficulties of following advice coming from two opposed quarters, brought him to his point. 'Many people', he explained, 'tell me: "Harlequin, you must speak in French; the ladies don't understand you and even the gentlemen have difficulty in following you." I thank them for their counsel and turn in the other direction, when several gentlemen tell me: "Harlequin, you mustn't speak French, you'll ruin your skill." I am at a loss. Shall I speak Italian? Shall I speak French? I put the question to you, sirs.' On this occasion a voice from the audience cried: 'Speak as you wish; you'll always be a delight.'* But the very fact that the question had to be put shows the force of the demand; and Riccoboni, bowing to it, started to revive some of the Franco–Italian pieces given at the old Théâtre Italien and to negotiate, as his predecessors had done, with French authors. Neither the out-of-fashion Gherardi material, however, nor the new works, based mainly on the type of farcical comedy popular at the fairs, satisfied either Riccoboni or the public. He stood, in fact, confronted by a dilemma. Anxious to keep up high standards, he himself prepared several scenarios, of which the first was *L'Italien marié à Paris* (1716), in which he sought to give a new character to the ancient forms and to bring these forms up to date; but the Italian dialogue, improvised by the actors, could make but faint appeal.* And, on the other hand, the imitation of the Gherardi plays, together with the imitation of the kind of pieces produced at the fairs, was alike distasteful to him and unpalatable to the spectators. It almost seemed that the new Théâtre Italien would be compelled to close.

Then a rather strange thing happened. A French painter, Jacques Autreau, who had never before produced a play, brought to Riccoboni in 1718 a comedy called *Le naufrage au Port-à-l'Anglais*. The provenance of the manuscript did not seem to promise much, but by some inner sense the elderly author had, in fact, devised exactly what the actors needed—a French play which introduced persons whose inadequate command of the language would still be acceptable and which presented scenes likely to interest and attract a Parisian audience. Autreau's story tells how a party of foreign voyagers have been forced by a storm to seek shelter at an inn in a French port. One of these is an Italian who is accompanied by his two daughters, both of whom, having been well educated, have some knowledge of French and who soon, inspired by love, do the best they can to improve their conversational abilities. The basic setting, then, was excellently appropriate for a company of which most members were still inadept in speaking a language not their own. Apart from this, the author had adroitly inserted various elements calculated to appeal to the Parisians—a good intrigue, central scenes discussing the subtleties of love and gallantry, various amusing pieces of business for the comic characters and a number of musical divertisements, not extraneous to, but built naturally into, the plot.

The result was an overwhelming success; there was no more talk among the comedians of leaving Paris; and a new tradition was set. Until the very end of their career in France, still half a century distant, the Italians never quite abandoned their improvised performances, and these served to keep them in contact with that from which they sprang; but from now on we may imagine how actively they applied themselves to the improvement of their conversational French and how thus they fitted themselves for the inclusion within their repertory of plays in that language. We may imagine, too, what encouragement Autreau's triumph gave to other authors and with what eagerness the Italians looked round for works by which that triumph might be repeated.

Nor were their expectations disappointed. Two years after the production of *Le naufrage*, in March 1720, two French authors presented a piece called *L'amour et la vérité*: one of the collaborators was of no importance, but the other was Marivaux, who some six months later brought out his *Arlequin poli par l'amour*. In looking at this play we realise that with subtle skill a new and harmonious dramatic form had been fashioned for what these players could offer. Here the dream of Watteau was being realised in actual stage performance. We have left the world of the Port-à-l'Anglais and entered a realm of the imagination—not the fantastic and absurd world delineated in so many of the Gherardi plays, but a world seemingly real which is yet enchanted and apart from actuality. In this play, and in the other plays of Marivaux which were to follow, the commedia dell'arte had found a new spirit, a new scope for the exercise of its talents.

While, however, we may recognise that this represents a development which can heartily be acclaimed, that in these comedies we stand far removed from the somewhat rough and clumsy experiments made by the earlier Comédie Italienne, we must at the same time acknowledge that the advent of Marivaux, even because of his artistic achievement, was destined in the end to submerge the Italian players in France. No danger came from his refinement of the love episodes and the cultivation of his exquisite sensibility; it was entirely legitimate for him to take Harlequin and show him in a new light; his atmosphere of enchantment was a proper modification of the romantic unreality of the earlier commedia dell'arte; yet in effect he destroyed, or laid the foundations for destroying, its very being. Improvisation became of less and less importance; and, if Harlequin was retained, his companions declined; instead of the bold vigour of the Gelosi, a genteel delicacy, characteristically French, enveloped the stage.

There need be no surprise, therefore, in seeing the Comédie Italienne during succeeding years at once advancing in esteem and losing the quality which was originally attached to its title. If it could have built a new being for itself on Marivaux' basis, something of great value might have resulted, but time cannot be arrested and the stage constantly demands variety. Some authors, it is true, sought to imitate his style, but without any signal success, while others tended to draw the Italian–French comedy further and further away from its original spirit. At the same time, the need of producing novelties induced the actors to fall back upon divertisements of various kinds in an endeavour to keep the audiences amused. In particular, they started to cultivate parodies or burlesques, a type of dramatic representation which evidently appealed to the public but which was ill-suited to preserve the best and most characteristic qualities of the Italian style. Ballet-pantomimes, vaudevilles and spectacular pieces all drew the theatre in the same direction. When, in 1729, Riccoboni left the stage and returned to Italy, the writing on the wall was clearly visible.

Gradually the company changed. Visentini retired in 1739 and his place was taken, first, by Antonio Costantini and, later, by Carlo, called Carlin, Bertinazzi, and these men kept the character of Harlequin vital. From time to time, notably when Carlo Antonio Veronese, who took the part of Pantalone, and his daughters Anna (Corallina) and Camilla, joined the company in 1744, there was a revival of interest in improvised scenarios, but for the most part parodies and the like formed the staple

F. M. Queverdo Pel   Dambrun Sculp

Tous les genres sont bons hors le genre
ennuyeux.

of the repertory. Not surprisingly, in 1762 the Comédie Italienne eventually amalgamated with the Opéra Comique, an outgrowth of the fairs, and its fate was finally
sealed. When Carlo Goldoni came to Paris, he tried—somewhat strangely in view of
a life-long struggle to substitute written dialogue for improvised—to keep the old
spirit alive by preparing various scenarios for the actors, but, as he himself records,
'in 1780 there came a sorry catastrophe for the comedians my compatriots. They
had admitted the Opéra Comique into their association and the new arrivals drove
out the old.' The comic opera alone survived and the days of the Italian spoken

Le bon Ménage

F.M. Queverdo inv del   1785   Delonquiel Sculp

Ah! papa, papa, c'est pour nous?

comedy were over; of the old players only Carlin Bertinazzi, the last of the great eighteenth-century Harlequins, was retained in the company. In such 'comédie-parades' and 'divertissements' as were turned out by authors like de Piis and Barré occasionally wisps of the ancient characters remain; but, if a single *Cassandre oculiste* preserves the wraiths of Pantalone in Cassandre himself, of Pierrot and of Colombine, most of these pieces preserve not the slightest trace of commedia dell'arte figures. Harlequin alone maintained a fitful existence—an existence which for one fleeting moment seemed as though it were to come once more to its pristine strength.

Between 1779 and 1783 Florian penned three plays—*Les deux billets, Le bon ménage* and *Le bon père*—which clearly showed that he both understood the character of Harlequin and appreciated the dramatic method responsible for establishing him in his pre-eminent position. Harlequin, he avers, echoing and modifying earlier judgements, 'is perhaps the only character who unites in himself wit and simplicity, shrewdness and folly. Harlequin, always good-natured, always easy to cheat, believes everything he is told, falls into all the traps set for him; nothing surprises him, everything puzzles him; he has no logic, no sensibility; he loses his temper, is appeased, grieves and is consoled all at the same moment; his joy and his sorrow are both delightful. He is, then, by no means a buffoon, nor is he a serious person; he is a great child; he has a child's grace, sweetness, cleverness; and children are so lovable that I count on success if I have been able to give to this child all the sense, all the wit and all the sensibility of a man.'* Then, still more significantly, he declares: 'These three plays form, so to say, the romance of my Harlequin, set forth in the three most interesting periods of life—those of the lover, the husband and the father. While always keeping his original character intact, I have made him speak differently in each of the three comedies, corresponding to his different affections and age in each.'

Here is the true commedia dell'arte procedure; but Harlequin cannot live alone, nor can he conserve his true spirit when he is fettered to words provided for him by another. By the time Florian was writing, the possibility of rehabilitating him among his proper companions was gone; the Comédie Italienne had lost its roots, and while these three plays were being composed its very name vanished from the roster of Parisian theatres.

COMMEDIA DELL'ARTE IN GERMANY, POLAND, RUSSIA AND ENGLAND

The establishment of a permanent theatre in Paris with the name 'Italian' attached to it has demonstrated the wide sweep of influence exerted by the commedia dell'arte, and this sweep of influence extended far beyond the area of France.

At the close of the seventeenth century perhaps the most distinguished and best organised company was that directed by Francesco Calderoni, known as Silvio, and his wife Agata, who acted under the name of Flaminia. Serious-minded, this pair endeavoured to preserve the best traditions, to follow Barbieri's advice and, by maintaining high standards, to avoid vulgar meaningless buffoonery in their productions. Because of this, special interest attaches to the fact that the greater part of their time was spent abroad; the company went to Munich in 1687 and remained there for four years; in 1697–8 it gave a season in Brussels; in 1699 it went to Vienna and, after giving some performances in Augsburg, returned to the Austrian capital in 1703.

III SCARAMOUCHE   II2 HARLEQUIN

Fresh theatrical territory was thus being opened up. Even more important were some developments immediately after the closing of the first Théâtre Italien in 1697. Within a few months, Angelo Costantini received a request from August II, Elector of Saxony and King of Poland, to form a good troupe which might be attached to his court. Costantini busily set to work, with the result that three years later an enormous company, including some hundred individuals, started trekking northwards to Dresden. The success of the visit was marred, however, by Costantini's own indiscretion in making love to the monarch's favourite mistress; as a result, he was arrested, and for twenty years he languished in prison. While he lay immured, however, another company, led by Tommaso Ristori, arrived at Warsaw in 1715 and there remained in court service for a period of fifteen years.

Already, some knowledge of the Italian style of playing had reached Poland. Under Sigismund III in 1592 three Italian actors are recorded, and by 1633 an author Piotr Baryka could familiarly refer in his *Z chłopa król* to Italian buffooneries and comedies. Later, there were amateur improvised plays with the familiar characters at the court of Ladisław IV; 'Arlekin' was introduced by G. A. Comenius into an intermezzo within his *Hercules monstrorum domitor* as this was acted at his gymnasium at Lesno; there was even a public for the translation by Kryzsztof Piekarski of Andreini's *Bravure* as *Bohatyr strazny*; an unidentified company gave delight to the king in 1688. The way had thus been prepared for the establishment of permanently settled troupes.*

192

13   113 HARLEQUIN   NWH

Trufaltin

114 TRUFFALDINO

Spinetina.

115 SPINETTINA

116 BRIGHELLA

After its fifteen years of service in Warsaw, the Italian company decided to penetrate even further afield, and in 1733, 1734 and 1735 the actors proceeded to Russia where they gave shows before the Empress Anna Ioannovna.* A record of their performances has come down to us in the form of forty scenarios in Russian, evidently prepared for the sake of those who could not understand Italian. Still a further record of interest in the Italian comedians is a manuscript, unfortunately not exactly datable, containing various intermedii with commedia characters. Harlequin is well represented there, sometimes under the guise of Kherlikin; as in other countries, his follies and his wit appear to have captured most attention. Meanwhile, in Poland King August III commanded two of the actors, Andrea and Marianna Bertoldi, to form a new company: he as Pantalone and she as Rosetta consequently became leaders of a troupe which had a lengthy career in Dresden and Warsaw from 1738 until the fifties of the century. Here too a tangible record of the comedians' activities has recently come to light in the form of certain programmes covering the years 1748 to 1754—particularly valuable in that they give information about several plays unrecorded elsewhere, and in that one of them in 1754 mentions the names of the actors, which included the great Pantalone of his time and the friend of Goldoni, Cesare D'Arbes.

Without doubt in these three lands, Germany, Poland and Russia, the Italian comedy was a force leading towards the development of native theatres and without doubt its characters were long remembered. We have only to look at the Dresden and Meissen ware with the exquisite figures executed by J. J. Kändler and others to recognise the imprint of the companies which performed at the Saxon–Polish courts. Elsewhere, as at the castle of Krumlov in Czechoslovakia, wall frescoes richly tell of the joy once taken in these shows. Nevertheless, it cannot be said that the commedia dell'arte took root in these lands. We may trace, if we will, an Italian influence leading through the work of men such as Gottfried Prehauser and Josef von Kurz on to the fantastic creations of Ferdinand Raimund; but such influence is tenuous. The strongest appeal made in the eastern countries seems to have been mainly in the direction of farce and buffoonery. When, for example, the 'Königliche Pohlnische und Khurfürstliche Sächsische Hoff-Comoedianten' presented a Julius Caesar play at Prague in 1718, they announced it as *Der mit 23 Wunden auf dem Capitolio zu Rom ermordete Julius Caesar, Erster Römischer Kayser; oder, Arlequin Der lustige Neapolitaner.** Such was the taste of the time.

The taste of the time was no better in England, where also for a short period the Italian comedy appeared to be extending its scope. During the Restoration period Fiorilli twice visited London, and in 1678 a Modena troupe gave a few performances before Charles II. That this last visit was not exactly a success is indicated by some complaints from the players; the Dottore in particular (G. A. Lolli) counted the days until he could escape from the vicinity of 'the miserable Thames'. During the early

117   ITALIAN CHARACTERS IN EASTERN EUROPE

118 HARLEQUIN IN POLAND   119 HARLEQUIN IN EASTERN EUROPE

part of the century following, however, French companies from the fairs arrived to give several seasons between 1720 and 1726 at the Haymarket and Lincoln's Inn Fields, while in 1726 a group of Italians presented a series of subscription performances for the public. From the titles of their offerings as announced in the newspapers their repertory seems to have consisted of a diversity of pieces among which old scenarios mingled with comedies from the Gherardi collection and with plays of the kind popular at the Parisian fairs.

The Italian actors and their French colleagues certainly helped to stimulate a new development, unfortunately not a very worthy one, in the English playhouse, but that development itself had been inaugurated several years previously. It would seem that in the first decade of the century several pairs or trios of performers started to arrive in London from overseas; their services were engaged at the theatres for entr'acte entertainments, and the nature of their turns can readily be guessed from the way in which they were announced: 'a Night Scene by a Harlequin and a Scaramouch, after the Italian manner' or 'a Mimic Night Scene after the Italian manner by a New Scaramouch and Harlequin'.

This soon led to imitation. Apparently John Weaver, Drury Lane's dancing-master, was earliest in the field, and the 'Italian model' was confessedly used by him in the first of English pantomimes. If originator of the new style, however, he soon found a rival whose fame shadowed his. John Rich, or Lun, eagerly turned to exploit

199

120 ITALIAN CHARACTERS AT A BALL

121 JOHN RICH AS HARLEQUIN   122 DAVID GARRICK AS HARLEQUIN

the pantomimic form and himself took the part of Harlequin. Before the visit of the French actors the pantomime had been made familiar to English audiences and by the time the Italians arrived in 1726 it had become one of the most popular of entertainments. Thus, in effect, what these Italians accomplished was merely an intensification of a theatrical form already well established, since for eighteenth-century audiences as for Elizabethan what they had to say meant nothing and only their 'tumbling' remained in men's minds.

Thus was set upon the English stage the ubiquitous pantomime. Although bitterly attacked by dramatists and critics, although made the subject of scores of satirical prints, it continued steadily to grow in popularity. During its lengthy career, to a period within living memory it kept the 'Harlequinade' as an integral part of its being; but the 'Harlequinade' stands far apart from the commedia dell'arte, and it was not long before the original Italian characters were vulgarised and transformed into the knockabout Pantaloon and Clown.

GOLDONI AND GOZZI

In spite, then, of an increased and lively interest in Italian actors, the various European theatres outside of Italy itself allowed, or forced, the commedia dell'arte to disappear or to lose its characteristic quality. England reduced it to pantomime, while France, although it held more closely to some important elements, brought it down to the levels of vaudeville and eventually crushed it out of existence.

Naturally, within Italy the story assumes a different form, even if the sequel is similar. While, as we have seen, various influences inimical to the basic nature of the original commedia dell'arte operated to twist and turn the comedies in a false direction, and while many companies of actors wandered from town to town offering performances of a debased kind, the tradition set by the Gelosi was still maintained by several of the more important troupes and, indeed, the accounts given of some individual performances suggest that all through the eighteenth century there were comedians fully able to vie with the most lauded actors of the past. That many troupes in Italian cities presented shows as wretched as those described by Garzoni is certain, and the enemies of the commedia dell'arte did not refrain from attacking the companies of players who purveyed such fare. Reading these records, one might well believe that nothing of value remained. On the other hand, against the references to actors 'insipid, ridiculous, downright bad' can be set the information which we have concerning the troupe led by Girolamo Medebach—a troupe which included a rich assemblage of brilliant comedians and with which Carlo Goldoni was so closely associated. When we read that Antonio Collalto, almost the last of the true Pantalones, could make 'the expression of grief, anger and joy pierce through his hideous mask' we realise that the old skill had by no means gone.* By

123 HARLEQUIN DR FAUSTUS

Behold how Arlequino disdaining Peers.
And tauntingly Snuffs up the Authors Cares.
His offerd wellmeant Piece thereby dascries.
Putting Him Off with Jeers, vFleers & Lies!
Jno: Cecilebus Fœtius

Next mark the Motley'd Buskin Sock
Bestowing on him an Arbitrary Mock.
Then View the Rubbish near em laid,
Then See the thriving Griping Sons of Trade.

him and by others the ancient technique of the improvised comedy was being carried on with distinction.

With the advent of Carlo Goldoni, however, came a change—not an alteration, as in France, due to the need of adjusting performances to alien public tastes, not a modification which came in gradual stages without any individual force directing it, but rather a deliberate metamorphosis dependent upon the firm ideas of one man. Towards the commedia dell'arte Goldoni's attitude was ambivalent. During his long career he composed many scenarios, and even at the close of his life he was prepared to write several of these for the Italian comedians in Paris. He admired and loved the vitality of the actors and towards them he was drawn, too, by patriotic affection. He was ready to meet their demands, and among his works are numerous musical pieces, mainly comic operas but also fantastic spectacular shows of a kind in which the players liked to indulge. On the other hand, his true devotion was to comedy, and his concept of the comic form led him ultimately to destroy the very fabric of the commedia dell'arte.

In his *Mémoires* Goldoni speaks frequently of the 'reform' in dramatic style which he slowly planned and which by stages he succeeded in establishing. This 'reform' involved deviations from the commedia dell'arte both in content and in form, the one inextricably bound up with the other, although an understanding of his aims demands separate consideration of these two elements. Basically, Goldoni was concerned with bringing character, social criticism and moral purpose to the stage, and for the achievement of this objective he required a realistic framework. By character, he meant individual, specialised character distinct from the wider, generalised character familiar in the commedia dell'arte; by social criticism, he meant the presentation of scenes of ordinary life such as were being cultivated by sentimental dramatists in France and England; and by moral purpose, he meant the exhibition of plots which should not merely please but should also instruct the audience.

Realism, the creation of a play-world which would give the spectators the illusion of seeing actuality presented before them, was clearly the prime requisite for the achievement of these ends. The stage picture and ordinary life were drawn together. 'The two books', he says, 'on which I pondered most, and of which I shall never repent having put to my use, were the World and the Theatre. The first offers to my view more and ever more human characters, paints them for me so naturally that they seem to be put there to provide me with endless themes for pleasing and instructive plays; it represents for me the outward signs, the power, the effects of all the human passions; it gives me strange episodes; it informs me about current habits; it instructs me concerning the vices and errors most common in our age and country —vices which deserve the disapproval or derision of wise men; and at the same time it points out for me in virtuous persons the means by which Virtue resists such corruptions. And from this book I make my collections, constantly turning over its pages and meditating upon them in whatever circumstances or actions I am involved, selecting whatsoever must certainly be known by anyone who wishes to make some success in this profession of mine. The second book, the book of the Theatre, as I practise it, tells me how I must present on the stage the characters, the passions, the events which I have read about in the book of the World—how to shade their tones so as to give them greater relief, how to choose those tints which may render them pleasing to the tender eyes of the spectators. Above all, I learn from the Theatre to

125 HARLEQUIN ATTACKED

distinguish what is more apt to make an impression on the sentiments, to arouse wonder or laughter or some such pleasing delight in the human heart, a delight which arises chiefly from discovering in the play errors and follies naturalistically depicted and put elegantly before the audience.'*

206

126   HARLEQUIN AS A REJECTED LOVER

For this reason he demanded a complete transformation of stage practice, a fundamentally different relationship between audience and actors. In the thesis-play *Il teatro comico* (1750) a young author-actor comes in reciting a soliloquy and Goldoni's spokesman Orazio enquires to whom he is speaking. 'Well,' says the actor,

'I'm talking to the public', and Orazio counsels him: 'Don't you see that you simply mustn't talk to the public? The actor must imagine, when he is alone, that no one hears or sees him. This speaking to the audience is an intolerable vice and must on no account be permitted.' The young author remarks that almost all the improvising comedians indulge in such procedure. 'They do ill, very ill,' replies Orazio, 'and they ought to be stopped.' They ought to be stopped, in Goldoni's opinion, from using unrealistic methods of this kind; but he went further and virtually demanded the stopping of improvisation entirely. In this same thesis-play he introduces satirically a foolish piece of improvised dialogue spoken by Brighella. 'You see?' comments Orazio, 'That's the reason why we must try to bind the actors to written parts; otherwise they easily fall back on antiquated and unrealistic dialogue.'

Still further, the use of masks, fundamental to the commedia dell'arte, he regarded as completely alien to the new endeavour, both because masks did not permit the audience to watch the play of emotions upon the actors' faces and because they emphasised general qualities instead of particular. Attempts are sometimes made to argue that Goldoni's reform was moralistic and not technical—that he did not object to improvisation as such, but merely to incompetent players, that he did not really propose to banish the masks entirely; but such a view runs manifestly counter to the evidence.* The change in content could not be effected without a change in form. Categorically he declares that in his view 'comedies without masks are always more natural and pithy'. 'The mask', he says, 'must always inhibit the actor in expressing both joy and grief. Whether the character is making love, irate or jesting he always has the same piece of leather on his face, and however much he gesticulates and varies the tones of his voice, he can never show, by means of those facial expressions which are the heart's interpreters, the diverse passions agitating his soul.' Masks admittedly were employed by the Greeks, but this was because the theatres of that time were enormous, and in any case 'the emotions and sentiments had not then been brought to such delicacy as is demanded today; we now want the actor to have a soul, and a soul under a mask is like fire under ashes. That is why I conceived the idea of reforming the masks of the Italian comedy and of substituting comedies for farces.' It will be observed that here the word 'reform' has the significance of 'destroy'. And so, when he started to write for Cesare D'Arbes, the Pantalone of Medebach's company, he deliberately set out to persuade this actor to appear 'à visage découvert'; that, he declares, 'was my project, that was my chief aim'.

At the start—and even later in his career—he encountered difficulties. When he put his ideas before the actors, 'some encouraged me to go on with my plan, others wanted me merely to write farces; the first consisted of the Lovers who wanted written dialogue, the second were the comic players, who, accustomed not to memorise any lines, were anxious to shine without going to the trouble of studying.'*

His first approaches towards securing the fulfilment of his aims were, therefore, tentative. By force of argument, he managed to persuade the actor playing Pantalone to abandon his mask and try a 'comedy of character' and, accordingly, in 1738 he wrote his first essay in the new style, *Momolo cortesan*, a piece which consisted mainly of a scenario with written lines only for the principal role. From this play he moved on to others until in *Il mercante fallito* (1741), 'there were many more scenes written out than in the two preceding plays, so that slowly, step by step, I came nearer to my goal of composing all my lines; and I had not long to wait before reaching that objective despite the comic masks who stood in my way'. Gradually the actors, realising the quality of his genius, took the bait, and each one, anxious to have a play specially written for him by this master, was prepared to accept his conditions. In the *Mémoires* there appears a brilliant scene which describes how, at Pisa, Goldoni received a visit from a tall man, broadly and stoutly built, who walked across his room with a malacca cane in his hand and a round English-style hat on his head. Goldoni rose from his chair, and his visitor made a sweeping gesture to indicate that he should not incommode himself. The author sat again and the tall man approached him. 'Sir,' he said, 'I have not the honour of your acquaintance, but you must know my father and uncle in Venice. I am your very humble servant, D'Arbes.'* As in a play, Goldoni then gives their conversation:

GOLDONI. What? Signor D'Arbes? The son of the master of posts at Friuli—that son who was thought lost, who was sought for so anxiously, and whose absence was so bitterly lamented?

D'ARBES. Yes, sir, that prodigal son who has not yet prostrated himself at his father's knees.

GOLDONI. But why do you delay giving him that consolation?

D'ARBES. My family, my relatives, my country will not see me again until my brows are gloriously crowned in laurel.

GOLDONI. What then is your position, sir?

At this question D'Arbes rises from his chair, pats his goodly stomach and, in a tone of mingled pride and buffoonery, says:

D'ARBES. Sir, I am an actor.

GOLDONI. All talents are worthy if he who possesses them knows how to use them.

D'ARBES. I am the Pantalone of the company at present in Livorno. I cannot call myself the least important of my companions, and the public does not disdain to crowd into the performances in which I play a part. Medebach, our director, has given me hundreds of opportunities; I am no dishonour to my parents, to my country, to my profession, and, without boasting, sir (*with another pat on the stomach*), if Garelli is dead, D'Arbes has taken his place.

At this moment, just as I am about to offer him my congratulations, he strikes such a comic attitude that I laugh and cannot get the words out.

D'ARBES. Do not think, sir, that it is in self-glorification that I have vaunted the high position I enjoy in my profession. I am an actor; I introduce myself to an author; and I have need of him.

GOLDONI. You have need of me?

D'ARBES. Yes, sir. Indeed, I have come here for the one purpose of asking you to write a play for me; I have promised my companions a comedy by Goldoni, and I wish to keep my word.

GOLDONI (*smiling*). You want to keep your word, then?

D'ARBES. Yes, sir, I know your reputation. I know you are as polite as you are accomplished. You will not say me nay.

GOLDONI. I am very busy. I cannot do it.

D'ARBES. I respect your business. You will write this play when you wish, at your convenience.

The result was *Tonin Bella Grazia* (1745), which led, through the first version of *Il servitore di due padroni* (1746), written for Sacchi, the Harlequin, on to *La vedova scaltra* (1748) and the later glories of the Goldoni canon. The author had won his battle: improvisation gave way to written dialogue; the masks were reduced in importance; and in some of the comedies even the very name of the commedia dell'arte characters vanished. Realism and social purpose had triumphed.

Once he had established his position, opposition from within the theatre was considerably less than opposition from without. There were still men, in the midst of the sentimental, moralising society for which Goldoni catered, who saw the follies and sensed the consequences of the new realism, and in Venice Count Carlo Gozzi stood out as their leader. At first glance, in looking at the bitter warfare in which Goldoni and Gozzi were the protagonists, it may seem as though the latter were a noble and disinterested champion who buckled on armour with the virtuous desire to defend the distressed commedia dell'arte. Such a view, however, must be recognised, when we look carefully at the facts, to lie far from the truth. Gozzi defended the commedia dell'arte, it is true, but he defended it, not because he appreciated its virtues and wished to preserve them, but only because his central purpose of attacking Goldoni was served by his so doing.

For the core of Gozzi's theatrical philosophy we must get down to the core of Goldoni's; the latter sought to establish a realistic, educative drama; to the former such a drama was anathema and to fight it he turned to satire and ridicule. Regarding the esteem in which the popular Goldoni was held as 'a fungus of human opinion', he gathered together a group of like-minded friends and loosely formed them into an academy called the Granelleschi, at the meetings of which verses and pamphlets

MADᴸᴱ COLUMBINE   MADᴸᴱ ARLEQUINE.   MADᴸᴱ LUCINDE, fille de GERONTE.   IL DOTTORE SCATALON BOLOGNESE.   IL CAPITANEO SPAVENTO NAPOLITANO.   IL ARLEQUIN   MONSᴿ OCTAVIO.

LA DONNA IULIA   LA CORINNE   LE SCARAMOUCHE   LE SIEUR PANTALON

Non oculos modo, sed loculos quoq; Comicus arte
Haud raro petulans vexat et evacuat.

Scaramuz und Arlequin kan manches thug ergözen.
Dabey Sie auch dasz Herz und Beutel offt verlesen.

Cum Pr.Sac.Cæs.Maj.   Mart. Engelbrecht excud. A.V.

LUCINDE.   DONNA PETRONELLA.   DONNA MARTINA.   LALAGE.   SIEUR ANSELMO.   SIEUR GERONTE   BRIGELLA.

LE SCAPINE.   DONNA ANGELICA   LISETTE   LE MESETIN.   LE ARLEQUIN BERGAMASEO.   LE FAMEUX CRISPIN.

Turba levis lepidos risus spectanda theatris
Excitat; ast caveat, seria quisquis amat.

Dem eiblen Hauss macht offt ihr Geberd u Spiel viel Lachen.
Wer aber ernsthafft ist, der meydet ihre Sachen.

Cum Pr.Sac.Cæs.Maj.   Mart. Engelbrecht excud. A.V.

were composed for the purpose of showing up Goldoni's follies and errors.* These finally resulted in a lengthy skit. Gozzi imagines that, as his companions are at an inn during carnival time, looking down at the crowds in the piazza, they see a monster, shaped like a man, but with four faces. They ask this monster to meet them, and boldly Gozzi challenges it. He shows that, in fact, it is the spirit of Goldoni's 'reform' and he proceeds to ridicule that author's styles of writing. The first face represents those scenarios to which Goldoni added some written parts; the second symbolises sentimental comedies such as *Pamela*; the third indicates the Venetian-set plays of gondoliers and common folk; the fourth reveals his semi-tragic oriental pieces. Despite this variety, Gozzi asserts, Goldoni puts himself forward as the proponent of plebeian realistic comedy imbued with a shallow morality. In the end, the monster confesses itself vanquished.

This is all very well, but, in so far as the commedia dell'arte is concerned, Gozzi's approach becomes clearly defined in a comment which he introduces into his ironically styled *Memorie inutili*. Goldoni's aim, he states, 'was to strangle the inno- cent improvised comedy which had been interpreted by several excellent players deservedly adored by the public—Sacchi, Fiorilli, Zannoni and D'Arbes—who diverted both the cultured and the uncultured and who spoilt the trade of poetic respectability'. As a consequence it occurs to him that 'nothing could better castigate' Goldoni's 'literary arrogance than the taking under my protection the sallies, the jests, the comic episodes of the improvised farces of our Truffaldinos, Tartaglias, Brighellas, Pantalones and Smeraldinas'. Thus, admittedly the object of the defence and protection was simply to use the commedia dell'arte for the purpose of castigating Goldoni's arrogance. Even more clearly is this object revealed when Gozzi turns to deal with the inception of the famous *Love of the Three Oranges*. Goldoni's supporters had pointed to their hero's success with the public, and Gozzi wrote his piece as a deliberately ironic exercise: 'Since Goldoni always obstinately referred to his crowded houses as a proof of the value of his theatrical compositions, one day I impenitently expressed the opinion that crowded houses did not demon- strate that the shows were good and that I could guarantee to draw still larger crowds than he did with his rubbish by working into dramatic form the fairy-tale of *The Love of the Three Oranges* which grannies narrate to their grandchildren.' The play was an enormous success, and consequently Gozzi publicly claimed that 'art in composition, careful building-up of episodes, skilful rhetoric and harmony of diction can give to a puerile impossible plot, if it be treated seriously, the illusion of truth.' His aim, then, in entering into this field was to demonstrate the absurdity of the 'realistic' endeavour and to refute Goldoni's arguments, not to cultivate the commedia dell'arte for its own sake. Thus came the series of fantastic pieces from *Il corvo* in 1761, through *Il re cervo* and *Turandot* (1762), on to *I pitocchi fortunati* in 1763 and *L'augellino Belverde* in 1765. Four things are to be observed concerning these dramas. First, Gozzi no less than Goldoni substituted written dialogue for improvised speech, and no less took pride in his literary talent. Second, he specifically rejected the accusation that the success of his plays depended largely upon the skill of the actors in interpreting the comic masks: 'everybody', he says, 'knows that the Italian masks to which I chose to give my support, both for show and for the legitimate recreation of the spectators who rightly took delight in them, do not appear in all my plays—only in a few, and even there they have only a minor part'. Thirdly, several of these plays introduce an element of literary satire such as was cultivated in the declining Comédie Italienne but was at odds with the original spirit of the commedia dell'arte; thus *L'amore delle tre melarance* forms, in effect, an attack on the 'new' drama, with the Mago Celio representing Goldoni, Fata Morgana ridiculing Chiari, Tartaglia depicting the Venetian public and Truffaldino standing for the commedia dell'arte itself. And finally, we must observe that the style of the plays which Gozzi produced was founded, not on the work of the early Italian companies, but upon that of the Gallicised Théâtre Italien and even upon that of the still more debased troupes located at the Parisian fairs. Despite their charm, therefore, Gozzi's *fiabe* cannot seriously be taken to be works designed to rehabilitate the commedia dell'arte, nor did they have any effect of this kind. Their ridicule gave them immediate popularity and eventually drove Goldoni from Venice; their delicacy and charm have kept some of them, in varying forms, alive in the theatre: but they mark in themselves a dead end. Perhaps we may decide that Gozzi was as responsible as Goldoni was for finally destroying the commedia dell'arte in Italy; and it is even possible to find agreement with those who claim to see more of its spirit preserved in the latter's comedies than can be found in the fantastic fables written by the former.

THE CULT OF PHILOSOPHY AND REALISM

Whatever our attitude may be to Gozzi and Goldoni, however, the fact remains that between them they indicate the end in Italy of a long and a great tradition. In England, the Italian comedy had lost itself in silent pantomimic entertainments; in France the Italian strength was made delicate and the spoken word was transformed into song. Yet neither of these two developments was so inimical to this comedy's spirit as what happened within Italy itself. The inner power of the comedy of skill came from improvisation, and now in place of the improvising actors was set the composing author. Actually, this represented merely the culmination of a lengthy movement. Even at the time when the Gelosi were celebrating their triumphs a playwright, Cristofero Castelletti, could come forward with a prologue expressing views closely akin to those of Goldoni a century and a half later, deploring the fact that written comedy, serious in intent, moral and profitable, was so little esteemed, while the public flocked to listen to the 'improvised and foolish prattling of an old man and his Bergamask servant'.* About a century after this Luigi Riccoboni was trying his best to shift the actors away from improvisation and to encourage the audiences to patronise performances of literary tragedy and comedy: indeed, his statue in Modena is inscribed with the words: 'Luigi Riccoboni introduced the Italian theatre to the age of Maffei and Goldoni'. Goldoni's reform, therefore, was not his own invention; it was the final and successful application of a dramatic philosophy long dreamed of.

The phrase 'dramatic philosophy' is by no means unwarranted, for the new style of realistic and educative comedy which Goldoni cultivated, however much it was adumbrated during earlier years, was built upon the concepts of the age of reason, as these became applied to theatrical representation. Over the whole of Europe spread the idea of a realistic theatre, founded on rationalism and sensibility, intimately intent upon social values, anxious, through comic reproof and the exercise of pathos, to play a moral and improving part within the community. The sentimental comedy and bourgeois tragedy in England, the sweep of the *'drame'* in France, Goldoni's reform in Italy, all were parts of one general irresistible movement.

It was a serious, a 'philosophic', movement; and quite clearly it looked with disdain and even disgust on any theatrical performances which did not have an educational value. No one could dream of saying that the commedia dell'arte was educational in this sense, and consequently it became the mission of this movement, not to infuse a new spirit into the old scenarios, but to banish them completely. When Goldoni took Samuel Richardson's *Pamela* and made it into a play, *Pamela fanciulla* (1750) he introduced a scene in which several gentlemen discuss the stage. The setting is, of course, London; Lord Bonfil, Lord Coubrech and Lord Artur are seated with 'Il Cavaliere Ernold', who has recently returned from the Grand Tour and through whom the author, by means of ironic commendations of puerile shows such as only the poorer Italian companies displayed, endeavours to win the public away from the improvised comedy. After making Ernold go into ecstasies over French gallantries, he causes him to turn to the theatre:

ERNOLD. English plays are critical, instructive, full of good characters and witty sallies, but they don't make you laugh. In Italy the public can enjoy bright and clever comedies. O, if you could have seen that lovely character Harlequin! It's a shame that London audiences will not accept masks on the stage. If we could introduce Harlequin into our comedies, it would be the most delightful thing in the world. He represents a servant stupid and witty at the same time. He has a most ridiculous mask; his costume is made up of many colours; he makes you die of laughter. Believe me, my friends, if you could see him, for all your seriousness you would be forced to laugh. He says the wittiest things. Instead of saying 'padrone' he'll say 'poltrone'. Instead of saying 'dottore' he'll say 'dolore'. For 'cappello' he'll say 'campanello', for 'lettera' he'll say 'lettiera'. He's always talking about eating, he flirts with all the girls. He beats his master terribly.

LORD ARTUR (*rising*). My lord, friends, goodbye. [*He goes out*]

ERNOLD. You're leaving? I've just remembered a magnificent jest; you can't help laughing at it. Harlequin one evening in a comedy wanted to cheat an old man called Pantalone, so he disguised himself as a Moor, then as a moving statue, then as a skeleton; and at the end of his tricks he beat the good old man with his stick.

LORD COUBRECH (*rising*). My friend, pray pardon me. I cannot stay longer. [*He goes out*]

ERNOLD (*to Bonfil*). Just see what it means not to have travelled!

BONFIL. Sir, if such things make you laugh, I do not know what to think of you. Surely you do not want me to believe that in Italy intelligent men, men of spirit, laugh at stupidities of this sort. Laughter is proper to man, but all men do not laugh at the same thing. There is a noble form of laughter which arises from a skilful use of words, from clever conceits, from brilliant witticisms. There is also a debased kind of laughter which comes from scurrilities, from stupidities. Forgive me for speaking to you as frankly as I should to a relative, a friend. You have travelled too soon; you should have prepared yourself for your travels by serious study. History, chronology, art, mathematics, philosophy are the subjects most essential for a traveller. Sir, if you had devoted yourself to study before leaving London, you would not have fixed your attention on the pastimes of Vienna, Parisian gallantries and Italy's Harlequin.*

That performances of the kind described by Ernold were being given is certain; in almost the same words an English journal of 1726, while discussing the Italians who visited London in that year, asserted that 'the great Machine of Wit, in all their Entertainments, is Harlequin's wooden Sword; and whenever the Mirth of the Audience begins to flag, Harlequin is to take Care to raise it again, by exercising the said Weapon upon the Prince, or Lover, or the embroider'd Gentleman of the Play, the drubbing of whom about the Stage never fails of having a good Effect.'* No one can object to those who during the eighteenth century condemned such vulgarities and absurdities; and without doubt the commedia dell'arte, by allowing itself to descend to such depths, was partly responsible for its own fate. But Goldoni's attack was directed at more than the wretched troupes who purveyed the vulgar follies; it was aimed at the improvised comedy as a whole, both good and bad. Goldoni knew and admired Sacchi, and Sacchi's Harlequin assuredly never relied for his effects upon the batonings described by Ernold; yet, in his desire to stamp out the improvised style, the author of *Pamela fanciulla* descends to the familiar device of the satirist, presenting the worse that he may cast ridicule on the whole.

The age of reason and sensibility had no use for the exercise of fantasy, and the actor's business came to be the presentation of the real, as adapted by the dramatist to inculcate a moral lesson. When he visited London in 1727, Goldoni's precursor Riccoboni wrote a verse essay *Dell'arte rappresentativa* in which he averred that 'the chief and necessary aim of the actor is to ensure that he does not depart from truth. . . . The natural ever dispenses to us that clear light called good-sense which has virtue alike at home, in the streets and on the stage.'

This in effect was Harlequin's death-knell. Gozzi might see the absurdities of the various kinds of 'realistic' plays, 'supposedly cultured and true to life, but most often devoid of culture and far from reality, one almost always precisely like the other, which flourished on our stage for three long decades';* but the realistic plays, as we know to our cost, had come to stay.

128   PANTALONE AND THE CAPITANO

216

EPILOGUE

In 1780 the Comédie Italienne was suppressed; nearly a century later, in 1860, appeared a two-volume work by Maurice Sand entitled *Masques et bouffons* giving a sketch of the commedia dell'arte's history. During the interim of eighty years, we may say that the Italian comedy completely vanished. Three tattered remnant relics remained, but none of these preserved more than a faint memory of that from which they sprang. The Harlequinade tradition in the English pantomime was nothing more than a farcical interlude involving comic types far removed from their originals; the Pierrot tradition in France as cultivated by Deburau had virtually no real connection either with the Pierrot of 1700 or the still earlier Pedrolino; the Pulcinella tradition in Naples travelled in a direction almost diametrically opposed to that taken by the Gelosi and their immediate descendants. These traditions, indeed, bore just about the same relation to Scala's scenarios as did the Restoration fair 'drolls'— *The Bouncing Knight*, *The Grave-Makers* and *Bottom the Weaver*—to *Henry IV*, *Hamlet* and *A Midsummer Night's Dream*, the plays from which they were derived.

Still more significant was the fact that virtually all memory of the commedia dell'arte disappeared. A few German romantics occasionally spoke of it with affection; but quite clearly what Tieck, Brentano and Grillparzer were thinking of was not the pristine Italian comedy but the fantastic works produced at the end of its career by Carlo Gozzi. Schiller translated *Turandot* and for it Karl von Weber composed some music; *L'amore delle tre melarance* was praised. It was felt that, in an age of reason and science, Gozzi stood out as a man championing the power of the imagination, and for this he was esteemed; but beyond the work of Gozzi little attention was paid by the romantic enthusiasts to the rest of the commedia dell'arte tradition. All the achievements of the actors from Giulio Pasquati to Antonio Collalto, from Tristano Martinelli to Carlin Bertinazzi were as though they never had been.

Maurice Sand's study of 1860 is not very important in itself, but it certainly has significance as a symbol. Romantically conceived and introducing many demonstrably false suppositions, it yet marked the beginning of a new movement in the commedia dell'arte's history—an attempt to survey the development of this theatre and to assess its value. Although Sand's pioneering effort was not immediately followed up, it led in the eighties of the century to a concentrated endeavour aimed at gathering information about the now-vanished stage and at providing a sound basis for an understanding both of its progress and of its essential spirit. From this period of the eighties, revived interest in the comedy of skill has never declined; indeed, we may well decide that as decade followed decade it has increased and deepened, and that, surveying the period from 1880 to 1960 we can watch its progress gathering strength in three major movements, from 1880 to 1914, from 1920 on to the thirties and, finally, from about 1950 to the present.

The first period was marked principally by the work of scholars. In 1880 appeared the earliest printing of some scenarios from manuscript, and this initial effort was followed by many others, so that, whereas Maurice Sand had been aware only of Scala's plays and of those presented at the Théâtre Italien, by 1914 numerous collections had been unearthed in various libraries and carefully described—producing a total of some seven hundred scenarios in all. The fortunes of the Italian players abroad began to be carefully documented; letters written by the comedians were gathered and, from these and from other documentary sources, their lives and professional careers were outlined; attempts were made to relate the growth of the improvised style to the general development of Italian Renaissance drama. Somewhat strangely, yet in itself a sign of the far-flung interest in the theme, this period closes with the appearance in 1914 at Petrograd of the first effort, and perhaps still one of the most important of many succeeding efforts, to delineate the form and capture the true spirit of the commedia dell'arte.

Konstantin Miklashevski's Russian study, written in 1914 but delayed in publication until 1917, has a double value, for itself and for what it reflects. While scholarly in its approach, it sprang from the theatre—and this means that at the very close of this period of research and exploration in libraries, the Italian comedy was beginning once more to attract those concerned with the stage, and particularly those who were intent upon establishing something fresh and vital. Gordon Craig, who stood as a symbol of the new spirit, enthusiastically turned to the comedy of skill; Jacques Copeau, who founded the Théâtre du Vieux Colombier in 1913, was equally a disciple of the commedia; and in Russia, the immediate source of Miklashevski's inspiration was to be found in the experiments which led on the one hand to Blok's *Balaganchik* (1906), with its Pierrot and Harlequin, and to Vsevolod Meyerhold's early experiments in the commedia dell'arte style.

Theatrical interest continued into the second period, that of the twenties and thirties. When Copeau went off with his young actors to Bourgogne, improvisation and gymnastics formed the basis of his instructional method, and the famous Compagnie

218

des Quinze originated from such performances (in which Michel Saint-Denis was actively engaged) as *La danse de la ville et des champs* (1928). Later, Léon Chancerel, both by his writings and by his practical experiments with the Comédiens Routiers and the Théâtre de l'Oncle Sébastien, carried on the tradition based on 'collective creation, fixed characters, wide scope left for actors' inventions, study of and practice in the traditional pieces of business, contact with the public, simplification of scenery, anti-naturalism, union of burlesque and poetry, use of the half-mask for some characters'. The time has arrived when the mask, so much disliked by Goldoni, comes into its own again, and Copeau can declare that 'the actor under the mask exceeds in power the performer whose face is seen by the audience. The mask lives. It has its own style and its sublime speech.'*

Nor was this development confined to France. During the early revolutionary period in Russia, the efforts made before 1914 were intensified, and almost all the noted producers of that time—Meyerhold, Komissarjevsky, Tairov, Radlov, Vakhtangov—acknowledged their indebtedness to the commedia dell'arte style. In 1922 Vakhtangov produced a magnificent *Turandot* in which the actors appeared in ordinary dress and, with the aid of a few wisps of brightly coloured cloth, transformed themselves in imagination into the oriental figures of Gozzi's fantasy; authors such as Evreinov found in this world an inspiration and an encouragement; musicians like Prokofiev, who composed music for Gozzi's *Love of the Three Oranges*, were drawn also into this sphere, and the ballet embraced the old Italian characters; on the evening of 14 January 1901 six opera houses presented simultaneously Mascagni's *Le maschere* in which the commedia characters dominated the stage; fifteen years later Hugo von Hofmannsthal and Richard Strauss collaborated in *Ariadne auf Naxos*, bringing Harlequin and four of his companions into association with the realm of Greek myth. Everywhere the movement spread, and we have only to glance at Paul Ernst's *Pantalon und seine Söhne* (1916) or consider the career of Max Reinhardt to recognise that this was, indeed, an international movement.

While all this was proceeding within the world of the theatre, the trickle of books on the commedia dell'arte grew into a steady stream. Some were of a journalistic kind and repetitive of errors; some, in their enthusiasm, submerged the commedia dell'arte within the wastes of pantomime and circus; but still numbers aided in the understanding and in the evaluating of the spirit which had thus caught the theatre's attention. A firm foundation was being laid, and it is not too much to say that by this time the work of the Gelosi and other associated troupes was better appreciated than at any period since the beginning of the seventeenth century.

A slight lull came in the forties, but the following decade of the fifties has witnessed a truly remarkable upsurge of interest in the subject. The commedia dell'arte, despite the fact that it can offer us no plays for the reading, is now familiarly and widely known; Harlequin's 'life' has been narrated not once but many times; a vast body of manuscript and un-reprinted material bearing on the fortunes of the Italian actors has been made available. Some producers, particularly in France and Italy, have shown direct inspiration from this source, while authors such as Achard, Romains and Anouilh have clearly found here suggestions for their work. Jacques Fabbri won success and acclaim for his production of Santelli's *La famille Arlequin* in 1955, and above all, Marcello Moretti by his magnificent Arlecchino in *The Servant of Two Masters* presented in the Piccolo Teatro of Milan, has shown us what Sacchi meant to audiences of the eighteenth century.

This production deserves very special mention because in it a living demonstration has been made of the quality inherent in the commedia dell'arte style. To read the 'lazzo of the fly' as described by Riccoboni leaves us unmoved; but when Moretti comes crawling out from under a table all is changed. Hat crushed in hand, he stalks the fly, hits out at it and misses. His subtle movements show it buzzing round his head and then settling at a corner of the stage. Stealthily, Harlequin edges towards it, indicating to the spectators that they should remain absolutely silent and, of course, stimulating their laughter still more. He pretends annoyance and again signals them to be quiet as cautiously he creeps towards the fly. Finally, with a sudden leap he catches it and one can almost see his mask smiling in triumph. Down he sits and swallows his prey. A moment later, the fly is buzzing up and down inside him and he bobs about with its movement until by a sudden punch at his own body it is quelled—and off Harlequin goes on another tack, the incident forgotten.

The close of this episode draws attention to that quality of Harlequin's which goes to the very core of his being—his ability to think of only one thing at a time and consequently to move easily and completely out of one situation into another. Of this, a second scene in *The Servant of Two Masters* may be taken as an illustration. Brighella has been commissioned to prepare a specially delectable dinner. Harlequin enters carrying in his hand a very important letter given him by his master to deliver. He forgets his mission at once on meeting Brighella, and when the latter seeks his advice concerning the dinner, the episode starts in a manner very close to that which has already been quoted from *La thèse des dames*. Each thinks of an idea for the banquet and then immediately afterwards rejects the idea as impractical or unfitting. Then they both squat on the stage while Brighella indicates what in his opinion should be the arrangement of the dishes. Harlequin disagrees, and, by now entirely forgetting both his master's command and the important contents of the missive, tears off several pieces from the letter to serve as symbols of the dishes and the arrangement which he believes is appropriate. Brighella objects and shifts some of the pieces of paper; Harlequin tears off other portions, and the pair start to move them about. Then suddenly in Harlequin's imagination the whole thing is transformed; the little pieces of paper become draughtsmen, and with a quick triumphant movement he picks up one of them and nimbly jumps it over his opponent's

129 MARCELLO MORETTI AS HARLEQUIN

pieces. Thereupon he rises with the air of saying 'The game's over, I've won'. Not for one moment does his mind go to the letter; it comes to his memory only when he is asked for it by his master—and then, in Moretti's playing, we can almost feel the shock that comes to him on realising what he has done.

Harlequin's comic pathos, too, comes to life. He has opened the trunks belonging to his two masters and, once more with only one thought in his mind, he tosses out the contents of each in turn. Then he hears someone coming and hastily starts putting back the various items; but, as he does so, he begins to be in doubt as to which piece of clothing belongs to which trunk. He hesitates, puts a jacket in one and then hurriedly takes it out again. At last he is satisfied; the job has been properly done; and he beams delightedly at one of his masters who enters upon the stage. Then he sees this man take from the trunk which belongs to him a cloak which, from his expression, clearly does not. At that moment, watching anxiously, Harlequin seems literally to contract and a blank despair grips his whole body. He is deflated, and, from being at the height of self-esteem, descends to utter dejection.

All of this, of course, is not commedia dell'arte, since such dialogue as is uttered had been written by Goldoni and memorised by the actors; but the skill exhibited is authentic, and we may again say with confidence that in the production of *The Servant of Two Masters* we are nearer to the plays of Martinelli and Sacchi than any audiences have been for the past century and a half. And the production demonstrates how much of pleasure the comedy of skill has yet in it to bring. Watching the adroitness of the movements and the split-second timing which carry us from episode to episode, we appreciate the joy derived by earlier audiences from seeing the same or similar plays repeated time and again. The content does not matter in comparison with the skill.

This leads to a final observation. The interest shown during the present century in the commedia dell'arte has come almost entirely from those dissatisfied with the realistic, naturalistic, propagandist theatre which is the descendant of those eighteenth-century sentimental dramas concocted by the age of reason. During the years from 1800 to 1900 the theatre tended to be either silly or serious—silly with its melodramas and farces, serious with its plays which sought to depict actuality and set the dramatists up as philosophers with a message. More and more, either trivial entertainment or heavy solemnity took possession of the stage. Against this, the young theatre-men during the earlier years of the present century revolted, and in their revolt they found in the comedy of skill something they could admire, something which might give them inspiration. The commedia dell'arte perhaps can never return in its full form, although there are actors still who, with encouragement and opportunity, could interpret its characters in the ancient style, and although the experiments already made promise we know not what achievement in the future; but at least it forms a prime touchstone by which producers and dramatists and critics may have their philosophies of the theatre tested and judged. Whether Shakespeare actually witnessed any performances given by the Italians we cannot say with certainty, but with assurance we can declare that the inner spirit of his early comedies closely approaches that of Scala's plays; and we can reasonably guess that commedia dell'arte performances would have appealed to him. With equal assurance can we assert that Ibsen, O'Neill and their successors, had they been able to see such performances, would have been as little amused as Queen Victoria.

130　THE TRIUMPH OF HARLEQUIN

BIBLIOGRAPHY

[Since various 'bibliographies' of essays and books written on the commedia dell'arte up to about 1930 are readily available, the references given here are, for the most part, restricted to studies published since that time.]

Fundamentally, our knowledge of the commedia dell'arte comes from four sources: (1) the scenarios, (2) the iconographic material showing characters and scenes, (3) the accounts given by contemporaries concerning methods of performance, and (4) the extant letters of the comedians themselves.

THE SCENARIOS

The various collections of scenarios, many of them brought to light within comparatively recent years, have been described and analysed as a whole by Kathleen M. Lea in *Italian Popular Comedy* (2 vols., Oxford, 1934), by Mario Apollonio in *Storia della commedia dell'arte* (Rome, 1930) and *Storia del teatro italiano* (3 vols., Florence, 1938–46), and by Vito Pandolfi in *La commedia dell'arte* (5 vols., Florence, 1957–60). Many specimens of individual texts are now available: a representative selection was included by Enzo Petraccone in his *La commedia dell'arte* (Naples, 1927); K. M. Lea reproduces several, mainly from the Corsini and Locatelli collections, and others from Scala's volume are presented in Vito Pandolfi's vast collection of documents related to this subject. The more important collections are:

FLAMINIO SCALA, *Il teatro delle favole rappresentative overo la ricreatione comica, boscareccia e tragica* (Venice, 1611). [The only early printed series, 50 texts in all.]

BASILIO LOCATELLI: two manuscript volumes in the Biblioteca Casanatense, Rome (1211, 1212), dated 1618 and 1622. [In all, over 100 texts, the importance of which, although considerable, is diminished by the fact that Locatelli's approach is rather that of the academic amateur than of the professional.]

CORSINI: two manuscript volumes in the Biblioteca Corsiniana, Rome (45 G. 5 and 6). [One hundred texts, most of them very short with only brief indications of the action, and many representing shortened versions of Locatelli texts; distinguished by the fact that each play is illustrated by a drawing.]

CORRER: manuscript volume in the Museo Correr, Venice (1040). [A collection probably made for the Teatro S. Cassiano, and, if so, earlier than 1630: 51 texts in all.]

BARTOLI: manuscript collection in the Biblioteca Nazionale, Florence (Cod. Magliabechiana, II. i. 190 and 80; printed by A. Bartoli in *Scenari inediti della commedia dell'arte*, Florence, 1880). [22 texts and one in the introduction.]

CASANATENSE: manuscript collection in the Biblioteca Casanatense, Rome (4186). [48 texts, mostly of mid-seventeenth-century style; apart from references in Lea and in *Masks, Mimes and Miracles* (1931) to plays printed from this collection, note may be made of several included by A. G. Bragaglia in his *Commedia dell'arte* (vol. 1 in the series called *Teatro*, Rome, 1943).]

NAPLES: two manuscript volumes in the Biblioteca Nazionale, Naples (XI. AA, 40 and 41). [183 scenarios in all, copied in 1700 by Antonio Passanti for the Conte di Casamarciano; evidently taken from various sources, but clearly of Neapolitan vintage.]

VATICAN I: manuscript in the Biblioteca Vaticana, Rome (Barb. lat. 10244). [12 texts, all peculiarly lengthy, belonging to the late seventeenth century.]

VATICAN II: manuscript collection in the Biblioteca Vaticana, Rome (Barb. lat. 3895). [12 scenarios, probably of the late seventeenth century.]

MODENA: manuscript plays in the Archivio di Stato and the Biblioteca Estense, Modena. [12 texts, of varying dates; one at least, *La schiava*, is very early.]

ADRIANI: manuscript volume in the Biblioteca Comunale, Perugia (A 20). [22 texts, dated 1734, an amateur collection.]

Several other single plays have been preserved, but are of little importance. Much is known concerning the pieces presented at the Théâtre Italien in Paris. Apart from those Franco–Italian works printed by Evaristo Gherardi in *Le théâtre italien* (Paris, 1694, in one volume; 1700, in six volumes; cited here from the edition of 1741, printed in Amsterdam) and from those in *Le nouveau Théâtre Italien* (8 vols., 1733, 9th vol. 1736; complete edition, Paris, 1753), there are several manuscript collections, of which the most important is that containing a series of notes made by G. D. Biancolelli (Bibliothèque de l'Opéra, Paris; copy in the Bibliothèque Nationale), while numerous pieces are recorded in such works as the *Dictionnaire des théâtres de Paris* (6 vols., Paris, 1756), C. and F. Parfaict, *Histoire de l'ancien Théâtre-Italien* (Paris, 1753) and J. A. J. Desboulmiers, *Histoire anecdotique et raisonnée du Théâtre-Italien* (7 vols., Paris, 1769), and elsewhere. Some forty plays given by the Italian company which acted in Russia between 1733 and 1735 are reproduced by V. N. Perettz in *Итальянскія комедіи* (Petrograd, 1917), while another collection, *Одиннадцать интермедій* XVIII *века* (Petrograd, 1915) gives texts of various eighteenth-century intermezzi; information concerning similar plays acted in Warsaw about the same time appears in Bohdan Korzeniewski's 'Komedia dell'arte w Warszawie' (*Pamiętnik teatralny*, 1954, 29–56).

ICONOGRAPHY

Illustrative material relating to the commedia dell'arte is rich, but no attempt has as yet been made to codify it. Charles Sterling interestingly discusses some 'Early Paintings of the Commedia dell'arte in France' (*Bulletin of the Metropolitan Museum of Art*, n.s. vol. II (1943), pp. 11–32); H. Adhemar has two essays—on 'French Sixteenth-century Genre Paintings' (*Journal of the Warburg and Courtauld Institutes*, vol. VIII (1945), pp. 191–5), and 'Sur quelques tableaux français représentant la Commedia dell'Arte XVI–XVIII siècle' (*Rivista di studi teatrali*, no. 9/10 (1954), pp. 107–13); A. C. Sewter, in 'Queen Elizabeth at Kenilworth' (*Burlington Magazine*, vol. LXXVI (1940), pp. 71–6) reproduces a picture showing a troupe arriving at a palace (this certainly does not depict the Elizabethan court; presumably it shows the Italian actors in France); René Thomas-Coèle, in 'Farceurs français et italiens' (*Revue d'histoire du théâtre*, vol. XII (1960), pp. 127–30) discusses three painted cloths of about 1700 now at the Musée des Arts Décoratifs; Helmut Vriesen, in 'Neue Theaterkupfer der Werkstatt von Martin Engelbrecht' (*Maske und Kothurn*, vol. VI (1960), pp. 276–9), draws attention to some hitherto unrecorded prints of the same period; in 'Notes on a Painting formerly attributed to Watteau' (*Burlington Magazine*, vol. CII (1960) 'advertisement supplement', pp. ii–iii) Marianne Roland Michel assigns an interesting 'Triumph of Harlequin' to Hubert Robert; the *Rivista di studi teatrali* (no. 9/10 (1954), pp. 55–68) includes a study by Valerio Mariani on 'Commedia dell'Arte e arti figurative' (pp. 55–68), concerned chiefly with eighteenth-century artists; and J. H. M'Dowell has a short article on 'Some Pictorial Aspects of Early Commedia dell'arte Acting' (*Studies in Philology*, vol. XXXIX (1942), pp. 47–64). Hundreds of drawings, prints and paintings are reproduced in various volumes: reference may be made particularly to Agne Beijer and P. L. Duchartre, *Recueil de plusieurs fragments des premières comédies italiennes* (Paris, 1928; the 'Recueil Fossard'); P. L. Duchartre, *La comédie italienne* (Paris, 1925; English translation, 1928), and *La commedia dell'arte et ses enfants* (Paris, 1955); *Masks, Mimes and Miracles* (1931); and Fausto Nicolini, *Vita di Arlecchino* (Milan, 1958). Numerous early woodcuts are facsimiled in Vito Pandolfi's volumes. The best account of the Trausnitz frescoes is that by Günter Schöne, 'Die Commedia dell'arte—Bilder auf Burg Trausnitz in Bayern' (*Maske und Kothurn*, vol. V (1959), pp. 74–7, 179–81).

CONTEMPORARY STUDIES

Two collections of texts provide reprints of most of the early source material—those edited by E. Petraccone and by V. Pandolfi. These make available the whole or portions of P. M. Cecchini, *Frutti delle moderne comedie et avisi a chi le recita* (Padua, 1628) and the manuscript *Discorso sopra l'arte comica*; N. Barbieri, *La supplica* (Venice, 1634); F. Andreini, *Le bravure del Capitano Spavento* (Venice, 1607); *Rodomontadas españolas* (Venice, 1627); Andrea Perrucci, *Dell'arte rappresentativa* (Naples, 1699); Luigi Riccoboni, *Histoire du théâtre italien* (Paris, 1728); together with passages from manuscript collections. In Pandolfi's volumes considerable space is devoted to texts of popular verses involving commedia dell'arte characters, to summaries of the so-called 'commedie mimiche' (written plays obviously based on knowledge of improvised performances) and to diverse writings by professional actors.

Although the scores of extant letters penned by comedians during the sixteenth and seventeenth centuries tell us little of their art, they are invaluable both for the picture they give of actors' relationships and for their information concerning the composition and movements of the various troupes. Most of these letters are to be found in Luigi Rasi's splendid *I comici italiani* (2 vols., Florence, 1897–1905) and in Alessandro D'Ancona's *Origini del teatro italiano* (2 vols., Turin, 1891). Summaries of the itineraries of the acting companies and much useful information on individual actors appear in the *Enciclopedia dello spettacolo* (Rome, 1954, in progress), while several volumes give fuller analysis of the players' travels.

GENERAL STUDIES

Of the numerous books on the subject, the best critical studies are those by Constant Mic, *La commedia dell'arte* (Paris, 1927: revised version of his volume in Russian, issued under his full name, Konstantin Miklashevski, *La Commedia dell'arte или театръ итальянскихъ комедіантовъ* XVI, XVII, *и* XVIII *столѣтіи*, Petrograd, 1914–17) and the 'histories' cited above, of Mario Apollonio. Two interesting essays are printed in the *Rivista di studi teatrali* (no. 9/10, 1954)—Mario Apollonio's 'L'improvvisazione nella commedia dell'arte' (pp. 13–28) and Eugenio Levi's 'La favola nel teatro comico e nella commedia dell'arte' (pp. 29–48). Of the general accounts published since 1930 may be mentioned: A. Cervellati, *Storia delle maschere* (Bologna, 1944); A. G. Bragaglia, *Le maschere romane* (Rome, 1947) and *Pulcinella* (Rome, 1953); P. Toschi, *Le origini del teatro italiano* (Turin, 1955); A. K. Djivelegov, *Итальянская народная комедия* (Moscow, 1954; German translation A. K. Dshiwelegow, *Commedia dell'Arte*, Berlin, 1958), a Marxist interpretation following the lines of that by S. Mokulskii in 'Комедия масок' (*Театр и Драматургия*, 1933). Most of these devote considerable space to the discussion of the ultimate origins of the Italian stage characters; the currently fashionable view rejects the supposed Roman sources and attributes the rise of the commedia to (*a*) the development of carnival elements, (*b*) the attempt to make popular the academic comedies of the time or (*c*) the desire to find a means of social satire. In many of these works historical evidence is strained, and Ireneo Sanesi does well, in his 'Note sulla commedia dell'arte' (*Giornale storico della letteratura italiana*, vol. CXI (1958), pp. 5–76), to emphasise the need of sticking to the facts and of carefully questioning a number of commonly repeated statements.

Here may be listed, too, a couple of 'lives' of Harlequin—that by Thelma Niklaus, *Harlequin* (1954), has only slight value, but the study by F. Nicolini, cited above, is important. Gustave Attinger examines 'L'évolution d'un type en France: Arlequin' (*Rivista di studi teatrali*, no. 9/10 (1954), pp. 78–96). Other articles on particular characters are referred to below in the notes. Like Thelma Niklaus' book on Harlequin, Kay Dick's sentimentally conceived *Pierrot* (1960) has hardly any value, and other writings on this character are concerned, not with the commedia dell'arte Pierrot but with the wholly different figure presented by Jean-Gaspard Deburau; on this mime-actor see L. Péricaud, *Le Théâtre des Funambules* (1897) and T. Rémy, *Jean-Gaspard Deburau* (1954).

THE COMMEDIA DELL'ARTE ABROAD

Especially valuable are several recent studies of the Italian actors' activities outside their own country. While some works, such as I. A. Schwartz' *The Commedia dell'arte and its Influence on French Comedy in the Seventeenth Century* (New York, 1933) are of little worth, others, of which G. Attinger's *L'esprit de la commedia dell'arte dans le théâtre français* (Paris, 1950) is chief, have opened up fresh vistas in fact and in critical thought. Raymond Lebègue's 'Les débuts de la Commedia dell'Arte en France' (*Rivista di studi teatrali*, no. 9/10 (1954), pp. 71–7) deals with the earlier period. Xavier de Courville's *Luigi Riccoboni, dit Lélio* (3 vols., Paris, 1943–58) gives a detailed account both of Riccoboni's life and of the theatre in his time. On the same subject Claudio Varese has an essay entitled 'Luigi Riccoboni, un attore tra letteratura e teatro' (*Bolletino* of the Centro di studi moratoriani, Modena, no. 6 (1957), pp. 47–59). Xavier de Courville examines 'La Commedia francisé de Marivaux: un renouveau de la scène française aux feux de la rampe italienne' (*Rivista di studi teatrali*, no. 9/10 (1954), pp. 97–106).

Recent writings on the Italians in Germany include: Heinz Kindermann, *Die Commedia dell'arte und das deutsche Volkstheater* (Leipzig, 1938), the same author's 'La Commedia dell'Arte und das deutsche Theater' (*Rivista di studi theatrali*, no. 9/10 (1954), pp. 143–71) and his *Theatergeschichte Europas* (vol. III (1959), 'Das Theater der Barockzeit'); Herbert Hohenemser, *Pulcinella, Harlekin, Hanswurst* (*Die Schaubühne*, vol.

XXXIII, 1940); and, of minor importance, Artur Kutscher, *Die Comedia dell Arte* [sic] *und Deutschland* (*Die Schaubühne*, vol. XLIII, 1955). R. Alewyn has a study of 'Schauspieler und Steigreifbühne des Barock' (*Mimus und Logos, Festgabe für Carl Niessen* (Emsdettern, 1915), pp. 1–18), and O. Rommel has contributed a valuable paper on 'Die Commedia dell'arte und ihr Verhältnis zur deutschen Wanderbühne zur Alt-Wiener Volkskomödie' (in *Die Alt-Wiener Volkskomödie*, Vienna, 1952). There is a note on early performances in Austria in E. C. Salzer's 'La commedia italiana dell'arte alla corte viennese' (*Rivista italiana del dramma*, vol. II (1938), pp. 184–5).

The second volume of Kathleen M. Lea's history deals with the impact of the Italian actors on the Elizabethan theatre, and she has made a further contribution to this topic in her 'Connections and Contrasts between the Commedia dell'Arte and English Drama' (*Rivista di studi teatrali*, no. 9/10 (1954), pp. 114–26). Sybil Rosenfeld's *Foreign Theatrical Companies in Great Britain* (1955) sums up the information available on this subject and presents some new material. Reference should also be made to A. L. Bader, 'The Modena Troupe in England' (*Modern Language Notes*, vol. L (1935), pp. 367–9); Alfredo Obertello, 'Su una compagnia di comici italiani a Londra nel 1678–79' (*Rivista di studi teatrali*, no. 9/10 (1954), pp. 138–42); I. K. Fletcher, 'Italian Comedians in England in the Seventeenth Century' (*Theatre Notebook*, vol. VIII (1954), pp. 86–91, and *Rivista di studi teatrali*, no. 9/10 (1954), pp. 127–37).

A useful survey of the evidence relating to the Italians in Spain (but clearly not based on exact knowledge of the commedia dell'arte) is N. D. Shergold, 'Ganassa and the "Commedia dell'arte" in Sixteenth-Century Spain' (*Modern Language Review*, vol. LI (1956), pp. 359–68). Reference may also be made to Gerardo Guerrieri, 'Lettera per un saggio su "Commedia dell'Arte e Spagna"' (*Rivista di studi teatrali*, no. 9/10 (1954), pp. 172–5), and E. B. Place's enquiry, 'Does Lope de Vega's *Gracioso* Stem in Part from Harlequin?' (*Hispania*, vol. XVII (1934), pp. 257–70). S. J. Gudlangsson has an interesting study of *De Komedianten tij Jan Steen en Zijn Tijdgenooten* (The Hague, 1945), and Ettore Lo Gatto surveys 'La Commedia dell'Arte in Russia' (*Rivista di studi teatrali*, no. 9/10 (1954), pp. 176–86).

Of special interest because of the fresh information presented are several contributions from Poland: besides the valuable article, cited above, by Bohdan Korzeniewski, these include: Mieczysław Brahmer, 'La commedia dell'arte in Polonia' (*Ricerche slavistiche*, vol. III (1954), pp. 184–95), *Z djiejów wlosko-polskich stosunków kulturalnych* (Warsaw, 1939) and 'Goldoni in Polonia' (*Civiltà Veneziana Studi*, vol. VI (1960), pp. 239–46); Julian Lewánski, 'Faust i Arlekin' (*Pamiętnik teatralny*, vol. VI (1957), pp. 76–120); and Zbigniew Raszewski, 'Porcelanowa Arlekinada' (*Pamiętnik teatralny*, vol. VI (1957), pp. 121–30). The last-mentioned essay adds to and corrects information given by Sacheverell Sitwell in *Theatrical Figures in Porcelain: German Eighteenth Century* (1943). On this subject Günther von Plechmann has a short study, *Franz Anton Bustelli: Die Italienische Komödie in Porzellan* (Berlin, 1947).

GOLDONI AND GOZZI

The literature on Goldoni is vast and most of the critical works deal directly or indirectly with his relationship to the commedia dell'arte. For these, the bibliographies in the *Enciclopedia dello spettacolo* may be consulted. The general tendency in Italy now is to decry the value of the commedia dell'arte in favour of Goldoni—as in Renato Simone's 'I comici dell'Arte' (*Rivista di studi teatrali*, no. 9/10 (1954), pp. 49–52). An important recent work is that by M. Dazzi, *Carlo Goldoni e la sua poetica sociale* (Turin, 1957). The recent success of *Il servitore di due padrone* as presented by the Piccolo Teatro di Milano has occasioned several critical essays on this subject: here may be noted Jaakko Ahokas, 'Commedia dell'arte' (*Parnasso*, Helsinki, no. 7 (1956), pp. 303–8), and Gherardo Marone, 'La comedia del arte y la reforma de Carlos Goldoni' (*Estudios Italianos en la Argentina* (Buenos Aires, 1956), pp. 277–81). The *Mémoires* (3 vols., Paris, 1787) are, of course, fundamental for an understanding of Goldoni's 'reform' and should be read in conjunction with Gozzi's *Memorie inutili* (ed. G. Prezzolini, 2 vols., Bari, 1910).

THE COMMEDIA DELL'ARTE TODAY

Numerous notes have been written on modern experiments in the commedia dell'arte style. Here may be consulted: Léon Chancerel, *Le théâtre et la jeunesse* (Paris, 1941; 4th edition, 1953), and his short essay 'Permanence et réveil de la Commedia dell'Arte en France' (*Rivista di studi teatrali*, no. 9/10 (1954), pp. 189–99); two other articles in the same periodical, Georges Lerminier, 'La Commedia dell'Arte et notre temps' (pp. 200–3) and Elisabeth Brock-Sulzer, 'Die Commedia dell'Arte und ihre Rolle im heutigen Theater' (pp. 204–15); the summary given by G. Attinger, cited above; and P. Blanchart, 'Survivance d'une tradition' (*Théâtre*, 4ème cahier (Paris, 1945), pp. 261–98). This issue of *Théâtre* also has other related contributions by Georges Jamati, Xavier de Courville and Paul Arnold under the general title of 'Une tradition théâtrale: de Scaramouche à Louis Jouvet'. S. Mokulskii, in the article cited above, notes the influence of this kind of comedy on various Russian producers. On the productions of the Piccolo Teatro della Città di Milano, see *Piccolo Teatro* (Milan, 1958).

NOTES

[Since this book aims rather at a critical assessment of the commedia dell'arte than at a factual 'history', references in the notes have been kept to a minimum. For scenarios mentioned by name in the text see the Index. 'Pandolfi' and 'Petraccone' allude to the collections of texts prepared by these editors; Apollonio's two studies are given as *Teatro italiano* and *Commedia dell'arte* respectively.]

PAGE

3 The earliest mention of Arlecchino occurs in a document of 1584, when he is associated with Pedrolino and Burattino; the following year he appears in an *Histoire plaisante des faictes et gestes de Harlequin*. But he does not come before us clearly until the publication of the *Compositions de rhetorique* in 1601 and of Scala's *Teatro* ten years later.

15 Cecchini, *Discorso* (Pandolfi, vol. IV, pp. 88–9); Barbieri, *Supplica* (Petraccone, pp. 26–7).

16 G. J. Casanova de Seingalt, *Confutazione della storia del governo veneto d'Amelot de la Hussaie* (Amsterdam, 1769), vol. III, pp. 285–8. Casanova does not here name Sacchi, but clearly this is the actor referred to.

17 Adriani (Petraccone, pp. 263–72).

18 Cecchini, *Discorso* (Pandolfi, vol. IV, pp. 88–9).

26 The description of the early Bavarian amateur performance is in Massimo Troiano, *Discorsi delli triomfi, giostre, apparati, e delle cose più notabili fatte nelle sontuose nozze, dell'Illustrissimo et Eccellentissimo Signor Duca Guglielmo* (Munich, 1568). For Salvator Rosa's activities see Benedetto Croce, *I teatri di Napoli del rinascimento alla fine del secolo decimottavo* (Naples, 1891; new edition (Bari, 1916), pp. 78, 100). The Warsaw performances are referred to by M. Brahmer in *Ricerche slavistiche*, vol. III (1954), pp. 184–95. On amateur productions in general see A. Valeri, 'Gli scenari di Basilio Locatelli' (*Nuova Rassegna*, vol. III (1894), pp. 525–8).

27 The quotation is from T. Garzoni, *La piazza universale di tutte le professioni del mondo* (Venice, 1589), p. 740.

28 For the letters, here and on p. 29, see Rasi, vol. I, pp. 141, 543, 579–81, 140, 171–6, 33, 202–3, 633. Gozzi's comment appears in his *Memorie inutili*, vol. I, p. 257.

31 Bruni (Pandolfi, vol. IV, pp. 59–60). The Modena letter is given in Rasi, vol. II, p. 694.

31 Evaristo Gherardi, *Le théâtre italien*, vol. I, signatures a2 verso–a3.

31 Desboulmiers, vol. I, p. 42.

32 Evaristo Gherardi, *Le théâtre italien*, vol. I, signature a2 verso.

32 Barbieri, *Discorso* (Pandolfi, vol. III, p. 376).

32 Bruni (Pandolfi, vol. IV, pp. 59–60).

32 N. Boindin, *Lettres historiques sur la Nouvelle Comédie Italienne* (Paris, 1717), vol. I, pp. 14–15.

33 Barbieri, *Discorso* (Pandolfi, vol. III, p. 376).

33 Perrucci (Petraccone, pp. 74–5, 84).

34 Goldoni, vol. I, p. 335.

34 On Vincenza Armani see F. Bartoli, *Notizie istoriche de' comici italiani* (Padua, 1781), vol. I, p. 51.

35 Gozzi, vol. I, p. 255.

36 Perrucci (Petraccone, pp. 107–9).

37 The quotation is from Desboulmiers, vol. I, pp. 33–4. Isabella Andreini, *Fragmenti* (Pandolfi, vol. II, pp. 48–68). Bruni, *Dialoghi scenici* (Pandolfi, vol. II, pp. 37–47).

37 Perrucci (Petraccone, pp. 95–8).

37 The two scenarios are *La vedova costante* (Bartoli, 1) and *La bellissima commedia in tre persone* (Bartoli, 3).

38 Perrucci (Petraccone, p. 178).

38 The quotation is from Desboulmiers, vol. I, pp. 34–5.

39 Barbieri, *Supplica* (Petraccone, pp. 26–7). Perrucci (Petraccone, p. 94).

39 Riccoboni, p. 61. Charles de Brosses, *Lettres d'Italie* (Dijon, 1927), vol. II, p. 258.

40 Riccoboni, pp. 49–50.

41 The modern director is A. G. Bragaglia, *Le maschere romane*, p. 63. The second quotation is from G. Attinger, p. 39.

41 Copeau is quoted from P. L. Duchartre, *Commedia dell'arte*, p. 52.

42 Apollonio, *Teatro italiano*, vol. II, p. 290, calls attention to the mirror effect.

47 The quotation is from Djivelegov, pp. 102, 107.

49 Cecchini, *Frutti* (Pandolfi, vol. IV, p. 100).

50 The scenarios are: *Il pedante* (Scala, 31), *Il fido amico* (Scala, 29) and *Le disgratie di Flavio* (Scala, 35).

51 The scenarios are: *Li tre fidi amici* (Scala, 19) and *Li quattro finti spiritati* (Scala, 33).

52 For the popular rimes see Pandolfi, vol. I, pp. 305–22.

52 See, for example, *Il portalettere* (Scala, 23), *La mancata fede* (Scala, 27), *Cavalier ingrato* (Correr, 17), *Due sorelle rivale* (Correr, 23), *Li duo vecchi gemelli* (Scala, 1), *Li due Venetiani* (Locatelli, II, 6). 'Tofano' appears in *Il furto amoroso* (Venice, 1613) and 'Tofano Beltrami' in *La fida fanciulla* (Bologna, 1629), both by C. Scaliggeri. 'Tofano Venitiano' is head of a household in *Il finto Tofano* (Scala, 24).

53 For Stefanello Bottarga in Spain see N. D. Shergold—who, however, seems to treat the name as that belonging to an actor (and not to a type) and who, following K. M. Lea, confuses the picture by stating that this player took the parts both of Zanni and Pantalone. This statement may be derived from a misinterpretation of some verses by 'Il Lasca' (Antonfrancesco Grazzini) published by Carlo Verzone in his edition of *Le rime burlesche* (Florence, 1882): 'ma or tra più lodati giovani d'oggi è più lodato che contraffà un Zanni e Stefanello'.

55 Leone Adorni appears in *Li finti servi* (Scala, 30); Zanobio in *La finta pazza* (Scala, 8), *Li scambi* (Corsini, I, 7), *Le due schiave* (Corsini, I, 16), *Sardellino invisibile* (Corsini, I, 40), *Le due sorelle schiave* (Locatelli, II, 9) and *Li furti* (Locatelli, II, 32); Piombino in *Il ritratto* (Scala, 39). Francesco Andreini, *Bravure* (Pandolfi, vol. I, p. 375) speaks of Salimbeni as one 'che faceva da Vecchio Fiorentino detto Zanobio, e da Piombino'; quite clearly the two characters, Zanobio and Piombino, are here kept distinct.

55 Ubaldo Lanterni is a father's name in the Bartoli collection; Ponsevere in Vatican I; Prospero in Adriani; Anselmo and Beltrano in Naples.

56 For names given to the Dottore see Rasi, vol. I, p. 407 and K. M. Lea, vol II, pp. 483–5.

56 Cecchini, *Frutti* (Pandolfi, vol. IV, p. 98).

56 The two episodes occur in *La schiava* (Modena), and the 'aphorisms' are in *Le cento e quindici conclusioni del plusquamperfetto Dottor Gratiano Partesana da Francolin* (1587; Pandolfi, vol. II, pp. 11–19).

60 The Dottore is described as rich and of noble family in *Li duo Capitani simili* (Scala, 17), as a physician in *Isabella astrologa* (Scala, 36) and *La pazzia d'Isabella* (Scala, 38) and as a charlatan in *La fortuna di Flavio* (Scala, 2).

60 The various roles assigned to the Dottore may be exemplified by reference to *La gran pazzia di Orlando* (Corsini, I, 1), *Li dui Trappolini* (Corsini, I, 32), *La commedia in commedia* (Corsini, I, 34), *Magior gloria* (Naples, I, 34), *Il cavaliere creduto pazzo* (Vatican, I, 2), *Li dispetti* (Corsini, II, 36), *Elisa Alii Bassa* (Corsini, II, 4), *Non può essere* (Naples, I, 33). For Michelino see *La fida infedeltà* (Correr, 10) and *L'amor costante* (Corsini, II, 11).

60 For Cassandro see *Li duo amanti furiosi* (Correr, 5) and *Li tre fidi amici* (Scala, 19).

61 Jan Potocki, *Recueil de parades représentées sur le théâtre de Łańcut dans l'année 1792* (Warsaw, 1793); annotated and translated into Polish by Julian Lewański (*Dialog*, vol. II (1956), pp. 6–26).

61 For Claudio or Claudione see *Li tappeti alessandrini* (Scala, 26), *La caccia* (Scala, 37) and *Claudione fallito* (Corsini, I, 30).

62 Coviello is a servant in N. Barbieri's *La Clotilde* (Perugia, 1649), an innkeeper in V. Verucci's *Ersilia* (Venice, 1611), a merchant in the same author's *La vendetta amorosa* (Viterbo, 1625), a 'dottore' in his *La Portia* (Venice, 1611). In S. Tomadoni's *Le scioccherie di Gradellino* (Venice, 1689) he is called 'Coviello Spaccamontagna'.

65 For 'Coviello Cetrullo Cetrulli' see Benedetto Croce, *I teatri di Napoli* (Bari, 1916), p. 33. A. G. Bragaglia, 'Coviello ragazzo di vita' (*Sipario*, no. 146 (June 1958), pp. 3–4), treats this character as a Captain and notes his success in the eighteenth century as interpreted by Gennaro Sacchi and Giacomo Raguzzino.

65 Perrucci (Petraccone, p. 130). For Cola associated with Arlecchino see K. M. Lea, vol. I, p. 281. Cola is a merchant in V. Verucci's *La moglie superba* (Viterbo, 1630), a lover in P. Veraldo's *L'anima dell'intrico* (Venice, 1626), a Neapolitan knight in N. Barbieri's *L'oristella*

(Perugia, 1649), a servant in G. B. Salviati's *Il tesoro* (Rome, 1676) and *Truffaldino medico volante* (Rome, 1672). His roles in the scenarios are multifarious.

65 Pasquariello's parts are equally various: he is a lover in *Nuovo finto principe* (Naples, I, 11) and a gardener in *Li ritratti* (Corsini, I, 17). Giambattista del Tufo in 1588 alludes to 'Pascariello Pettola' (B. Croce, *I teatri di Napoli* (Bari, 1916), p. 32); hence his part may be the same as that of Pettola in some Corsini scenarios wherein he appears both as a father and as a servant—*Li tre Turchi* (I, 18), *Li consigli di Pantalone* (I, 36), *Sardellino invisibile* (I, 40), *Il torneo* (I, 42), *Horatio burlato* (I, 44), *Il Proteo* (I, 45), *L'innocente rivenduta* (II, 12), *Il Pantaloncino* (II, 16), *Li finti mariti* (II, 27).

66 A. G. Bragaglia has a short essay on 'La maschera di Tartaglia' (*Sipario*, March 1955, pp. 3–4).

69 Apollonio, *Teatro italiano*, II, 271, notes the 'loose' and 'tight' costumes but runs the 'patched' in with these. His survey does not quite accord with the available facts.

70 Visentini's feat is recorded by Desboulmiers, vol. I, p. 70.

72 The episodes appear in the Biancolelli manuscript.

73 For the reference to a chameleon see the *Calendrier historique des théâtres* (Paris, 1751), quoted in P. L. Duchartre, *La commedia dell'arte*, p. 127. For the Marmontel passage see his *Œuvres complètes* (Paris, 1819), vol. IV, p. 418.

74 K. M. Lea, vol. I, p. 71, alludes, without reference, to Zan Bagattino. In Domenico Balbi's *Il Bagattino disgratiato* (Venice, 1698) both Bagattino and Bagolino appear—the one as 'first' and the other as 'second' zanni.

75 On Callot see A. Glikman, Жак Калло (Leningrad–Moscow, 1959): this reproduces many of the original drawings.

77 See F. Bartoli: *Notizie istoriche de' comici italiani* (Padua, 1781), vol. II, p. 283, A. G. Bragaglia, *Lazzi di Brighella* (Rome, n.d.) and, for the *Motti* (or *Generici*), Pandolfi, vol. IV, p. 304.

77 Parfaict, p. 83.

79 Rasi, vol. I, p. 461.

84 T. Nashe, *The Works*, ed. R. B. McKerrow (1905), vol. III, p. 342.

87 K. M. Lea, vol. I, pp. 88–9, draws attention to the way in which Punch has been identified with Naples, England and France. Similarly, A. G. Bragaglia ('Pulcinella in Europa', *Sipario*, no. 134 (June 1957), pp. 8–9) notes the way this character has been shaped to the needs of different countries.

88 K. M. Lea, vol. I, p. 99, reproduces a seventeenth-century woodcut showing a school of Punches.

89 For Pedrolino see particularly in the Scala collection *La fortunata Isabella* (3), *Il vecchio geloso* (6), *Li duo fidi notari* (20) and *Li quattro finti spiritati* (33).

89 See the woodcut on the title-page of G. C. Croce, *La gran vittoria di Pedrolino* (Bologna, 1621).

96 For the servetta's remark see Perrucci (Petraccone, p. 153).

101 The episode appears in the Biancolelli manuscript. Cecchini, *Frutti* (Pandolfi, vol. IV, pp. 100–1).

101 F. Andreini, *Bravure* (Pandolfi, vol. I, pp. 359–60).

101 Perrucci (Petraccone, p. 134). The scenarios cited are: *Il marito* (Scala, 9), *Il ritratto* (Scala, 39), *Flaminio disperato* (scenario in the Biblioteca Nazionale, Rome).

105 For the verses on the supposed death of Fiorilli, see Rasi, vol. I, p. 896.

107 See A. G. Bragaglia, *Giangurgolo ovvero il calabrese in commedia* (n.d., Ente Provinciale Turismo di Cosenza), and also Perrucci (Petraccone, p. 134).

112 For the parts taken by the Lover see *Li tre fidi amici* (Scala, 19), *La forza dell'amicitia* (Vatican, I, 9), *Cintio giuocatore* (Vatican, I, 6), *L'amante volubile* (Vatican, I, 7), *L'incauto ovvero l'inavvertito* (Bartoli, 7).

115 Niccoletto is in *Li quattro finti spiritati* (Scala, 33).

115 In connection with 'Chocholi' compare Coccalino in *Clarinda perseguitata* (Casanatense, 15) and *Il segno fatale* (Casanatense, 21) and Coco in *Il Gratiano innamorato* (Corsini, II, 41).

116 There is a puzzle about this comment by Martello. Constant Mic quotes it in French with a reference, 'Lettre à Recanati' (pp. 29–31); in his original Russian volume the reference is 'Lettera a G. B. Recanati in *Seguito del Theatro italiano* di Pierjacopo Martello. Bologna 1723' (p. ix). Apparently no such letter is printed in that set of volumes, nor have I been able to track it down in any other volume.

116 J. W. Goethe, *Gedenkausgabe der Werke, Briefe und Gespräche*, ed. Ernst Beutler (Zürich, 1949), *Gespräche mit Goethe*, p. 719.

120 *Gli honesti amori della Regina d'Inghilterra con la morte del Conte di Sessa* (Casanatense, 48). See Winifred Smith, 'The Earl of Essex on the Stage' (*PMLA*, vol. XXXIX (1924), pp. 147–73). The scenario may be derived from a Spanish play.

124 On the 'corago' see Perrucci (Petraccone, pp. 193–6).

125 Desboulmiers, vol. I, p. 41.

137 On night scenes see Perrucci (Petraccone, pp. 183, 196).

139 The scenarios cited are: *La gelosa Isabella* (Scala, 25), *La vedova costante* (Bartoli, 1). The episode referred to occurs in *Li duo fidi notari* (Scala, 20). See also *La finta notte di Colafronio* (Bartoli, 2).

144 For the comment by the Duke of Guise see Perrucci (Petraccone, p. 184).

145 The scene of thievery appears in *La finta notte di Colafronio* (Bartoli, 2).

145 The scene of Pantalone outside his house occurs in *Li tappeti alessandrini* (Scala, 26).

146 The trick of the basket of fruit is in *Le burle d'Isabella* (Scala, 4).

148 The scene of Pantalone, Graziano and Harlequin appears in *Il ritratto* (Scala, 39), that of the attempted murder in *Il padre crudele* (Bartoli, 6). For Pulcinella's folly see the 'lazzo' cited in Petraccone, 264.

148 Ottonelli, vol. I, p. 29.

149 Attinger, p. 51.

150 Perrucci (Petraccone, pp. 182–3).

150 Djivelegov, p. 102, and see also pp. 99, 112, 113.

150 Djivelegov (on Harlequin) p. 128, (on realism) p. 199.

151 Desboulmiers, vol. I, pp. 33–4. The reference to 'vividity and truth' is made by Charles de Brosses, *Lettres d'Italie* (Dijon, 1927), vol. II, p. 258.

152 For other examples of scenarios presenting episodes similar to that in *Il vecchio geloso* see *Li duo amanti furiosi* and *Il mastro di Terentio* in the Correr series (nos. 5 and 31).

152 Saint-Évremond, *Œuvres* (Amsterdam, 1739), vol. III, p. 272.

152 The quotation is from Emilio Del Cerro, *Nel regno delle maschere* (Naples, 1914), p. 279.

152 Apollonio, *Teatro italiano*, vol. II, p. 283. On the question of realism and anti-realism see Attinger, pp. 434–6.

155 On the 'plastique du théâtre' see Attinger, p. 433.

156 On the use of colour see Apollonio, *Teatro italiano*, vol. II, p. 274.

158 For Gabrielli see Pandolfi, vol. IV, pp. 111–17. The musical element is dealt with by Nino Pirrotta, 'Commedia dell'Arte and Opera' (*Musical Quarterly*, vol. XLI (1955), pp. 305–24).

160 For Aaron Hill's remarks see Sybil Rosenfeld's *Foreign Theatrical Companies in Great Britain* (1955), p. 19.

163 The Paduan contract is discussed by Ester Cocco, 'Una compagnia comica nella prima metà del secolo XVI' (*Giornale storico della letteratura italiana*, vol. LXV (1915), pp. 55–70).

166 Isabella Andreini's letters are printed by D'Ancona, vol. II, pp. 490–2.

166 Lord Buckhurst's letter is cited in the *Calendar of State Papers: Foreign Series* (1569–71), p. 413. For the comment regarding the success of the Gelosi in 1577 see A. Baschet, *Les comédiens italiens à la cour de France sous Charles IX, Henri III, Henri IV et Louis XIII* (Paris, 1882), p. 74.

167 Baschet, p. 90; D'Ancona, vol. II, pp. 484–5.

167 The Earl of Lincoln's letter is given in J. Nichols, *The Progresses of Queen Elizabeth* (1823), vol. I, pp. 302–3. The fortunes of Alberto Naseli are usefully summarised by N.D. Shergold in 'Ganassa and the "Commedia dell'arte" in Sixteenth-century Spain' (*Modern Language Review*, vol. LI (1956), pp. 359–68).

168 For Drusiano Martinelli in England see Sir E. K. Chambers, *The Elizabethan Stage* (Oxford, 1923), vol. II, pp. 262–3, and for the other visits see K. M. Lea, vol. II, pp. 352–3.

169 I owe the 'Curtesse' reference to Professor F. P. Wilson, but this had already been cited in the *Enciclopedia dello spettacolo*, vol. III, p. 1215.

171 For the connections between Martinelli and Marie de' Medici see Baschet, pp. 202 ff. The letter from Henri IV is cited pp. 157–8.

172 The letter of 1615 is given by A. Saviotti, 'Feste e spettacoli nel seicento' (*Giornale storico della letteratura italiana*, vol. XLI (1903), pp. 63–4).

172 For the letter from Giovanni de' Medici see Baschet, p. 169; other epistles are cited in his work and in Rasi.

173 For the letter of 1620 see Rasi, vol. III, pp. 517–19.

174 For Borromeo and Ottonelli see Pandolfi, vol. III, pp. 405 and 431.

175 Andreini's 'sonnets' are given by Pandolfi; the 'prayer' appears at vol. III, p. 350.

181 The allusion to Scapino's abandoning of his mask is in *Annales du Théâtre Italien* (Paris, 1788), vol. I, p. 36, cited by Attinger, p. 336.

182 Gherardi, *Le Théâtre Italien*, vol. I, 'Avertissement', signature 2 v verso.

182 The scene quoted appears in vol. V, pp. 422–9.

232

183 *Le Théâtre Italien*, vol. IV, p. 75.

184 J. W. Goethe, *Gedenkausgabe der Werke, Briefe und Gespräche*, ed. Ernst Beutler (Zürich, 1949), *Gespräche mit Goethe*, p. 719.

186 Desboulmiers, vol. I, pp. 185–6.

187 For *L'Italien marié à Paris* see *Dictionnaire des théâtres de Paris* (1756), vol. III, pp. 226–34.

191 *Théâtre de M. de Florian* (Paris, 1786), 'Avant-propos', vol. I, pp. 13–14, 20.

192 See M. Brahmer, 'La commedia dell'arte in Polonia' (*Ricerche slavistiche*, vol. III (1954), pp. 184–95), and 'Su una compagnia di comici italiani a Varsavia in metà del settecento' (*Atti del secondo congresso internazionale di studi italiani* (1958), pp. 355–9); Kazimierz Konarski, 'Teatr warszawski w dobie saskiej' (*Pamiętnik teatralny* (1952), pp. 15–36); and Julian Lewański, 'Faust i Arlekin' (*Pamiętnik teatralny* (1957), pp. 76–120).

197 For the Italian actors in Russia, see the references cited in the bibliography and P. N. Berkov, *Русская народная драма XVII–XX веков* (Moscow, 1953). For the Warsaw repertoire see the articles by Bohdan Korzeniewski and Zbigniew Raszewski cited above.

197 The title of the Prague play is given by Jean Braber in *Revue d'histoire du théâtre*, vol. XI (1959), p. 49.

203 On Collalto see Attinger, p. 355, referring to *Annales du Théâtre Italien* (Paris, 1788), vol. II, p. 124.

206 Goldoni's statement about the World and the Theatre appears in the preface to the first (Bettinelli) collection of his comedies in 1750 (see Pandolfi, vol. IV, p. 343; *Opere*, ed. Filippo Zampieri (Milan, 1954), pp. 191–2). For the passages in *Il teatro comico* see the *Collezione completa* (Prato, 1819), vol. I, pp. 55–6, 43.

208 A. G. Bragaglia, in 'Goldoni und die Commedia dell'arte' (*Maske und Kothurn*, vol. III (1957), pp. 302–11), attempts to argue that Goldoni's reform was not technical. Goldoni's remarks on the mask appear in a letter to Francesco Vendramin, 11 July 1763 (Dino Mantovani, *Carlo Goldoni e il Teatro di San Luca a Venezia* (Milan, 1885, p. 191)), and in *Mémoires*, vol. II, pp. 196–7.

208 *Mémoires*, vol. III, pp. 16–17; vol. I, pp. 325, 340.

209 *Mémoires*, vol. I, pp. 405–7.

212 The remark concerning the 'fungus' is in *Memorie inutili*, ed. Giuseppe Prezzolini (Bari, 1910), vol. I, p. 207; that on Gozzi's own aims, vol. I, p. 221; that on *The Love of the Three Oranges*, vol. I, p. 230; that on the public declaration, vol. I, p. 247; that on his use of masks, vol. I, p. 250.

214 C. Castelletti, *I torti amorosi* (Venice, 1581), preface.

215 For the passage from *Pamela fanciulla* see Goldoni's works (Prato, 1819), vol. II, pp. 31–3.

215 The reference to the Italians in London is cited in S. Rosenfeld, pp. 15–16.

216 Gozzi's remarks are in *Memorie inutili*, vol. I, p. 265.

219 For Léon Chancerel's statement see Attinger, p. 446. Copeau's declaration is quoted by Léon Chancerel (*Le théâtre et la jeunesse* (1941), p. 131).